Machine Learning Fundamentals in Action

A Step-by-Step Guide to Implementing Machine Learning Solutions

KONSTANTIN TITOV

ISBN: 979-8-3438-0297-9

TABLE OF CONTENTS

1. INTRODUCTION TO MACHINE LEARNING

1.1 What is Machine Learning?

Machine learning (ML) is a powerful tool that allows computers to learn from data. Instead of being explicitly programmed for every task, machines use algorithms to analyze and interpret patterns in the data. From this, they can make decisions, predictions, or recognize patterns with little or no human intervention. In simple terms, machine learning is about teaching computers to learn and improve over time, similar to how humans do.

The Origin of Machine Learning

The concept of machine learning dates back to the 1950s. At its core, it was based on the idea that machines could recognize patterns, and by doing so, they could "learn." One of the earliest examples of machine learning was a program created by Arthur Samuel in 1959. It allowed a computer to play checkers. The program would improve its performance over time by learning from its mistakes. This was a significant breakthrough, as it demonstrated that computers could be taught to improve and make better decisions based on experience.

The Essence of Learning in Machines

Learning in machines is not unlike human learning, but it operates differently. While humans learn from direct experience, machines learn from data. The more data the machine processes, the more patterns it can recognize. The machine doesn't need explicit instructions for every scenario. It relies on algorithms to find relationships in the data, adjust its internal processes, and improve its performance on a given task.

Think of machine learning as baking. Instead of following a fixed recipe, you experiment with ingredients (data), tweak the recipe (algorithm), and eventually, you create a delicious cake. Over time, you refine the process and become more efficient. Machine learning works similarly, but with data and algorithms instead of flour and sugar.

Why is Machine Learning Important?

Machine learning has become a cornerstone of modern technology. It's used in almost every field today—from healthcare and finance to entertainment and e-commerce. Its importance lies in the ability to process vast amounts of data quickly and make decisions or predictions without constant human oversight.

For example, every time you use a recommendation system on Netflix or Amazon, you're interacting with machine learning. The system analyzes your past behavior, compares it with millions of other users, and suggests what you might like next. This kind of personalized experience was impossible a few decades ago.

In healthcare, machine learning can help doctors predict diseases, based on patterns in medical data. It can detect early signs of cancer in images or predict how a patient might respond to a specific treatment. These insights allow professionals to make better decisions faster, often with life-saving outcomes.

In finance, machine learning models are used for fraud detection. They can monitor transactions, detect unusual patterns, and alert banks before any money is lost. This is done at a scale and speed that no human team could achieve.

How Does Machine Learning Work?

At its core, machine learning relies on algorithms. An algorithm is a set of instructions that the machine follows to solve a problem. Think of it as a recipe or a formula. However, in machine learning, the algorithm doesn't remain static. It adapts based on the data it encounters.

Machine learning typically involves three main types of learning:

1. **Supervised Learning**: This is the most common type. In supervised learning, the machine is given a set of labeled data. For example, you might give it pictures of cats and dogs, labeled accordingly. The machine then learns to identify cats and dogs by finding patterns in the images. Once it's trained, you can give it new, unlabeled pictures, and it will predict whether they contain a cat or a dog.

2. **Unsupervised Learning**: In this case, the machine isn't given labeled data. Instead, it must find patterns or structure in the data on its own. A common use of unsupervised learning is clustering, where the algorithm groups similar data points together. For example, it might

group customers with similar shopping habits, even though we haven't explicitly told it what those habits are.

3. **Reinforcement Learning**: This type of learning is more dynamic. The machine interacts with its environment and learns by trial and error. It receives rewards or penalties for the actions it takes, and it adjusts its behavior accordingly. Reinforcement learning is often used in robotics or games, where an agent learns to take actions that maximize its rewards.

Machine Learning vs. Traditional Programming

One way to understand machine learning better is by comparing it to traditional programming. In traditional programming, we give the computer a set of instructions to follow step by step. For example, if you're writing a program to identify spam emails, you might manually define certain rules.

"If the email contains the word 'win,' mark it as spam." But as we know, spammers get creative. They might use words like "w1n" or "prize" instead, and your program becomes ineffective.

In machine learning, instead of writing rules, we give the machine data—lots of it. We feed it thousands of spam and non-spam emails, and the machine learns the characteristics of each category. It builds its own rules based on patterns it finds in the data. The machine can then generalize from the training data and make predictions on new emails.

This approach is not only more flexible, but it's also much more powerful. Machine learning systems can adapt to new patterns over time. Traditional programs, on the other hand, would need to be updated manually whenever something changes.

The Future of Machine Learning

The future of machine learning is incredibly promising. We are only scratching the surface of what these systems can do. As computing power increases and more data becomes available, machine learning models will become even more accurate and efficient.

Today, machine learning powers chatbots, self-driving cars, voice assistants, and recommendation systems. But its potential goes far beyond these applications. In the future, we may see machine learning integrated into almost every aspect of life—from personalized education to smarter cities and even better medical diagnoses.

However, with great power comes responsibility. As machine learning becomes more prevalent, concerns about data privacy, bias, and ethics also rise. It's essential to ensure that the systems we build are transparent, fair, and accountable.

Machine learning is changing the world in profound ways. It allows machines to learn from data, adapt, and improve over time. Whether it's making recommendations, detecting fraud, or improving healthcare, machine learning is at the forefront of technological innovation. And while there are challenges ahead, the possibilities are nearly limitless.

It is essential to not only understand how machine learning works but also to recognize its potential and its limitations. After all, the more we know about this technology, the better equipped we'll be to harness its power responsibly.

1.2 The Role of Data in Machine Learning

Data is the lifeblood of machine learning. Without it, machine learning algorithms would be useless. Data provides the raw material that enables machines to learn, improve, and make predictions. In fact, the success of any machine learning model depends largely on the quality, quantity, and variety of the data it's trained on. So, to fully understand machine learning, we must first grasp the critical role that data plays in the process.

Data is the Foundation

Machine learning works by finding patterns in data. The machine doesn't "think" or "understand" like a human, but instead, it analyzes the data, looking for relationships, structures, and patterns that it can use to make decisions. The more data it has, and the more relevant that data is to the task at hand, the better it can learn.

Think of data as the fuel in a car. The more fuel you have, the farther the car can go. But if the fuel is of poor quality, the car's performance will suffer. The same is true for machine learning. Good data allows a model to reach its full potential, while bad data can lead to poor results.

Types of Data in Machine Learning

Not all data is the same, and different types of data serve different purposes in machine learning. Broadly speaking, data used in machine learning falls into three categories:

1. **Structured Data**: This is data that is highly organized and easily searchable. Think of it as data stored in a spreadsheet or a database. Examples include customer names, transaction amounts, and product IDs. Structured data is typically labeled and can be used for tasks like classification or regression.

2. **Unstructured Data**: This is data that doesn't follow a specific format. It's often more challenging to analyze, but it can also provide richer insights. Examples of unstructured data include images, videos, text files, and audio recordings. Unstructured data is becoming increasingly important as we develop models for tasks like image recognition, speech-to-text, and natural language processing.

3. **Semi-Structured Data**: This is a hybrid of structured and unstructured data. It has some organization but isn't as rigidly formatted as structured data. JSON files or XML data are examples of semi-structured data. This kind of data is often used in web applications or APIs.

The Importance of Quality Data

In machine learning, the saying "garbage in, garbage out" holds true. No matter how sophisticated your algorithms are, if the data you feed them is flawed, incomplete, or biased, the model's predictions will be equally flawed. Quality data is essential for building accurate models.

Quality data means that the information must be:

- **Accurate**: The data should represent the real-world situation as closely as possible. Inaccurate data leads to incorrect predictions.

- **Complete**: Missing data can mislead a model, causing it to make inaccurate decisions. For example, if you're predicting customer behavior and half the customer records are missing, the model won't be able to generalize well.

- **Relevant:** The data must be relevant to the problem you're trying to solve. Irrelevant data adds noise and can confuse the model.

- **Unbiased:** Bias in the data can lead to biased models. For example, if your training data only includes data from a specific demographic, your model might struggle to generalize to other groups.

A common challenge in machine learning is ensuring that the data you're using is both high-quality and representative of the problem you're trying to solve.

Data Collection

Before a machine learning model can learn, it needs data. Collecting data is often one of the most time-consuming parts of the machine learning pipeline. Depending on the problem, data might come from various sources:

- **Databases:** Companies store massive amounts of data in relational databases. These can provide valuable structured data for models.

- **APIs:** Many services provide APIs (application programming interfaces) that allow you to collect data programmatically. For instance, Twitter provides an API for collecting tweets, while financial APIs offer market data.

- **Web Scraping:** When data isn't readily available through an API, web scraping can be used to collect information from websites. However, this must be done ethically and in line with legal guidelines.

- **Sensors and IoT Devices:** In industries like manufacturing or healthcare, sensors and devices continuously generate real-time data. Machine learning models can be trained on this data to monitor processes, predict failures, or optimize performance.

- **Public Datasets:** There are many freely available datasets, such as the UCI Machine Learning Repository or Kaggle, which can provide a wealth of data for experimentation and model training.

Data Preprocessing

Once data is collected, it's rarely ready for use in a machine learning model right away. It needs to be cleaned, transformed, and organized—a process known as data preprocessing. Data preprocessing is one of the most critical steps in machine learning because it ensures that the data fed into the model is suitable for learning.

Steps in Data Preprocessing:

1. **Data Cleaning:** This involves handling missing values, correcting errors, and filtering out irrelevant information. For example, if a dataset has missing entries, you might fill those gaps with average values or remove incomplete records.

2. **Normalization and Standardization:** This step ensures that the data falls within a similar range. Some machine learning algorithms perform better when the input values are scaled. For example, a dataset with values ranging from 0 to 100,000 might need normalization to bring all the values into a range between 0 and 1.

3. **Feature Engineering**: This process involves creating new features from existing data. For instance, if you have a dataset with customer birth dates, you might create a new feature that calculates the customer's age. Feature engineering is crucial because it can reveal hidden patterns in the data.

4. **Encoding Categorical Variables**: If the dataset contains categorical variables (e.g., "male" or "female"), these need to be converted into a numerical format that machine learning models can process. One-hot encoding or label encoding are common methods for this.

5. **Splitting the Dataset**: To build a robust model, the data is usually split into three parts: training, validation, and test sets. The model learns from the training set, fine-tunes itself using the validation set, and is evaluated on the test set. This ensures that the model generalizes well to unseen data.

Data Variety and Volume

When it comes to machine learning, **more data is usually better**—but only up to a point. Having a large volume of data helps models learn more patterns and perform better. However, simply increasing the volume isn't enough. The variety of the data is equally important.

For example, if you're training a self-driving car, the data should include images of roads under various conditions—sunny, rainy, foggy, etc. If the model is only trained on sunny days, it will fail when it encounters fog. Diverse data ensures that the model can generalize better and handle a wide range of real-world scenarios.

Data variety also helps avoid overfitting, where the model becomes too specialized in the training data and struggles to perform on new data.

Data Augmentation

In some cases, collecting more data might be difficult or expensive. This is where **data augmentation** comes in. Data augmentation techniques artificially increase the size of the dataset by modifying the existing data. In image recognition, for example, images might be flipped, rotated, or cropped to create new training examples. This helps the model learn to recognize objects in various orientations or conditions.

Data plays a fundamental role in machine learning. It provides the foundation on which models are built and determines how well those models perform. The quality, quantity, and variety of data are all crucial factors. Collecting and preparing data is one of the most challenging but vital parts of any machine learning project.

Without good data, even the most advanced algorithms will fail to produce meaningful results. But with the right data, machine learning has the potential to transform industries and solve complex problems. Therefore, as machine learning practitioners, we must prioritize data quality and make informed decisions about how we collect, clean, and use our data.

1.3 Types of Machine Learning: Supervised, Unsupervised, and Reinforcement Learning

Machine learning can be broken down into different types based on how the algorithm learns from the data. The three primary types of machine learning are **supervised learning**, **unsupervised learning**, and **reinforcement learning**. Each of these types has a unique approach to learning and solving problems. Let's explore them in detail to understand their differences and when they are most useful.

Supervised Learning

Supervised learning is the most commonly used type of machine learning. In supervised learning, the model learns from labeled data. This means that for each input (such as a picture, sentence, or number), the correct output is already known (like a label or category). The algorithm's job is to learn the relationship between the inputs and outputs, so it can predict the correct output for new, unseen data.

How It Works

Imagine you're trying to teach a child to recognize different animals. You show the child pictures of cats and dogs, and for each picture, you tell them if it's a cat or a dog. Over time, the child learns the differences between the two animals based on the features in the pictures—things like the shape of the ears or the length of the fur. Once the child has learned enough, they can identify a new picture of a cat or dog correctly.

In supervised learning, the computer model works in the same way. The labeled dataset is the training material that the model uses to learn. The algorithm makes predictions on the training data, and each time it gets something wrong, it adjusts itself until it becomes accurate enough.

Examples of Supervised Learning Algorithms

- **Linear Regression**: Used for predicting a continuous value (e.g., house prices).

- **Logistic Regression**: Used for binary classification (e.g., spam or not spam).

- **Decision Trees and Random Forests**: Models that make decisions by splitting the data into smaller subsets.

- **Support Vector Machines (SVM)**: Used for classification tasks with a clear margin of separation between classes.

When to Use Supervised Learning

Supervised learning is ideal when you have a large dataset of labeled examples and a clear idea of the desired output. It's commonly used in situations like:

- **Email classification**: Is the email spam or not?

- **Fraud detection**: Is a financial transaction fraudulent or legitimate?

- **Medical diagnosis**: Based on symptoms and medical history, what is the diagnosis?

Unsupervised Learning

Unsupervised learning takes a different approach. Here, the data is **unlabeled**, meaning the algorithm has to figure out patterns and relationships on its own. The goal of unsupervised learning is to identify hidden structures or groupings in the data without any human-provided labels. This type of learning is often used when we don't know what we're looking for but want the machine to uncover insights.

How It Works

Let's return to our child example, but this time, imagine you give the child a set of animal pictures without telling them which animals are cats, and which are dogs. The child will start to notice similarities between certain pictures and group them together.

Over time, they might realize that pictures with pointy ears and whiskers seem to belong to one group (cats), while the ones with floppy ears and wagging tails belong to another group (dogs). This is what unsupervised learning does—it looks for patterns and similarities without any specific instructions.

Examples of Unsupervised Learning Algorithms

- **Clustering (e.g., k-Means)**: Groups similar data points together (e.g., grouping customers based on purchasing behavior).

- **Dimensionality Reduction (e.g., PCA)**: Reduces the number of features in a dataset while preserving as much information as possible.

- **Anomaly Detection**: Identifies unusual data points or outliers (e.g., detecting abnormal network activity).

When to Use Unsupervised Learning

Unsupervised learning is useful when you have a large amount of data but don't have predefined labels. It's especially helpful in the following scenarios:

- **Customer segmentation**: Grouping customers based on purchasing patterns without predefined categories.

- **Market basket analysis**: Finding associations between products in shopping carts (e.g., customers who buy bread often also buy butter).

- **Anomaly detection**: Identifying fraud or outliers in datasets, such as unusual activity in banking transactions.

Reinforcement Learning

Reinforcement learning is a completely different paradigm

compared to supervised and unsupervised learning. In reinforcement learning, an agent (which could be a software program or a robot) learns by interacting with an environment. It takes actions, receives feedback in the form of rewards or penalties, and uses this feedback to learn the best strategy for achieving its goals.

How It Works

Think of reinforcement learning like training a dog to fetch. You throw a ball, and if the dog brings it back, you give it a treat (reward). If the dog doesn't fetch, it gets no reward. Over time, the dog learns that fetching the ball results in a positive outcome (the treat), and it gets better at the task. The dog doesn't get explicit instructions; it learns through trial and error.

In the case of machine learning, the agent might be a self-driving car learning how to navigate a road. It takes actions (e.g., turning left, speeding up), observes the outcome (e.g., staying on the road, crashing), and learns to adjust its behavior to maximize its rewards (e.g., getting to the destination safely).

Examples of Reinforcement Learning Algorithms

- **Q-Learning**: A type of reinforcement learning where the agent learns the value of actions in a specific state.

- **Deep Q-Networks (DQN)**: Combines reinforcement learning with deep learning to handle complex environments like video games.

- **Policy Gradient Methods**: Learn the best policy (set of actions) by directly optimizing for it.

When to Use Reinforcement Learning

Reinforcement learning is most commonly used in environments where an agent can take sequential actions and learn from the results. It's useful in situations like:

- **Game AI**: Teaching agents to play complex games like Chess or Go, where each move has consequences.

- **Robotics**: Training robots to complete tasks like picking up objects or navigating through an environment.

- **Self-driving cars**: Learning how to drive by adjusting actions based on the car's environment and the results of its decisions.

Key Differences Between the Types of Learning

- **Data Requirement**: Supervised learning requires labeled data, while unsupervised learning doesn't. Reinforcement learning doesn't rely on labeled data, but on feedback from interactions with its environment.

- **Nature of the Task**: Supervised learning is often used for prediction and classification, unsupervised learning for discovery of hidden patterns, and reinforcement learning for decision-making in dynamic environments.

- **Learning Process**: Supervised and unsupervised learning typically involve analyzing data to find patterns, while reinforcement learning is about learning through trial and error in an environment.

Each type of machine learning—supervised, unsupervised, and reinforcement learning—has its strengths and ideal use cases. **Supervised learning** is excellent when you have a well-labeled dataset and a clear goal in mind. **Unsupervised learning** shines when you want to uncover hidden patterns or groupings in data. **Reinforcement learning** is perfect for dynamic, decision-making environments where actions must be taken, and feedback is received over time.

Whether you're building a recommendation system, creating a self-driving car, or uncovering hidden customer insights, understanding which type of machine learning to use is crucial for success.

1.4 Real-World Applications of Machine Learning

Machine learning (ML) has moved from academic research to being a key player in shaping industries worldwide. Today, machine learning powers technologies we use daily, making systems smarter, more adaptive, and capable of learning from data to perform better over time.

From personalized recommendations on streaming platforms to revolutionizing healthcare, the practical applications of machine learning are far-reaching. Let's explore some of the most impactful real-world applications of machine learning across various sectors.

1. Healthcare: Revolutionizing Diagnosis and Treatment

Healthcare is one of the most promising areas where machine learning is making a profound difference. Medical professionals now leverage ML algorithms to analyze large amounts of patient data, diagnose diseases earlier, and provide more personalized treatment plans.

- **Medical Imaging**: Machine learning models are trained to analyze X-rays, CT scans, and MRIs to detect anomalies that may indicate diseases like cancer, fractures, or other conditions. Deep learning models, particularly convolutional neural networks (CNNs), are exceptionally good at recognizing patterns in images. For example, Google's

DeepMind has developed an AI system that can detect over 50 eye diseases by analyzing retina scans with an accuracy comparable to that of expert ophthalmologists.

- **Predictive Analytics**: Machine learning can predict patient outcomes by analyzing past medical records. For instance, it can predict which patients are at risk of developing complications after surgery or which individuals may be prone to certain chronic diseases, allowing doctors to take preventative measures.

- **Drug Discovery**: The process of discovering new drugs is lengthy and expensive. Machine learning speeds up this process by predicting how different compounds interact with specific proteins in the body, reducing the time it takes to develop effective treatments.

2. Finance: Automating and Securing Financial Services

The financial industry has been an early adopter of machine learning, using it for tasks like fraud detection, algorithmic trading, and credit scoring. Machine learning has become indispensable for financial institutions seeking to improve efficiency and reduce risks.

- **Fraud Detection**: Machine learning algorithms are capable of scanning millions of transactions in real-time to detect fraudulent activities. By identifying patterns associated with fraud—such as unusual spending behavior or strange locations—ML systems can flag potentially fraudulent transactions. These systems adapt as they learn from new data, making them more effective over time.

- **Algorithmic Trading:** Financial institutions use machine learning to develop models that predict stock price movements and automatically execute trades. High-frequency trading platforms rely on ML algorithms to analyze market data and make decisions in milliseconds, far faster than any human trader.

- **Risk Assessment and Credit Scoring:** Machine learning models analyze financial histories to predict whether a borrower is likely to default on a loan. This makes credit scoring more accurate and inclusive, as it can consider a broader range of factors than traditional models.

3. Retail and E-commerce: Personalization at Scale

E-commerce platforms like Amazon, Netflix, and Spotify owe much of their success to machine learning. ML has enabled these companies to personalize user experiences, optimize their logistics, and improve customer satisfaction.

- **Recommendation Systems:** One of the most visible applications of machine learning is in recommendation engines. These algorithms analyze user behavior, such as search queries, browsing history, and purchase records, to recommend products or content that a user is likely to enjoy. For instance, Netflix's recommendation system accounts for nearly 80% of the content watched on the platform, using machine learning to analyze viewer preferences and predict what they want to see next.

- **Dynamic Pricing:** Machine learning is also used to optimize pricing strategies. E-commerce platforms adjust prices in real-time based on supply, demand, customer behavior, and competitor pricing. This dynamic pricing ensures that businesses remain competitive while maximizing profits.

- **Inventory Management and Demand Forecasting**: Retailers use ML algorithms to forecast demand for specific products, allowing them to manage their inventory more effectively. This helps to reduce overstocking or understocking situations, improving operational efficiency and reducing costs.

4. Transportation: Powering Autonomous Vehicles and Route Optimization

Machine learning is at the heart of the transportation revolution, particularly in the development of autonomous vehicles and optimizing logistics.

- **Self-Driving Cars**: Companies like Tesla, Waymo, and Uber are using machine learning to power their self-driving vehicles. ML algorithms process vast amounts of sensor data from cameras, lidar, and radar systems to detect objects, recognize road signs, predict pedestrian movement, and make real-time driving decisions. Machine learning enables these vehicles to improve over time as they gather more data from the road.

- **Route Optimization**: Machine learning helps companies like Uber, Lyft, and delivery services optimize routes for drivers. By analyzing traffic patterns, road conditions, and real-time data, ML algorithms suggest the fastest or most efficient routes, saving both time and fuel.

- **Predictive Maintenance**: ML is used in fleet management to predict when vehicles will need maintenance before they break down. This reduces downtime and maintenance costs while improving vehicle longevity and safety.

5. Manufacturing: Enhancing Efficiency and Reducing Costs

In manufacturing, machine learning plays a crucial role in improving processes, reducing waste, and ensuring quality control. By automating tasks and predicting equipment failures, manufacturers can operate more efficiently.

- **Predictive Maintenance**: Similar to transportation, manufacturing companies use ML to predict when machines are likely to fail. By analyzing sensor data, the system can detect signs of wear and tear or other anomalies, prompting maintenance before a breakdown occurs. This reduces costly downtime and ensures smoother operations.

- **Quality Control**: Machine learning models are used to monitor product quality during the manufacturing process. These systems can analyze images or other data to detect defects in products in real-time, ensuring that only items meeting quality standards move forward in the production line.

- **Supply Chain Optimization**: Machine learning helps manufacturers optimize their supply chains by forecasting demand, managing inventory, and predicting logistics needs. This leads to cost savings, better resource allocation, and reduced lead times.

6. Entertainment: Personalizing Content and Enhancing Creativity

Machine learning is also making waves in the entertainment

industry, where it's used to create personalized experiences for users and even generate creative content.

- **Content Recommendations**: As mentioned earlier, platforms like Netflix, Spotify, and YouTube use machine learning algorithms to recommend content based on user behavior. These recommendations help keep users engaged by showing them content they are likely to enjoy based on their preferences and the behavior of similar users.

- **Content Creation**: Machine learning is also being used to create new content. AI-generated music, art, and even scripts are becoming more common. For instance, OpenAI's GPT-3 model can generate human-like text, allowing it to write articles, stories, and even poetry with minimal human input.

- **Gaming**: In the gaming industry, machine learning helps create more intelligent and adaptive opponents. Games use ML algorithms to learn from player behavior, making the gameplay more challenging and personalized. Additionally, procedural content generation powered by machine learning creates new game environments, levels, and challenges dynamically.

7. Agriculture: Optimizing Farming Practices

Agriculture is embracing machine learning to optimize farming practices and increase productivity while reducing resource consumption.

- **Precision Agriculture**: Machine learning helps farmers monitor crop health, predict yields, and manage resources more efficiently. Drones and sensors collect data on soil conditions, moisture levels, and crop growth.

ML algorithms then analyze this data to provide actionable insights, such as when to water or apply fertilizers.

- **Crop Disease Detection**: Machine learning models can analyze images of crops to detect diseases early. By identifying patterns that humans might miss, these systems help farmers take preventive action before diseases spread, reducing crop loss and improving food security.

- **Automated Harvesting**: Machine learning is also used in robotic systems that can harvest crops automatically. These systems use computer vision to identify ripe crops and pick them efficiently, saving time and labor.

Machine learning is transforming industries, making systems smarter, more efficient, and better at adapting to real-world conditions. From healthcare to entertainment, transportation to agriculture, machine learning applications are enhancing the way we live, work, and interact with technology. As data continues to grow and algorithms become more sophisticated, the future of machine learning looks incredibly promising. It's not just about solving today's problems but opening up new possibilities for innovation across the globe.

1.5 Key Challenges and Opportunities in Machine Learning

Machine learning (ML) is a transformative technology with immense potential to revolutionize industries and solve complex problems. However, along with its vast opportunities, machine learning also faces several significant challenges. These challenges range from technical hurdles to ethical concerns, and addressing them is essential for the continued growth and success of ML applications. On the other hand, overcoming these obstacles unlocks new opportunities, enabling machine learning to thrive in even more areas of life and industry. In this section, we'll explore the key challenges and opportunities in machine learning.

Key Challenges in Machine Learning

1. Data Quality and Availability

Data is the foundation of machine learning, but obtaining high-quality data is a significant challenge. Many organizations struggle with data that is incomplete, inconsistent, or noisy. If the data is biased or lacks diversity, it can lead to skewed results and poor model performance.

- **Incomplete Data**: Missing data points can prevent the model from learning effectively. This often happens when data collection methods are flawed or when records aren't kept consistently. Handling missing data through imputation or discarding incomplete rows can work, but it's not always ideal.

- **Imbalanced Data**: Many datasets are imbalanced, meaning that certain categories are overrepresented while others are underrepresented. For example, in fraud detection, the number of non-fraudulent transactions vastly outweighs the number of fraudulent ones. This imbalance makes it harder for the model to learn from the minority class, and special techniques like oversampling, undersampling, or synthetic data generation are needed.

- **Data Accessibility**: Many industries, especially those that handle sensitive information (such as healthcare or finance), face issues with data privacy and regulations.

Strict data-sharing regulations (e.g., GDPR) make it difficult for machine learning projects to access the data they need. Organizations often have to anonymize or aggregate their data, which can reduce its utility for machine learning tasks.

2. Interpretability and Explainability

Machine learning models, particularly deep learning models, can be complex and difficult to interpret. While these models often provide accurate predictions, understanding why they make certain decisions remains a challenge. This is especially problematic in critical sectors like healthcare, finance, and legal fields, where trust in the model's decisions is crucial.

- **Black Box Models**: Many machine learning models, like neural networks, operate as "black boxes," where it's hard to understand how they arrived at a particular decision. For example, a neural network might predict that a person is at risk of developing a disease, but it's not clear which factors contributed to that decision.

- **Regulatory Compliance**: In fields like finance or healthcare, models often need to comply with regulations that require transparency. Companies must be able to explain how their models make decisions, which is difficult with opaque models.

3. Overfitting and Underfitting

Model performance is one of the most significant challenges in machine learning. Overfitting and underfitting are two common problems that can result in poor generalization.

- **Overfitting**: Overfitting happens when a model learns the training data too well, capturing noise and irrelevant details instead of general patterns. As a result, the model performs exceptionally well on training data but poorly on unseen data.

- **Underfitting**: Underfitting occurs when a model is too simple and fails to capture the underlying patterns in the data. This typically happens when the model is not complex enough or when it hasn't been trained for long enough.

Balancing between underfitting and overfitting is crucial, and finding that balance requires careful tuning of the model, along with cross-validation and regularization techniques.

4. Computation and Scalability

Training machine learning models, particularly deep learning models, requires immense computational resources. As data grows in size and complexity, so do the computational demands. For large-scale tasks, models need powerful hardware like GPUs (Graphics Processing Units) or TPUs (Tensor Processing Units), which can be expensive.

- **Training Time**: Some models, particularly in deep learning, can take days or even weeks to train on large datasets. This slows down innovation and the ability to test new ideas quickly.

- **Energy Consumption**: The computational cost of training models also translates into high energy consumption. This is becoming a growing concern in terms of sustainability, especially as AI usage expands.

- **Scalability**: Scaling machine learning models to work with massive amounts of data is challenging. Distributed computing frameworks like Hadoop or Spark help, but they add complexity to the pipeline, requiring specialized knowledge to implement and manage.

5. Ethical Issues and Bias

Machine learning models are only as good as the data they are trained on, and if that data contains biases, the models will learn and perpetuate those biases. This can lead to unfair or discriminatory outcomes, especially in sensitive areas like hiring, lending, or law enforcement.

- **Bias in Data**: Historical data often reflects societal biases. For example, a hiring algorithm trained on resumes from a predominantly male workforce may learn to favor male candidates, even though that's not the intended outcome. Identifying and correcting these biases is a complex task.

- **Fairness and Accountability**: Ensuring that machine learning models treat all individuals or groups fairly is critical. There's also a growing need to hold companies accountable for the outcomes their algorithms produce. If an algorithm makes a discriminatory decision, who is responsible?

Key Opportunities in Machine Learning

1. Personalized Experiences

One of the most exciting opportunities in machine learning is the ability to create personalized experiences for users. Personalization can improve customer satisfaction, loyalty, and engagement across many industries.

- **E-commerce**: Machine learning algorithms can recommend products to customers based on their browsing history, past purchases, and preferences, improving the user experience and boosting sales.

- **Entertainment:** Platforms like Netflix and Spotify use machine learning to provide personalized content recommendations, keeping users engaged and helping them discover new content tailored to their tastes.

- **Healthcare:** Machine learning can be used to develop personalized treatment plans for patients by analyzing their medical histories and genetic profiles, which can lead to better health outcomes.

2. Automation and Optimization

Machine learning offers immense potential for automating repetitive tasks and optimizing processes across industries. This leads to increased efficiency, reduced operational costs, and the ability to make better, data-driven decisions.

- **Manufacturing:** Machine learning can optimize supply chain management, predict equipment failures, and automate quality control processes. This results in reduced downtime, lower costs, and improved product quality.

- **Finance:** In the financial industry, machine learning can be used to automate tasks such as credit scoring, fraud detection, and algorithmic trading. These applications lead to faster, more accurate decisions and can save businesses money.

- **Healthcare:** Automation in medical imaging and diagnostics can help doctors process more data in less time, leading to faster diagnoses and treatments. ML-powered systems can also assist in drug discovery, speeding up the time to market for new medicines.

3. New Insights from Big Data

As data becomes more abundant, machine learning provides the tools to extract meaningful insights from it. The ability to process vast amounts of data quickly and efficiently means organizations can make smarter decisions and discover patterns that were previously hidden.

- **Predictive Analytics**: Machine learning enables organizations to make predictions about future events based on historical data. For example, predictive analytics can help retailers forecast demand for products, improving inventory management and reducing waste.

- **Healthcare**: In medicine, machine learning can analyze patient data to predict the likelihood of developing certain diseases, enabling earlier interventions and improving patient outcomes.

4. Advanced AI and Autonomous Systems

Machine learning is driving advances in artificial intelligence (AI), enabling systems to perform tasks autonomously. From self-driving cars to autonomous drones, the possibilities for automation are expanding.

- **Autonomous Vehicles**: Machine learning algorithms process real-time data from sensors and cameras in autonomous vehicles, allowing them to navigate complex environments, avoid obstacles, and make safe driving decisions.

- **Robotics**: In manufacturing and logistics, robots powered by machine learning are capable of performing intricate tasks, such as assembling products or managing warehouse inventories.

- **Smart Cities**: ML can optimize energy usage, traffic management, and waste collection, improving the efficiency of urban areas and making them more sustainable.

Machine learning presents a mix of challenges and opportunities that will shape its future and influence how it's adopted across industries. While technical difficulties such as data quality, interpretability, and computational demands remain hurdles, the potential for ML to drive innovation in areas like personalized experiences, automation, and autonomous systems is undeniable.

Addressing ethical concerns and ensuring fairness will be critical in building trustworthy and equitable systems. By navigating these challenges, we unlock endless possibilities for improving business processes, healthcare, transportation, and more, ultimately leading to a smarter, more efficient world.

Chapter 2: Preparing Data for Machine Learning

2.1 Understanding Data Sources and Formats

In machine learning, data is everything. It's the foundation that enables models to learn, predict, and improve. But to make the most of data, you need to understand where it comes from, what formats it can take, and how to work with it. The better you understand the various data sources and formats, the more effectively you can prepare and use data for machine learning models. Let's dive into the essential aspects of data sources and formats.

What Are Data Sources?

A **data source** is simply the origin or place from where data is collected. Data can come from a wide variety of sources, and in modern machine learning projects, accessing data from multiple sources is common. Each data source has its own characteristics, and understanding these is crucial for managing data quality, privacy, and structure.

Here are some common types of data sources:

1. Databases

Databases are one of the most structured and reliable sources of data. They are commonly used in businesses to store vast amounts of information in an organized manner. In databases, data is usually stored in tables that consist of rows and columns, which makes it easy to access and manipulate for machine learning tasks.

- **Relational Databases (SQL)**: Relational databases like MySQL, PostgreSQL, and Oracle are structured, using tables with rows and columns. Data is stored in a relational format, meaning that different tables can be linked through foreign keys. These databases are ideal for structured data like customer information, financial transactions, and product inventories.

- **NoSQL Databases**: NoSQL databases such as MongoDB or Cassandra store data in a more flexible format like documents (JSON), key-value pairs, or graphs. These are suitable for handling large volumes of unstructured data, like user activity logs or real-time sensor data.

2. APIs (Application Programming Interfaces)

APIs allow machine learning systems to interact with other systems and gather data. Many companies provide APIs that allow access to their data for specific purposes. For example:

- **Social Media APIs**: Twitter, Facebook, and Instagram provide APIs that allow developers to access public posts, trends, and user data.

- **Financial APIs**: Services like Alpha Vantage or Quandl offer APIs that provide financial data such as stock prices, historical market data, or currency exchange rates.

APIs are powerful because they allow you to pull real-time data, but working with APIs often requires authentication, rate-limiting management, and handling different formats such as JSON or XML.

3. Web Scraping

Sometimes, data isn't readily available via a database or API. This is where **web scraping** comes in. Web scraping involves extracting data from websites. Python libraries such as BeautifulSoup and Scrapy are commonly used to automate this process, gathering information from HTML pages.

For example, web scraping can be used to collect data on product prices across multiple e-commerce sites for competitive analysis or gather news articles for sentiment analysis. However, web scraping must be done responsibly and within legal constraints, as not all websites allow scraping.

4. Sensor Data and IoT Devices

With the rise of the Internet of Things (IoT), sensor data is becoming a major source of information for machine learning models. IoT devices such as smart thermostats, wearables, or industrial machines constantly generate data. This real-time data can be used to monitor equipment, predict maintenance needs, or optimize energy usage.

Examples of sensor data include:

- **Temperature**: From weather stations or smart home devices.

- **Motion and Proximity**: From security systems, smartphones, or fitness trackers.

- **GPS**: From navigation systems or mobile applications.

5. Public Datasets

There are countless public datasets available online, provided by organizations, governments, or research institutions. These are often used for educational purposes, experimentation, and to benchmark machine learning models.

Some popular sources of public datasets include:

- **UCI Machine Learning Repository**: Contains a large collection of datasets for various tasks like classification and regression.

- **Kaggle**: A data science community that provides thousands of datasets and challenges for ML practitioners.

- **Google Dataset Search**: A specialized search engine that helps find datasets from across the web.

Public datasets are highly valuable because they are often well-documented and widely used, making them perfect for testing models and learning new techniques.

Data Formats in Machine Learning

Once you have your data, you need to understand its format. Different machine learning models require different types of data formats, and choosing the right format ensures your data can be easily processed and analyzed. Let's go over the most common data formats you'll encounter in machine learning projects.

1. CSV (Comma-Separated Values)

The **CSV format** is one of the most popular data formats, especially for structured data. CSV files store data in a tabular form, with each line representing a record, and each field separated by commas. CSVs are easy to read, write, and parse, making them ideal for datasets with rows and columns.

- **Advantages**: CSV files are lightweight and human-readable. They can be opened in text editors or spreadsheet programs like Excel. Machine learning libraries like pandas make it easy to work with CSV files.

- **Disadvantages**: Since CSV files are plain text, they lack metadata and cannot store complex data types like images or videos. Additionally, if the dataset is large, CSV files can become inefficient in terms of storage and processing speed.

2. JSON (JavaScript Object Notation)

JSON is a flexible, human-readable format that is widely used for transmitting structured data, especially when working with APIs. It represents data as key-value pairs and is easy to parse into programming languages like Python.

- **Advantages**: JSON is excellent for representing semi-structured data. It is widely supported in modern web services and can easily handle nested structures (e.g., lists of objects).

- **Disadvantages**: JSON can be harder to work with than CSV for flat, tabular data. Also, JSON can be more storage-heavy than CSV due to its verbose nature.

3. XML (eXtensible Markup Language)

XML is another format commonly used for exchanging data between systems, especially in legacy systems and web services. XML is hierarchical, meaning it allows for a tree-like structure to represent nested data.

- **Advantages**: XML is flexible and supports complex data structures. It can handle metadata and allow for validation using schemas like XSD.

- **Disadvantages**: XML files tend to be larger and more difficult to parse compared to JSON. For machine learning, it's less common due to its verbosity.

4. Image Formats (JPEG, PNG, etc.)

When working with computer vision tasks, you'll deal with **image formats** like JPEG, PNG, and TIFF. These formats store pixel data, which machine learning models can use for tasks like object detection or image classification.

- **Advantages**: These formats are standardized and widely supported. Tools like OpenCV or PIL in Python make it easy to load, manipulate, and process image data for machine learning models.

- **Disadvantages**: Image files can be large, and working with high-resolution images can require substantial computational resources.

5. HDF5 and Parquet

For handling **large datasets** efficiently, formats like **HDF5** and **Parquet** are often used. These formats are optimized for reading and writing large amounts of data quickly, which makes them popular for big data and scientific computing.

- **HDF5**: Hierarchical Data Format is commonly used for large-scale datasets. It can store various types of data (including images, tables, or even complex multidimensional arrays) and allows for faster I/O operations than CSV or JSON.

- **Parquet**: Parquet is an efficient, columnar storage format often used in distributed computing systems like Apache Spark. It's highly efficient for reading and processing large datasets.

6. Time Series Data

Time series data consists of sequences of data points indexed in time order, typically collected at regular intervals. Common formats include CSV, JSON, or specialized formats like **TSV** (Tab-Separated Values). Examples include stock prices, sensor data, or web traffic over time.

- **Advantages**: Time series data is essential for any predictive analysis involving time, such as forecasting sales or predicting system failures.

- **Disadvantages**: Handling time series data can be complex, particularly when dealing with irregular intervals or missing timestamps.

Choosing the Right Format for Your Task

The choice of data format depends on your project's requirements and the type of data you're working with. For example:

- If you're working with structured, tabular data, **CSV** is often the easiest format to manage.

- For semi-structured or hierarchical data from web APIs, **JSON** is highly suitable.

- For large-scale data, especially in distributed computing environments, **Parquet** or **HDF5** might be more efficient.

- When dealing with images or video, you'll need formats like **JPEG** or **MP4**, and you might also need to preprocess them for compatibility with machine learning models.

Understanding data sources and formats is critical for successful machine learning projects. The diversity of data sources—from databases and APIs to sensor data and public datasets—offers immense possibilities, but each source brings its own set of challenges. Similarly, working with different data formats—whether CSV, JSON, or image files—requires knowing the strengths and limitations of each.

Choosing the right data source and format ensures that your machine learning model has the right foundation to succeed, leading to better predictions, faster processing, and more robust solutions.

2.2 Data Preprocessing: Cleaning, Normalization, and Transformation

Data preprocessing is a crucial step in the machine learning pipeline. Before feeding data into machine learning algorithms, it must be cleaned, normalized, and transformed to ensure that it's suitable for model training.

Poorly preprocessed data can lead to inaccurate models, unreliable predictions, and suboptimal performance. In this section, we'll explore the key steps in data preprocessing: **data** cleaning, normalization, and transformation.

What is Data Preprocessing?

Data preprocessing involves preparing raw data for machine learning models by transforming it into a clean and usable format. This process includes identifying and correcting errors, handling missing values, normalizing or scaling data, and transforming features to enhance the model's performance.

Machine learning algorithms rely on high-quality data to produce accurate predictions. Data preprocessing improves the quality of the input data, making it more meaningful and accessible for the learning algorithms.

Step 1: Data Cleaning

Data cleaning is the first and most critical step in preprocessing. The real-world data collected from various sources is often messy, incomplete, or full of errors. It's common to encounter missing values, duplicate records, or irrelevant information. Cleaning the data ensures that it is accurate, consistent, and free of errors.

1. Handling Missing Data

Missing data is one of the most frequent problems in datasets. It can occur due to human errors, technical glitches, or simply because some information wasn't available at the time of data collection. Machine learning models typically struggle with missing values, so they must be handled appropriately.

- **Removing Missing Data**: If the number of missing values is small and doesn't significantly impact the dataset, you can remove the rows or columns containing missing data. However, this can result in the loss of valuable information, so it's only recommended when the missing data is minimal.

- **Imputation**: A more common approach is to fill in missing data with reasonable values. For numerical features, you can replace missing values with the **mean**, **median**, or **mode** of the column. For categorical features, missing values can be filled with the **most frequent** category.

- **Predictive Imputation**: In more complex cases, machine learning models can be used to predict missing values based on other features in the dataset. This is done using algorithms like k-nearest neighbors (KNN) or regression models.

2. Removing Duplicates

Duplicate records can skew model training, especially if the same observation appears multiple times. Duplicate rows often arise from data entry errors, merging datasets, or incorrect logging of events. Removing duplicates ensures that each record in the dataset is unique and contributes equally to the model.

3. Handling Outliers

Outliers are data points that differ significantly from the rest of the dataset. These extreme values can distort model training, especially for algorithms that are sensitive to the range of data, like linear regression or k-means clustering.

- **Identify Outliers**: Outliers can be detected visually using plots like box plots or scatter plots, or statistically using methods like the Z-score or interquartile range (IQR).

- **Handling Outliers:** Depending on the situation, you can remove outliers, cap them to a maximum or minimum value, or treat them separately by creating new features. However, outliers should only be removed if you are confident they represent errors or irrelevant anomalies; otherwise, they may contain valuable insights.

4. Dealing with Inconsistent Data

Inconsistent data can arise from data entry errors, different measurement units, or variations in how data is collected. For example, a dataset might have entries for "United States" and "USA," which should be standardized to avoid treating them as different categories. Similarly, ensuring consistent measurement units (e.g., converting all temperature values to Celsius or Fahrenheit) is crucial for accurate modeling.

Step 2: Data Normalization

Normalization is an essential step in preprocessing numerical data. It ensures that all features contribute equally to the model, which is particularly important for algorithms that rely on distances between data points, such as **k-nearest neighbors (KNN)**, **support vector machines** (SVM), and **neural networks**.

Why Normalize Data?

When features in a dataset have different scales, some features may dominate the learning process, leading to biased models. For example, in a dataset containing income (measured in thousands of dollars) and age (measured in years), the income feature might have values in the range of thousands, while age is typically in the range of 20–100.

Without normalization, the machine learning algorithm might

give more importance to income simply because its values are larger, even though age might be equally or more relevant.

Methods of Normalization

1. Min-Max Scaling

Min-max scaling transforms the values of features to a fixed range, typically [0, 1]. This is done using the following formula:

$$X_{scaled} = \frac{X - X_{min}}{X_{max} - X_{min}}$$

Where:

- X is the original feature value,

- X_{min} is the minimum value of the feature, and

- X_{max} is the maximum value of the feature.

Min-max scaling preserves the relationships between the original data points but compresses the values into a fixed range. It is especially useful when you know the minimum and maximum bounds of your data.

2. Z-Score Standardization

Z-score standardization (also known as standardization or z-normalization) transforms the data so that it has a mean of 0 and a standard deviation of 1. The formula is:

$$X_{standardized} = \frac{X - \mu}{\sigma}$$

Where:

- XXX is the original feature value,

- $\mu \backslash mu\mu$ is the mean of the feature, and

- $\sigma \backslash sigma\sigma$ is the standard deviation of the feature.

Z-score standardization is particularly useful when the dataset contains features with a Gaussian (normal) distribution. It makes the data easier for certain algorithms, like logistic regression or neural networks, to process.

3. Robust Scaler

The robust scaler is useful when the data contains outliers, as it uses the **interquartile range (IQR)** instead of the minimum and maximum values. It scales the data based on the median and IQR, which makes it more robust to outliers:

Xscaled=X−medianIQRX_{scaled} = \frac{X - \text{median}}{IQR}Xscaled=IQRX−median

This method ensures that outliers don't unduly influence the scaling process.

Step 3: Data Transformation

Data transformation involves altering or creating new features from the existing data to improve model performance. Transformation techniques are especially helpful when the original data does not follow a normal distribution or when relationships between variables are non-linear.

1. Feature Encoding

When working with **categorical data**, machine learning models require that these categories be represented numerically. There are several ways to encode categorical features:

- **Label Encoding:** Converts each category into a unique integer. For example, if you have a "color" feature with categories "red," "blue," and "green," they could be encoded as 1, 2, and 3, respectively. This method is simple but can introduce ordinal relationships between categories that don't exist (e.g., is "green" > "blue"?).

- **One-Hot Encoding:** Creates a binary column for each category, assigning a 1 to the corresponding category and 0 elsewhere. For example, "red," "blue," and "green" would become three separate columns, each indicating the presence or absence of the color. This avoids introducing ordinal relationships and is widely used for categorical features with no inherent ranking.

2. Log Transformation

When a feature has a **skewed distribution**, a log transformation can help normalize it. For example, income data often has a right-skewed distribution, with most people earning modest amounts and a few earning very high incomes. Applying a log transformation can compress the range and make the distribution more normal, which some algorithms handle better.

The formula for a log transformation is:

$$X_{transformed} = \log(X + 1)$$

(We add 1 to avoid taking the log of zero or negative values.)

3. Polynomial Features

If the relationship between the input features and the target variable is non-linear, **polynomial transformations** can help capture this relationship. This technique generates new features that are powers of the original features. For example, for a feature XXX, polynomial transformation might create new features like X2X^2X2 or X3X^3X3, enabling the model to fit more complex patterns.

4. Discretization

Sometimes, continuous variables can be discretized into **bins** or **intervals**. For example, age could be split into groups like 0–18, 19–35, 36–50, and so on. Discretization simplifies the model, reduces noise, and can be useful when dealing with features that do not have a linear relationship with the target variable.

5. Interaction Terms

Interaction terms are created when two or more features are combined to capture their joint effects. For instance, if you have features for both **age** and **income**, their interaction might provide new insights into customer behavior. Adding interaction terms can improve the model's ability to capture complex relationships between features.

Data preprocessing is essential to ensure that your machine learning model receives high-quality data that's ready for analysis. Through data cleaning, we eliminate errors, missing values, and inconsistencies. By normalizing, we ensure that features are scaled correctly for the model to process. And through transformation, we create or modify features in ways that better represent the patterns.

2.3 Handling Missing Data and Outliers

Handling missing data and outliers is a critical aspect of **data**

preprocessing, which plays a significant role in machine learning. In real-world datasets, missing values and outliers are common issues that can degrade the performance of machine learning models if not addressed properly. Incorrectly handling these issues can lead to biased results, reduced accuracy, and overfitting.

In this section, we will discuss how missing data and outliers occur, the techniques used to handle them, and their importance in building robust machine learning models.

Understanding Missing Data

Missing data refers to the absence of a value in a dataset where one would normally be expected. Missing values can occur for various reasons, such as sensor failures, data collection errors, or users not providing certain information. Regardless of the cause, handling missing data appropriately is crucial for accurate analysis and modeling.

Types of Missing Data

There are three primary types of missing data:

1. **Missing Completely at Random (MCAR)**:

   o In this case, the missing data is entirely independent of any variables in the dataset. The missing values occur purely by chance. For instance, if a sensor randomly fails to record data at certain times, the data may be considered MCAR. Since the missing data is unrelated to other variables, removing or imputing the data is less likely to introduce bias.

2. **Missing at Random (MAR)**:

   o Data is missing based on some known factors, but the missingness is unrelated to the specific value of the missing data. For example, in a survey, younger respondents might be more likely to skip a question about income. In this case, the missingness is related to age but not to the actual income itself.

3. **Missing Not at Random (MNAR)**:

   o When data is missing because of the value itself, it is considered MNAR. For instance, people with lower income might be less likely to report their income on a survey. MNAR is more challenging to handle because the reason for the missing data is directly related to the missing values.

Strategies for Handling Missing Data

Handling missing data requires careful consideration. Simply removing rows with missing values is often not ideal, especially in datasets where missingness is common.

Here are several techniques for addressing missing data:

1. Removing Data (Deletion)

- **Listwise Deletion**: In this approach, any row (or instance) with a missing value is removed from the dataset. While this is a simple method, it can result in a significant loss of data if many rows contain missing values. It is suitable only when missing values are rare or the dataset is large enough that removing some rows does not negatively impact the analysis.

- **Pairwise Deletion**: Instead of removing an entire row, pairwise deletion removes only the specific instances where missing data affects the analysis. For example, in a correlation matrix, it uses all available data pairs without discarding entire rows. This approach preserves more data but can result in inconsistencies across analyses.

2. Imputation

Imputation involves filling in the missing values with reasonable estimates based on the available data. It allows for retaining as much of the dataset as possible while ensuring the continuity of machine learning workflows.

- **Mean/Median/Mode Imputation**: A common approach for numerical data is to replace missing values with the mean or median of the non-missing values. For categorical variables, the mode (most frequent category) is used.

  o Example: If the feature "age" has missing values, replace those with the mean or median age of the available data.

  o **Pros**: Simple and easy to implement.

  o **Cons**: Can introduce bias and reduce variance, especially if the percentage of missing values is high.

- **K-Nearest Neighbors (KNN) Imputation**: In this approach, the missing value for a data point is imputed by considering the values of its k-nearest neighbors. The idea is that similar instances in the dataset are likely to have similar values.

    o **Pros**: More sophisticated than mean/median imputation, as it accounts for patterns in the data.

    o **Cons**: Computationally expensive for large datasets, especially when using a large value of k.

- **Multivariate Imputation by Chained Equations (MICE)**: MICE is a more advanced technique that imputes missing data in a multivariate fashion. It uses regression models to predict missing values based on other variables in the dataset.

    o **Pros**: Accounts for the relationships between variables and provides a more robust imputation.

    o **Cons**: Complex to implement and computationally expensive.

- **Predictive Model Imputation**: A machine learning model (e.g., linear regression, decision tree) is trained to predict missing values based on the other variables in the dataset. This method is especially useful when the missingness is related to other variables.

    o **Pros**: Can produce highly accurate imputations.

    o **Cons**: May require significant computational resources and can be complex to implement.

- **Interpolation**: For time series data, missing values can be filled in using interpolation techniques, such as linear or polynomial interpolation, where the missing values are estimated based on adjacent data points in the series.

    o **Pros**: Suitable for time-dependent data.

    o **Cons**: Limited to specific types of data, such as time series.

3. Flagging Missing Data

In some cases, it can be beneficial to add an additional feature that flags whether a value is missing. This flag can then be used by machine learning algorithms to account for the fact that certain values were originally missing.

- **Pros**: Provides transparency and allows models to learn patterns in the missingness itself.

- **Cons**: Can lead to increased model complexity.

Understanding Outliers

Outliers are data points that significantly deviate from the other observations in the dataset. Outliers can occur due to measurement errors, data entry errors, or natural variability in the data. While outliers can provide valuable insights (e.g., identifying rare events or fraud), they can also skew model results and degrade performance if not handled properly.

Types of Outliers

There are generally two types of outliers:

1. **Univariate Outliers**: These outliers are detected by looking at one variable at a time. For example, in a dataset of house prices, a house with an extremely high price compared to the others might be considered an outlier.

2. **Multivariate Outliers**: These outliers are detected when considering the relationships between two or more variables. For example, if most houses with three bedrooms are priced between $300,000 and $400,000, but one house with three bedrooms is priced at $1 million, this could indicate a multivariate outlier.

Techniques for Handling Outliers

Outliers can significantly impact machine learning models, especially models sensitive to the distribution of data, such as linear regression. Here are several techniques for handling outliers:

1. Removing Outliers

- **Manual Inspection**: For small datasets, outliers can sometimes be identified and removed through manual inspection, based on domain knowledge or visualizations like box plots and scatter plots.

- **Z-Score**: The Z-score is a common method for identifying outliers in normally distributed data. The Z-score measures how many standard deviations a data point is from the mean. A Z-score greater than a certain threshold (commonly 3) indicates an outlier.

  - **Formula**: $Z=(X-\mu)\sigma Z$ = \frac{(X - \mu)}{\sigma}Z=\sigma(X-\mu)$ Where:

    - XXX = individual data point

    - $\mu\mu\mu$ = mean of the dataset

    - $\sigma\sigma\sigma$ = standard deviation of the dataset

  - **Pros**: Simple and widely used.

  - **Cons**: Assumes the data follows a normal distribution, which is not always the case.

- **IQR Method**: The interquartile range (IQR) is a measure of statistical dispersion, and outliers are identified as points that fall below the lower bound (Q1 - 1.5 * IQR) or above the upper bound (Q3 + 1.5 * IQR), where Q1 and Q3 are the 25th and 75th percentiles, respectively.

- o **Pros**: Works well for data that is not normally distributed.

- o **Cons**: Sensitive to the choice of threshold.

2. Transforming Outliers

- **Log Transformation**: If outliers are due to skewed data, applying a **log transformation** can compress the range of the data, reducing the impact of extreme values.

  - o **Pros**: Effective for reducing the influence of outliers in right-skewed data.

  - o **Cons**: Can only be applied to positive values.

- **Winsorization**: Winsorization involves capping extreme values to reduce the impact of outliers. For instance, the top and bottom 1% of data points might be capped at the 99th and 1st percentiles, respectively.

  - o **Pros**: Preserves the dataset by reducing the impact of extreme values rather than removing them.

  - o **Cons**: May introduce bias if applied indiscriminately.

- **Box-Cox Transformation**: The **Box-Cox transformation** is a more general transformation that can handle both positive and negative values. It seeks to make data more normally distributed, which can help in reducing the effect of outliers.

  - o **Pros**: Versatile transformation method.

o **Cons**: May be difficult to interpret.

3. Robust Models

Some machine learning algorithms are inherently robust to outliers. For example:

- **Decision trees** and **random forests** are relatively unaffected by outliers because they split data based on conditions rather than fitting coefficients.

- **Gradient boosting** models can handle outliers better than linear models.

For models that are sensitive to outliers (like linear regression or k-nearest neighbors), feature scaling methods such as **robust scaling** (which uses the median and IQR) can help reduce the impact of outliers.

Real-World Examples of Handling Missing Data and Outliers

- **Financial Services**: In fraud detection, missing data may occur in transaction records, while outliers (such as unusually large transactions) could signal fraudulent activity. Properly handling missing data ensures a more accurate fraud detection model, while dealing with outliers helps to identify potential fraud cases.

- **Healthcare**: In medical datasets, missing patient information (e.g., missing test results or demographic details) is common. In these cases, imputing missing data with appropriate techniques ensures better disease prediction models. Additionally, outliers in medical records (e.g., unusually high blood pressure readings) may indicate potential errors or rare medical conditions that require special attention.

- **Retail**: In e-commerce, missing customer preferences or outlier purchasing behaviors can distort personalization algorithms. Properly handling these data issues improves recommendation systems and customer segmentation strategies.

Handling missing data and outliers is a fundamental step in data preprocessing for machine learning. Whether it's imputing missing values using advanced techniques like KNN or MICE, or managing outliers through transformations or robust models, addressing these issues ensures that machine learning models are trained on high-quality data. By carefully managing missing data and outliers, you can build more accurate, reliable, and robust models that generalize well to real-world scenarios.

2.4 Feature Engineering: Extracting Meaningful Features

Feature engineering is one of the most critical aspects of building successful machine learning models. It involves creating new input features from existing data to enhance the performance of your model. Essentially, the goal of feature engineering is to extract meaningful features that can help the model better understand the patterns in the data, improving both accuracy and interpretability.

In many cases, a machine learning model is only as good as the features it's trained on. Even with advanced algorithms, poor feature selection or irrelevant features can significantly hurt model performance. In this section, we'll explore what feature engineering is, why it matters, and practical techniques for extracting meaningful features from your data.

What is Feature Engineering?

Feature engineering is the process of transforming raw data into informative and relevant features that better represent the underlying problem for the machine learning model. These new features, or modified versions of existing ones, are often derived from domain knowledge, mathematical transformations, or statistical insights.

The right features can help models make accurate predictions by highlighting the relationships between the data and the target variable. When done correctly, feature engineering can drastically improve the model's performance.

Why is Feature Engineering Important?

Machine learning models don't inherently understand the meaning of data. Instead, they look for patterns within numerical or categorical representations of that data. For example, raw data about a customer's shopping behavior might include timestamps, product IDs, and amounts spent.

While these raw inputs provide information, transforming them into features such as "total spend per visit" or "average number of products bought per visit" can make patterns much easier for the model to capture.

Effective feature engineering improves model accuracy, simplifies the problem, and reduces the need for complex algorithms. It can also help overcome issues such as:

- **Irrelevant Features**: Removing or modifying irrelevant features reduces noise in the model, allowing it to focus on the most important information.

- **Non-linear Relationships**: Transformations, like taking the logarithm or square root, can help capture non-linear relationships between variables.

- **Class Imbalance or Sparse Data**: Feature engineering techniques like grouping or aggregating categories can help deal with sparse or imbalanced data.

Key Feature Engineering Techniques

1. Feature Creation

Feature creation involves generating new features from existing ones. This can be as simple as creating a new column or as complex as combining multiple features based on domain-specific knowledge.

1.1 Polynomial Features

Polynomial features are useful when there are non-linear relationships between the features and the target variable. This technique involves creating new features by raising the original feature values to a power (e.g., $X2X^2X2$, $X3X^3X3$) or by creating interaction terms between features (e.g., $X1*X2X\_1 * X\_2X1*X2$).

For example, if you're predicting house prices and have features for the number of bedrooms and square footage, you might create interaction terms like:

- **Number of bedrooms squared** (Bedrooms2Bedrooms^2Bedrooms2)

- **Square footage times number of bedrooms** (Bedrooms*SquareFootageBedrooms * SquareFootageBedrooms*SquareFootage)

This allows the model to capture more complex relationships that might not be apparent in the raw data.

1.2 Aggregation

Aggregation is commonly used when you have time-based data or data with multiple instances for a single entity (e.g., multiple transactions for one customer). Aggregating these values over a period of time can help create meaningful features, such as:

- **Average spend per customer** over a given time period.

- **Total number of transactions** per customer.

- **Maximum/minimum value** for a specific variable.

For instance, in an e-commerce dataset, creating features like "total items purchased" or "average spend per order" can provide the model with a clearer understanding of customer behavior.

1.3 Date and Time Features

Date and time fields often contain useful information that can be transformed into more meaningful features. Raw timestamps may not be directly useful for machine learning models, but breaking them down into components can provide valuable insights. You can extract features like:

- **Day of the week** (e.g., Monday, Tuesday).

- **Time of day** (morning, afternoon, evening).

- **Month** or **quarter** (e.g., January, Q1).

- **Seasonality** (e.g., Summer, Winter).

For example, in sales forecasting, identifying trends based on the day of the week or season can help models better understand customer patterns.

2. Feature Transformation

Feature transformation modifies the existing data to make it more suitable for model training. This often involves scaling, normalizing, or altering the distribution of features to help the machine learning model work more effectively.

2.1 Log Transformation

Log transformation is commonly used to handle **skewed distributions**. Many real-world datasets, such as income or transaction amounts, are right-skewed, meaning that a small number of values dominate the distribution. By applying a log transformation, you can compress the range of these values and reduce the influence of outliers.

For example:

Xtransformed=logf_0(X+1)X_{transformed} = \log(X + 1)Xtransformed=log(X+1)

(Adding 1 avoids issues with zero values.)

This transformation can be helpful in linear regression, where normally distributed features often result in better model performance.

2.2 Binning or Discretization

Binning involves converting continuous numerical variables into categorical groups or bins. This technique is particularly useful for simplifying complex relationships and making patterns more apparent.

For example, a variable like **age** can be divided into bins like:

- 0–18: Child

- 19–35: Young Adult

- 36–50: Middle-Aged

- 51+: Senior

Binning allows the model to focus on general patterns within each group, rather than treating every unique age value as a separate entity.

2.3 Scaling and Normalization

Scaling and normalization are essential when your dataset contains features with vastly different ranges. For example, one feature might represent income in thousands, while another represents age in years. Machine learning models, especially those based on distance metrics (like k-nearest neighbors or support vector machines), can become biased toward features with larger ranges.

- **Min-Max Scaling**: This method scales the values of each feature between 0 and 1 using the formula:

$$X_{scaled} = \frac{X - X_{min}}{X_{max} - X_{min}}$$

This ensures that all features contribute equally to the model.

- **Z-Score Standardization**: This method standardizes features by subtracting the mean and dividing by the standard deviation:

$$X_{standardized} = \frac{X - \mu}{\sigma}$$

\mu}{\sigma}Xstandardized=σX−μ

This transformation is particularly useful when features are normally distributed and ensures that all features have a mean of 0 and a standard deviation of 1.

3. Handling Categorical Features

Categorical features are often more challenging to work with than numerical ones because most machine learning models require numerical input. Converting categorical data into numerical form while preserving the underlying information is critical.

3.1 One-Hot Encoding

One-hot encoding is one of the most common methods for dealing with categorical features. It converts each category into a separate binary column (1 or 0), with a 1 indicating the presence of that category.

For example, for a "Color" feature with three categories—Red, Blue, and Green—one-hot encoding would create three new columns:

Color	Red	Blue	Green
Red	1	0	0
Blue	0	1	0
Green	0	0	1

One-hot encoding prevents the model from interpreting ordinal relationships between categories (e.g., thinking Red > Blue), which would happen if we used simple numerical labels.

3.2 Label Encoding

Label encoding assigns a unique integer to each category. While this is simpler than one-hot encoding, it can introduce unintended ordinal relationships between categories.

For example:

Color Label

Red 1

Blue 2

Green 3

Label encoding is suitable for ordinal features where the order matters (e.g., ratings like "low," "medium," "high").

4. Feature Selection

Feature selection involves choosing the most relevant features to use in model training. Selecting the right subset of features reduces noise, improves model performance, and decreases computational complexity.

4.1 Correlation Analysis

One of the simplest ways to select features is by examining their correlation with the target variable. Features that have a strong correlation with the target are likely to be more useful for model training. You can use techniques such as **Pearson correlation** for numerical variables or **Chi-square tests** for categorical variables.

4.2 Recursive Feature Elimination (RFE)

RFE is an automated feature selection technique that recursively removes the least important features, based on a machine learning model's performance. It helps identify which features have the most significant impact on the model's predictions.

4.3 Principal Component Analysis (PCA)

PCA is a dimensionality reduction technique that transforms the original features into a smaller set of uncorrelated components while retaining most of the variance in the data. This can help reduce overfitting and improve computational efficiency in high-dimensional datasets.

Feature engineering is a powerful technique for improving machine learning models by transforming raw data into meaningful and informative features. By creating new features, transforming existing ones, and selecting the most relevant variables, you can significantly enhance the performance and interpretability of your models.

Effective feature engineering requires domain knowledge, creativity, and a deep understanding of the data. While it can be time-consuming, the rewards are worth it—better features often lead to more accurate models and better predictions.

2.5 Splitting the Dataset: Training, Validation, and Testing Sets

Splitting a dataset into **training**, **validation**, and **testing** sets is a crucial step in building a reliable machine learning model. This process ensures that the model is trained effectively, validated to prevent overfitting, and tested to evaluate its performance on unseen data. By dividing your dataset properly, you help the model generalize well and avoid common pitfalls such as overfitting or underfitting.

In this section, we'll explore the importance of splitting the dataset, how to divide it effectively, and the role each set plays in the machine learning pipeline.

Why Split the Dataset?

In machine learning, the goal is to develop models that perform well not only on the data they are trained on but also on unseen data. This is known as **generalization**. To achieve this, we need to simulate how the model will perform in real-world scenarios, which means testing it on data it hasn't seen during training. This is where splitting the dataset becomes essential.

Without splitting the dataset:

- The model would be tested on the same data it was trained on, leading to **overfitting**, where the model memorizes the training data but fails to generalize to new data.

- The model's accuracy would be misleading, as it wouldn't account for how the model performs on data it hasn't encountered before.

A proper split enables:

- **Training** the model on a subset of data.

- **Validating** the model to tune its parameters and prevent overfitting.

- **Testing** the model on a completely unseen set to evaluate its performance.

Types of Dataset Splits

Typically, the dataset is divided into three main sets:

1. **Training Set**: Used to train the machine learning model.

2. **Validation Set**: Used to fine-tune model parameters and evaluate its performance during training.

3. **Testing Set**: Used to assess the model's final performance on unseen data after training and tuning.

1. Training Set

The **training set** is the portion of the dataset used to teach the model. The model analyzes the patterns and relationships within this data to build its understanding and learn how to make predictions.

- **Purpose**: The training set is where the actual learning happens. The model adjusts its internal parameters (like weights in neural networks or coefficients in linear regression) based on this data.

- **Size**: The training set is typically the largest portion of the dataset, usually comprising around 60-80% of the total data. The larger the training set, the better the model can learn to recognize patterns.

During training, the model tries to minimize the error (or loss) between its predictions and the actual outcomes by adjusting its internal parameters through optimization techniques like gradient descent.

2. Validation Set

The **validation set** plays a crucial role in **model selection** and **hyperparameter tuning**. It helps to evaluate the model's performance during the training process and ensures that the model isn't overfitting to the training data.

- **Purpose**: The validation set is used to fine-tune the model's hyperparameters (such as learning rate, number of layers, regularization strength, etc.) and to make decisions like early stopping. It provides a way to monitor how well the model generalizes to data that it hasn't directly trained on, but that still comes from the same source as the training data.

- **Size**: Typically, the validation set takes up 10-20% of the total dataset. It should be large enough to provide reliable insights into the model's performance but not so large that it reduces the size of the training set significantly.

- **Hyperparameter Tuning**: Hyperparameters are settings that are not learned by the model but set manually, such as the depth of a decision tree or the learning rate in gradient descent. The validation set helps in choosing the optimal hyperparameters by testing different values and seeing which performs best on the validation set.

- **Early Stopping**: Early stopping is a technique used to prevent overfitting. The model's performance on the validation set is monitored during training, and training is stopped when performance no longer improves. This helps avoid situations where the model becomes too specialized to the training data and begins to overfit.

3. Testing Set

The **testing set** is used only after the model has been trained and validated. It provides a final, unbiased evaluation of the model's performance on unseen data. The key here is that the testing data is never used during training or tuning, making it the true measure of how well the model generalizes to new data.

- **Purpose**: The testing set assesses how well the model generalizes to real-world data that it hasn't seen before. The performance metrics obtained on the testing set (e.g., accuracy, precision, recall, F1 score, etc.) provide an objective measure of the model's quality and robustness.

- **Size**: Like the validation set, the testing set usually comprises 10-20% of the total dataset. It should be kept separate from the training and validation sets to provide an unbiased estimate of performance.

Once the model is tested on this unseen data, no further changes should be made to the model. The testing set serves as a final checkpoint to ensure the model is ready for deployment.

Splitting Strategies

There are different methods for splitting datasets depending on the type and size of the data. The choice of strategy depends on the size of your dataset, whether it's time-dependent, and how much computational power you have.

1. Holdout Method

The **holdout method** is the simplest and most common strategy for splitting the dataset. Here, the data is randomly divided into three sets: training, validation, and testing. The model is trained on the training set, fine-tuned using the validation set, and evaluated on the testing set.

- **Advantages**: Simple and easy to implement. Works well for large datasets where random sampling is representative of the underlying population.

- **Disadvantages**: May not be reliable for small datasets, as random sampling could lead to a non-representative split. Performance can vary based on the specific split.

Example:

- 70% of the data for training,

- 15% for validation,

- 15% for testing.

2. K-Fold Cross-Validation

K-fold cross-validation is a more robust method for training and evaluating models, particularly when the dataset is small. Instead of creating separate validation and testing sets, the data is split into **k** equally sized subsets (or "folds"). The model is trained **k** times, each time using a different fold as the validation set and the remaining folds as the training set.

The final performance is the average of the performance across all folds.

- **Advantages**: More reliable than the holdout method, especially for small datasets. It provides a better estimate of model performance and reduces variance caused by a single split.

- **Disadvantages**: Computationally expensive, as the model is trained and evaluated multiple times.

Example: If you use 5-fold cross-validation, the data is split into 5 subsets. The model is trained 5 times, each time using 4 subsets for training and 1 for validation.

3. Stratified Sampling

In cases where your dataset is **imbalanced** (for example, when one class is much larger than the other, like in fraud detection), it's important to ensure that each split maintains the same distribution of classes as the original dataset. This is where **stratified sampling** comes in.

Stratified sampling ensures that each of the training, validation, and testing sets contains approximately the same proportion of each class. This prevents the model from being biased towards the dominant class and ensures more reliable evaluation metrics.

4. Time Series Splitting

For **time-series data**, random splitting is not appropriate, as it would violate the temporal order of the data. Instead, you should use a **time-based split**, where the data is split chronologically.

In this case, the training set consists of data from earlier time periods, while the validation and testing sets consist of data from later time periods. This approach ensures that the model is evaluated on future data, which reflects real-world scenarios.

Avoiding Data Leakage

Data leakage occurs when information from the testing or validation set accidentally leaks into the training process, causing the model to perform better on the test data than it should. This can happen when features that won't be available during actual predictions are included in the training data.

For example, if you're predicting customer churn and the dataset includes a feature like "has the customer canceled their account?"—including this feature in the training set would give the model an unfair advantage, since it already knows the outcome.

To avoid data leakage:

- Ensure the testing data is completely unseen by the model during training.

- Be cautious about features that are related to the target variable in ways that wouldn't exist in a real-world scenario.

Splitting the dataset into **training, validation,** and **testing sets** is essential for building machine learning models that generalize well to new data. The training set allows the model to learn, the validation set helps tune the model's hyperparameters, and the testing set provides an unbiased evaluation of the model's performance.

Different strategies, such as the holdout method, k-fold cross-validation, and stratified sampling, offer flexibility depending on the dataset and problem. By carefully splitting the data and avoiding data leakage, you ensure that your machine learning model is robust, reliable, and ready for real-world deployment.

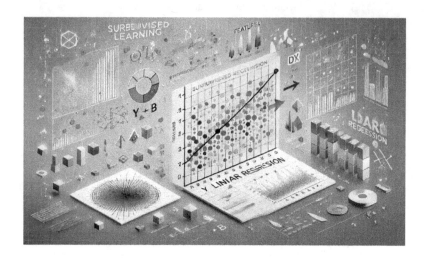

Chapter 3: Supervised Learning Algorithms

3.1 Linear Regression: Theory and Implementation

Linear regression is one of the most fundamental and widely used machine learning algorithms for predictive modeling. It's a simple, interpretable model that aims to establish a relationship between a dependent variable (the target) and one or more independent variables (the features). This method assumes that the relationship between the variables is linear, meaning that changes in the independent variables will result in proportional changes in the dependent variable.

What is Linear Regression?

Linear regression attempts to model the relationship between two variables by fitting a straight line to the data. This line, also known as the regression line, represents the predicted values of the dependent variable based on given values of the independent variables.

The basic formula for linear regression is:

$$y = \beta_0 + \beta_1 x_1 + \beta_2 x_2 + \ldots + \beta_n x_n + \varepsilon$$

Where:

- y is the dependent variable (the value we want to predict),

- x_1, x_2, ... x_n are the independent variables (the input features),

- β_0 is the intercept, representing the value of y when all x values are zero,

- β_1, β_2, ... β_n are the coefficients (weights) associated with each independent variable,

- ε represents the error term, accounting for the difference between the predicted and actual values of y.

Simply put, linear regression tries to find the best-fit line that minimizes the error between the predicted values and the actual values.

Types of Linear Regression

1. **Simple Linear Regression**: This involves one independent variable and one dependent variable. The relationship is represented by a straight line in a two-dimensional space.

Example: Predicting house prices based solely on the size of the house.

2. **Multiple Linear Regression**: This involves two or more independent variables used to predict the dependent variable. The relationship is represented in an n-dimensional space, where n is the number of features.

Example: Predicting house prices based on the size of the house, number of bedrooms, and location.

Assumptions of Linear Regression

Linear regression works well when certain assumptions are met. These assumptions include:

1. **Linearity**: The relationship between the independent and dependent variables is linear, meaning that changes in the target variable are proportional to changes in the features.

2. **Independence**: Observations should be independent of each other. This means that the value of one observation should not influence another.

3. **Homoscedasticity**: The residuals (or errors) should have constant variance across all levels of the independent variables.

4. **Normality**: The residuals of the model (the differences between the predicted and actual values) should follow a normal distribution.

5. **No Multicollinearity**: In multiple linear regression, the independent variables should not be highly correlated with each other. High correlation between features can make it difficult for the model to distinguish the individual effect of each variable.

The Cost Function

To fit the best possible regression line to the data, linear regression minimizes a **cost function** that quantifies the error in the model's predictions. The most commonly used cost function in linear regression is the **Mean Squared Error (MSE)**, which measures the average squared difference between the actual values and the predicted values:

$$\text{MSE} = (1/m) \, \Sigma \, (y_i - \hat{y}_i)^2$$

Where:

- y_i represents the actual value,

- $\hat{y}_i$ represents the predicted value,

- m is the total number of data points.

The goal of the linear regression algorithm is to minimize the MSE by adjusting the values of the coefficients (β_1, β_2, ..., β_n) so that the regression line fits the data as closely as possible.

Gradient Descent

One of the most popular methods for minimizing the cost function is **gradient descent**. Gradient descent is an iterative optimization algorithm that adjusts the model's coefficients in the direction that reduces the MSE.

Here's how gradient descent works:

1. **Initialization**: Start with random values for the coefficients.

2. **Compute Predictions**: Use the current coefficients to calculate the predicted values for the training data.

3. **Calculate Error**: Compute the MSE by comparing the predicted values with the actual values.

4. **Update Coefficients**: Adjust the coefficients in the direction that reduces the error. The size of each

adjustment is controlled by a parameter called the **learning rate**.

The update rule for each coefficient is:

$$\beta_j = \beta_j - \alpha \ (\partial / \partial \beta_j \ \mathbf{MSE})$$

Where:

- β_j is the coefficient being updated,

- α is the learning rate, controlling the step size for each iteration.

This process is repeated until the cost function converges, meaning the change in MSE between iterations becomes negligible.

Implementation of Linear Regression

While we won't include coding in this explanation, let's briefly outline the steps for implementing linear regression in a machine learning environment:

1. **Import Libraries**: You would typically import libraries like NumPy for numerical operations, pandas for data manipulation, and scikit-learn for the machine learning model.

2. **Create a Dataset**: Prepare your dataset with features and target values, such as house size and house price.

3. **Split the Data**: Divide the data into training and test sets. This allows the model to learn from one portion of the data and be evaluated on another portion that it hasn't seen.

4. **Train the Model**: Using a linear regression algorithm, fit the model on the training data to adjust the coefficients and minimize the error.

5. **Make Predictions**: Once the model is trained, use it to make predictions on the test data.

6. **Evaluate the Model**: After predictions are made, calculate metrics like Mean Squared Error (MSE) to determine how well the model performs on the test data.

7. **Visualize Results**: If you're working with simple linear regression, you can visualize the regression line and the actual vs predicted data points on a graph to see how well the model fits.

Multiple Linear Regression Example

Multiple linear regression involves using more than one feature to predict the target variable. For instance, to predict house prices, you could include variables like the size of the house, number of bedrooms, and distance from the city center.

The steps for multiple linear regression are similar to simple linear regression, but you'll be working with more than one independent variable. After training the model, you'll get multiple coefficients corresponding to each feature, which can provide insights into the importance of each feature in making predictions.

Linear regression is a simple yet powerful tool for modeling relationships between variables. It works best when there is a clear linear relationship between the features and the target variable. By ensuring that assumptions like linearity and independence are met, you can achieve accurate predictions using linear regression.

While it may seem basic compared to more complex machine learning models, linear regression is a great starting point and often provides valuable insights into how features relate to a target. Additionally, its simplicity and interpretability make it a popular choice in various industries, from finance to real estate and beyond.

Once trained and evaluated, the model can be deployed to make predictions, and further tuning can be performed to improve accuracy. Linear regression remains one of the most widely used algorithms due to its ease of use and effectiveness.

3.2 Logistic Regression for Classification Problems

Logistic regression is a widely used machine learning algorithm designed for **classification problems**, particularly when the target variable is binary (i.e., it can take only two values such as 0 or 1, True or False, Yes or No). Despite its name, logistic regression is used for classification rather than regression tasks. Its simplicity, interpretability, and efficiency make it a go-to model for solving binary classification problems.

What is Logistic Regression?

Logistic regression is a predictive analysis algorithm based on the concept of probability. While **linear regression** predicts continuous numerical values, logistic regression predicts the probability of a particular class or event, such as whether a customer will buy a product (yes/no) or whether an email is spam (spam/not spam). Logistic regression outputs a probability value that lies between 0 and 1, which is then converted into a binary outcome.

At its core, logistic regression models the relationship between a dependent binary variable and one or more independent variables by using a logistic function (also known as the sigmoid function). The logistic function maps the output of the linear equation (which can range from negative infinity to positive infinity) to a value between 0 and 1.

The basic formula for logistic regression is:

$$P(y = 1 \mid x) = 1 / (1 + e^{-(\beta_0 + \beta_1 x_1 + \beta_2 x_2 + \ldots + \beta_n x_n)})$$

Where:

- $P(y = 1 \mid x)$ is the probability that the target variable y equals 1 (i.e., the event happens) given the features x_1, x_2, ..., x_n.

- β_0 is the intercept (the bias term).

- β_1, β_2, ..., β_n are the coefficients (weights) corresponding to each feature.

- e is the base of the natural logarithm.

This function outputs a probability between 0 and 1, which can then be used to predict the class by applying a threshold (usually 0.5). If the probability is greater than 0.5, the predicted class is 1 (positive class); otherwise, it is 0 (negative class).

The Sigmoid (Logistic) Function

The sigmoid function is the heart of logistic regression. It transforms the linear combination of the input features into a value between 0 and 1, which represents the probability of belonging to one of the two classes.

The sigmoid function is given by:

$$f(z) = 1 / (1 + e^{(-z)})$$

Where:

- **z** is the output of the linear equation $(\beta_0 + \beta_1 x_1 + \beta_2 x_2 + \ldots + \beta_n x_n)$.

The sigmoid function is an S-shaped curve that maps any real-valued number to a value between 0 and 1. When the output of the sigmoid function is closer to 1, it means the model is more confident that the instance belongs to the positive class. Conversely, when the output is closer to 0, the model is more confident that the instance belongs to the negative class.

Logistic Regression Assumptions

Similar to linear regression, logistic regression comes with a set of assumptions that must be met to ensure the model works effectively:

1. **Binary Output**: Logistic regression is primarily designed for binary classification. If you have more than two classes, you would need to use extensions like multinomial logistic regression.

2. **Independence of Observations**: The observations in the dataset should be independent of each other.

3. **Linearity of Features and Log Odds**: Logistic regression assumes that the independent variables are linearly related to the log odds (the logarithm of the probability that the outcome is 1).

4. **Little or No Multicollinearity**: The independent variables should not be highly correlated with each other, as multicollinearity can make it difficult for the model to distinguish between the effects of different variables.

5. **Large Sample Size**: Logistic regression works best with large datasets, as small datasets may lead to overfitting and poor generalization.

Cost Function: Log Loss

In logistic regression, the model is trained to minimize a cost function called **log loss** (also known as binary cross-entropy). Log loss measures how well the model's predicted probabilities match the actual binary labels. The goal is to find the values of the coefficients (β_0, β_1, ..., β_n) that minimize the log loss.

The formula for log loss is:

Log Loss $= -(1/m) \Sigma [y_i \log(p_i) + (1 - y_i) \log(1 - p_i)]$

Where:

- **m** is the number of observations.

- y_i is the actual class label for the i-th observation.

- p_i is the predicted probability that y_i equals 1 (the positive class).

Log loss penalizes both overconfident and incorrect predictions, making it a suitable cost function for probabilistic classifiers like logistic regression.

Decision Boundary

In logistic regression, the **decision boundary** is the threshold at which we classify the predicted probability as either 0 or 1. By default, this threshold is set at 0.5, meaning:

- If the predicted probability $P(y = 1 \mid x)$ is greater than 0.5, the model predicts $y = 1$ (positive class).

- If the predicted probability $P(y = 1 \mid x)$ is less than 0.5, the model predicts $y = 0$ (negative class).

The decision boundary is linear, similar to the line in linear regression. However, instead of predicting continuous values, logistic regression uses this boundary to separate the data into different classes.

Applications of Logistic Regression

Logistic regression is used in various domains for binary classification tasks. Some common applications include:

1. **Spam Detection**: Logistic regression is often used to classify emails as spam (1) or not spam (0) based on features like word frequency, sender information, and formatting.

2. **Medical Diagnosis**: Logistic regression can be applied to predict the likelihood of a patient having a certain disease (1 = has disease, 0 = no disease) based on medical tests and patient history.

3. **Credit Scoring**: Financial institutions use logistic regression to determine whether a loan applicant is likely to default (1 = default, 0 = no default) based on factors like income, credit score, and debt.

4. **Customer Churn Prediction**: Logistic regression is used to predict whether a customer will stay (0) or leave (1) based on their transaction history, engagement metrics, and interaction patterns with a company.

5. **Binary Sentiment Analysis**: In text analysis, logistic regression can classify whether a given review or sentence is positive (1) or negative (0).

Evaluating Logistic Regression Models

Once the logistic regression model is trained, it's important to evaluate its performance. The following metrics are commonly used to assess logistic regression models:

1. **Accuracy**: Accuracy measures the proportion of correctly classified instances. However, accuracy can be misleading in imbalanced datasets, where one class dominates the other.

2. **Precision and Recall**: Precision measures the proportion of positive predictions that are correct, while recall measures the proportion of actual positives that were identified correctly. Both are crucial metrics for imbalanced classification problems.

3. **F1 Score**: The F1 score is the harmonic mean of precision and recall. It balances the trade-off between the two and is particularly useful when the dataset is imbalanced.

4. **ROC Curve and AUC**: The **Receiver Operating Characteristic (ROC)** curve shows the trade-off between the true positive rate (recall) and the false positive rate. The **Area Under the Curve (AUC)** measures the overall ability of the model to discriminate between the positive and negative classes.

5. **Confusion Matrix**: A confusion matrix provides a summary of the prediction results, showing the counts of true positives, true negatives, false positives, and false negatives.

Regularization in Logistic Regression

In some cases, logistic regression can overfit the training data, especially when there are many features. To prevent overfitting, regularization techniques such as **L2 regularization** (also known as Ridge regularization) can be applied.

Regularization adds a penalty to the cost function for large coefficient values, encouraging the model to find simpler relationships in the data. In logistic regression, regularization is controlled by a parameter called **lambda (λ)**, which determines the strength of the penalty. A larger λ applies a stronger penalty, while a smaller λ applies a weaker one.

Logistic regression is a powerful and widely used classification algorithm that is both simple and efficient. It's particularly effective when dealing with binary classification problems, such as spam detection, medical diagnosis, and customer churn prediction. Logistic regression's ability to provide probabilistic outputs makes it an excellent choice for tasks where understanding the probability of an outcome is important.

By understanding its assumptions, cost function, and how to evaluate the model using metrics like accuracy, precision, and recall, logistic regression can be applied effectively across various domains. Furthermore, with regularization techniques, logistic regression can handle large datasets and complex relationships without overfitting.

Whether you're starting with machine learning or need a robust solution for classification problems, logistic regression remains a reliable and interpretable option.

3.3 Decision Trees and Random Forests

Decision Trees and Random Forests are popular and powerful machine learning algorithms used for both classification and regression tasks. While Decision Trees offer a simple, visual method of decision-making, Random Forests provide more robustness and accuracy by using an ensemble of Decision Trees. These models are widely used in real-world applications, such as credit scoring, fraud detection, and customer segmentation.

Decision Trees: What Are They?

A **Decision Tree** is a supervised machine learning algorithm that splits data into different branches based on decision rules derived from the input features. The goal of a Decision Tree is to learn the decision rules that predict the target variable as accurately as possible. The tree is made up of **nodes** (decision points), **branches** (outcomes of the decision), and **leaves** (final predictions or outcomes).

Each internal node represents a test on a feature (e.g., is income greater than $50,000?), each branch represents the outcome of the test (e.g., yes or no), and each leaf node represents the final prediction (e.g., class or value). The decision-making process flows from the root node to the leaves.

How Decision Trees Work

1. **Root Node:** The root node is the starting point of the tree, where the data is initially split based on the feature that provides the highest information gain or the best split. The choice of the first feature is crucial because it sets the stage for the rest of the tree.

2. **Splitting:** At each node, the data is divided into subsets based on a feature. The goal is to split the data in a way

that improves the homogeneity of the target variable within the resulting groups. This process continues recursively for each subset of the data.

3. **Decision Rules**: At each node, the algorithm chooses the best feature to split the data by measuring criteria such as **Gini impurity** or **information gain**. These criteria help the algorithm determine which feature most effectively separates the data based on the target variable.

4. **Leaf Nodes**: When the data can no longer be split or meets a stopping condition (such as reaching a maximum depth or having only one class left), the algorithm assigns a prediction to the leaf node. For classification problems, the leaf node predicts the most common class. For regression, it predicts the average value of the target.

Criteria for Splitting the Data

Decision Trees use different criteria to decide where to split the data:

1. **Gini Impurity**: Used in classification tasks, Gini impurity measures the likelihood of incorrectly classifying a randomly chosen element from the dataset. The goal is to minimize the Gini impurity at each split.

Gini Impurity formula: Gini $= 1 - \Sigma\ (p_i)^2$, where p_i is the probability of an element belonging to a particular class.

2. **Information Gain**: This is based on **entropy**, a measure of randomness in the data. Information gain represents the reduction in entropy after the dataset is split on an attribute. The feature that provides the highest information gain is chosen for splitting.

Information Gain formula: Information Gain = Entropy (before split) - Entropy (after split)

3. **Mean Squared Error (MSE)**: In regression tasks, Decision Trees minimize MSE, which measures the average squared difference between the actual and predicted values. The goal is to split the data in a way that minimizes the MSE of the resulting groups.

Advantages of Decision Trees

1. **Interpretability**: Decision Trees are easy to understand and interpret, as the model can be visualized and explained in terms of decision rules.

2. **Non-linear Relationships**: Decision Trees can model non-linear relationships between the features and the target variable without requiring feature transformation.

3. **Handles Both Categorical and Numerical Data**: Decision Trees can work with both types of data, making them versatile.

4. **No Need for Feature Scaling**: Decision Trees do not require the data to be normalized or standardized.

Disadvantages of Decision Trees

1. **Overfitting**: Decision Trees are prone to overfitting, especially when they grow deep. Overfitting occurs when the model becomes too complex and starts capturing noise in the data rather than the actual patterns.

2. **Instability**: Small changes in the data can result in entirely different trees, making the model unstable.

3. **Bias**: Decision Trees can be biased towards features with many levels or categories, which can dominate the splitting process.

Random Forests: What Are They?

A **Random Forest** is an ensemble learning algorithm that combines multiple Decision Trees to create a more powerful and accurate model. The key idea behind Random Forests is to build multiple Decision Trees on different subsets of the data and average their predictions. By averaging the results of many trees, Random Forests reduce the risk of overfitting and improve generalization.

Each Decision Tree in a Random Forest is trained on a random subset of the data, and at each split, the algorithm only considers a random subset of the features. This randomness reduces the correlation between the trees, ensuring that the individual trees make different errors. The final prediction is made by aggregating the predictions of all the trees, either by majority voting (for classification) or averaging (for regression).

How Random Forests Work

1. **Bootstrap Aggregation (Bagging)**: Random Forests use a technique called **bagging**, where multiple subsets of the original data are created by sampling with replacement. Each Decision Tree in the Random Forest is trained on a different subset of the data. This ensures diversity among the trees and reduces the likelihood of overfitting.

2. **Random Subset of Features**: At each node, Random Forests consider only a random subset of the features to decide the best split. This randomness reduces the

correlation between trees and helps the model generalize better.

3. **Voting or Averaging**: For classification problems, each Decision Tree in the forest predicts a class, and the final prediction is made by taking a majority vote. For regression tasks, the predictions of all the trees are averaged to produce the final result.

Advantages of Random Forests

1. **Reduced Overfitting**: Random Forests reduce the problem of overfitting, which is common with single Decision Trees, by averaging the results of multiple trees.

2. **Improved Accuracy**: By combining the results of many Decision Trees, Random Forests typically achieve higher accuracy than individual trees.

3. **Handles Missing Data**: Random Forests can handle missing data by averaging over the predictions of trees that don't require the missing features for their predictions.

4. **Feature Importance**: Random Forests provide a measure of feature importance, helping you understand which features contribute most to the prediction.

5. **Versatility**: Random Forests work well for both classification and regression tasks and can handle high-dimensional data effectively.

Disadvantages of Random Forests

1. **Complexity**: Random Forests are more complex than single Decision Trees and require more computational resources, particularly for large datasets.

2. **Lack of Interpretability**: While individual Decision Trees are easy to interpret, the ensemble of many trees in a Random Forest makes the model less interpretable.

3. **Training Time**: Random Forests require more time to train compared to single Decision Trees, especially as the number of trees increases.

Applications of Decision Trees and Random Forests

1. **Credit Scoring**: Both Decision Trees and Random Forests are commonly used in the financial industry to assess credit risk by predicting whether a borrower will default on a loan.

2. **Fraud Detection**: Random Forests are effective in identifying fraudulent transactions by analyzing patterns in transaction data.

3. **Customer Segmentation**: Businesses use Decision Trees and Random Forests to segment customers based on their behavior, purchase history, and demographics.

4. **Medical Diagnosis**: In healthcare, Random Forests are used to predict the likelihood of a disease based on patient data and medical history.

5. **Recommendation Systems**: E-commerce platforms use these algorithms to recommend products to users based on their browsing and purchase behavior.

Key Differences Between Decision Trees and Random Forests

1. **Overfitting**: Decision Trees are prone to overfitting, especially with deep trees, whereas Random Forests

mitigate overfitting by averaging the results of multiple trees.

2. **Accuracy**: Random Forests generally provide more accurate predictions than individual Decision Trees, especially in complex tasks.

3. **Interpretability**: Decision Trees are more interpretable and easier to explain, whereas Random Forests, being an ensemble of many trees, lose interpretability.

4. **Stability**: Random Forests are more stable and less sensitive to small changes in the dataset, while Decision Trees can be highly sensitive to the specific data they are trained on.

Both Decision Trees and Random Forests are powerful machine learning algorithms, each with its strengths and weaknesses. **Decision Trees** are simple to understand, easy to visualize, and highly interpretable, making them a great choice for smaller datasets or when transparency is important. However, they can overfit easily and are sensitive to small changes in the data.

On the other hand, **Random Forests** provide better accuracy and robustness by aggregating multiple Decision Trees, making them ideal for large and complex datasets. While they are less interpretable than single Decision Trees, they offer a more stable and generalizable model.

In practice, if you need a simple, interpretable model and overfitting isn't a major concern, a Decision Tree might be sufficient. But if you require higher accuracy, robustness, and reduced risk of overfitting, Random Forests are typically the better choice.

3.4 Support Vector Machines: Margin-Based Classification

Support Vector Machines (SVMs) are powerful supervised learning algorithms used primarily for classification tasks, though they can also be applied to regression. SVMs are well-known for their ability to handle both linear and non-linear classification problems. They work by finding the best decision boundary, or **hyperplane**, that separates different classes in the dataset while maximizing the margin between them. The concept of margin is what makes SVM unique—it focuses on creating the largest possible distance between data points of different classes, which leads to better generalization.

What is a Support Vector Machine?

A Support Vector Machine is a classification algorithm that seeks to find the optimal hyperplane that separates the data points into different classes. The **hyperplane** is a decision boundary that divides the space into two (or more) classes. For binary classification, SVM finds the hyperplane that best separates the two classes by maximizing the margin between the nearest data points of each class. These nearest points are called **support vectors**, and they play a critical role in defining the hyperplane.

In a two-dimensional space, a hyperplane is a straight line, while in higher dimensions, it becomes a flat, linear surface. The goal of SVM is to identify the hyperplane that not only separates the classes but does so with the maximum margin between them. This margin is the distance between the hyperplane and the nearest data points from either class, and the larger the margin, the better the model generalizes to unseen data.

How Support Vector Machines Work

1. **Hyperplane**: In SVM, the hyperplane is the decision boundary that separates the classes. There can be many hyperplanes that separate the data, but the optimal hyperplane is the one that maximizes the margin between the two classes.

2. **Support Vectors**: The data points that are closest to the hyperplane are called **support vectors**. These points are critical because the position of the hyperplane depends on them. The rest of the points that are farther from the hyperplane do not influence its position.

3. **Margin**: The **margin** is the distance between the hyperplane and the nearest data points (the support vectors). SVM attempts to maximize this margin, as a larger margin reduces the risk of misclassification and improves the model's ability to generalize to new data.

The basic idea behind SVM is to minimize classification error by finding the hyperplane that gives the maximum margin between the two classes.

Linear SVM

In **linear SVM**, the data is linearly separable, meaning that a straight hyperplane can divide the classes perfectly. The goal of the SVM algorithm is to find the optimal hyperplane that separates the classes while maximizing the margin.

For a binary classification problem, the hyperplane can be defined by the equation:

$$\mathbf{w} \cdot \mathbf{x} + b = 0$$

Where:

- **w** is the weight vector (perpendicular to the hyperplane),

- **x** is the input feature vector,

- **b** is the bias term.

The decision rule for classifying a new data point is based on which side of the hyperplane it falls. If the result of $\mathbf{w} \cdot \mathbf{x} + \mathbf{b}$ is positive, the point is classified into one class (e.g., class 1), and if it is negative, it is classified into the other class (e.g., class 0).

Non-Linear SVM and the Kernel Trick

Not all data is linearly separable. For complex datasets where the classes cannot be separated by a straight line (or hyperplane), SVM uses a technique called the **kernel trick**. The kernel trick enables SVM to operate in a **higher-dimensional space** where the data becomes linearly separable.

The kernel trick works by transforming the original input space into a higher-dimensional feature space using a kernel function. Instead of manually adding new dimensions, the kernel function does this implicitly, allowing the algorithm to create more complex decision boundaries.

There are several commonly used kernel functions:

1. **Linear Kernel**: Suitable for linearly separable data. The linear kernel is equivalent to the regular linear SVM.

2. **Polynomial Kernel**: Allows for more complex relationships by adding polynomial terms. This kernel is useful when the relationship between the features and the target variable is non-linear.

3. **Radial Basis Function (RBF) Kernel**: The most commonly used kernel, it maps the data into a higher-dimensional space using radial basis functions. It is particularly effective when the decision boundary is highly non-linear.

4. **Sigmoid Kernel**: This kernel behaves like a neural network activation function and is sometimes used for specific non-linear problems.

The choice of the kernel depends on the problem and the distribution of the data. For most cases, the **RBF kernel** is a good starting point when the data is not linearly separable.

The Objective: Maximizing the Margin

The primary objective of SVM is to maximize the margin between the hyperplane and the support vectors. The larger the margin, the better the SVM is at generalizing to new, unseen data. This leads to a model that performs well not only on the training data but also on the test data.

The optimization problem for SVM is to minimize the following:

Minimize $(1/2) \, ||w||^2$ subject to $y_i \, (w \cdot x_i + b) \geq 1$ for all i

Where:

- $||w||$ represents the norm of the weight vector (to minimize the margin).

- y_i is the class label for the i-th training example (either +1 or -1).

- x_i is the feature vector for the i-th training example.

This formulation is called a **convex optimization problem** and can be solved efficiently using quadratic programming techniques.

Soft Margin SVM

In real-world datasets, perfect separation of classes is often not possible, especially when there is noise or overlapping data. To address this, SVM introduces the concept of a **soft margin**, which allows some misclassification of data points while still trying to maximize the margin.

The **soft margin SVM** introduces a penalty for misclassified points. The degree to which misclassified points are tolerated is controlled by a parameter called **C**. The **C parameter** balances the trade-off between maximizing the margin and minimizing classification errors:

- **Low C value**: Allows more misclassifications to increase the margin size, leading to a more generalizable model.

- **High C value**: Penalizes misclassifications more heavily, leading to a smaller margin and potentially overfitting the training data.

The soft margin approach enables SVM to handle non-separable data while still achieving good generalization.

Advantages of Support Vector Machines

1. **Effective in High-Dimensional Spaces**: SVM works well in situations where the number of features is greater than the number of data points, making it ideal for high-dimensional datasets such as text classification or gene expression data.

2. **Handles Non-Linear Relationships**: By using the kernel trick, SVM can model non-linear relationships

between features and the target variable, making it more flexible than linear models.

3. **Robust to Overfitting**: SVM, particularly with the use of soft margins and regularization (parameter **C**), can handle noise and avoid overfitting to the training data.

4. **Versatile for Classification and Regression**: While mainly used for classification, SVM can also be adapted for regression tasks (known as **Support Vector Regression**).

5. **Works Well with Small to Medium-Sized Datasets**: SVM is particularly effective when the dataset is not very large, yet has many features.

Disadvantages of Support Vector Machines

1. **Computationally Expensive**: SVM can be slow, particularly for large datasets, as the training process involves solving a quadratic optimization problem.

2. **Difficult to Interpret**: While SVMs can produce accurate models, they are not as interpretable as simpler models like decision trees or logistic regression, especially when using non-linear kernels.

3. **Choice of Kernel**: The performance of SVM is highly dependent on the choice of the kernel function. Finding the right kernel and tuning hyperparameters like **C** and the kernel coefficient (for the RBF kernel) can be challenging.

4. **Memory-Intensive**: Since SVM relies on support vectors, it can become memory-intensive when dealing with large datasets, as all support vectors must be stored in memory.

Applications of Support Vector Machines

1. **Text Classification:** SVM is commonly used in natural language processing tasks, such as spam detection and sentiment analysis, where the input data is high-dimensional.

2. **Image Recognition:** SVMs are used in image classification tasks, including handwritten digit recognition and object detection.

3. **Bioinformatics:** SVM is widely used in gene expression analysis and protein classification, where datasets are often high-dimensional and complex.

4. **Financial Forecasting:** In the finance sector, SVM can be used to predict stock prices, detect fraud, and assess risk.

5. **Handwriting Recognition:** SVM has been successfully used to classify handwritten characters by analyzing pixel intensity.

Evaluating the Performance of SVM

To assess the performance of an SVM model, common evaluation metrics include:

1. **Accuracy:** The proportion of correctly classified instances. However, accuracy alone can be misleading in imbalanced datasets.

2. **Precision and Recall:** Precision measures the proportion of positive predictions that are correct, while recall measures the proportion of actual positives that are identified correctly.

3. **F1 Score:** The harmonic mean of precision and recall, which balances the trade-off between them.

4. **ROC Curve and AUC:** The **Receiver Operating Characteristic (ROC)** curve plots the true positive rate against the false positive rate. The **Area Under the Curve (AUC)** measures the overall ability of the model to discriminate between classes.

Support Vector Machines are a powerful tool for both linear and non-linear classification problems. By focusing on maximizing the margin between classes and using techniques like the kernel trick, SVM achieves excellent performance even in complex datasets. The ability to handle high-dimensional data, combined with robust generalization properties, makes SVM a valuable algorithm in fields like text classification, image recognition, and bioinformatics.

Although SVM can be computationally expensive and harder to interpret than some other models, it remains a popular and highly effective method for a wide range of machine learning tasks. When properly tuned, SVM can deliver high accuracy and robust predictions, particularly in problems where data is not linearly separable.

3.5 k-Nearest Neighbors: A Simple but Powerful Algorithm

k-Nearest Neighbors (k-NN) is one of the simplest yet highly effective machine learning algorithms used for both classification and regression tasks. It's a **lazy learning algorithm**, meaning it doesn't explicitly build a model during training. Instead, it memorizes the training data and makes predictions based on the similarity between new data points and the stored examples. The algorithm classifies new instances by considering the **k** closest neighbors (data points) in the training set and making a decision based on the majority class or average value of these neighbors.

The simplicity of k-NN lies in the fact that it doesn't involve complex training processes, but it can still perform remarkably well, especially for small to medium-sized datasets.

How k-Nearest Neighbors Works

The basic idea behind k-NN is that similar points are likely to have similar outputs. Therefore, to classify or predict the outcome for a new data point, k-NN looks at the **k** nearest points (neighbors) in the training data and uses their labels or values to determine the outcome for the new point.

The steps for k-NN are as follows:

1. **Choose k**: Select the number of neighbors (k) to consider.

2. **Calculate Distance**: Compute the distance between the new data point and all the training data points. The most commonly used distance metric is **Euclidean distance**, but other metrics like **Manhattan distance** or **Minkowski distance** can also be used.

3. **Find Nearest Neighbors**: Identify the k closest training points to the new data point based on the calculated distances.

4. **Vote or Average**: For classification tasks, the majority class of the nearest neighbors is used to classify the new data point. For regression tasks, the average value of the k neighbors is used to make a prediction.

Euclidean Distance Formula

For two points (x_1, y_1) and (x_2, y_2) in two-dimensional space, the

Euclidean distance is calculated as:

$$\text{Distance} = \sqrt{(x_2 - x_1)^2 + (y_2 - y_1)^2}$$

In higher dimensions, the formula generalizes to:

$$\text{Distance} = \sqrt{\Sigma \, (x_i - y_i)^2}$$

This metric gives the straight-line distance between two points in a multidimensional space, which is used to determine the similarity between data points.

Choosing the Value of k

The parameter **k** is critical in determining the performance of the k-NN algorithm. Choosing the right value of k can significantly affect the model's accuracy and ability to generalize.

1. **Small k**: When k is small (e.g., k = 1 or 2), the model can be highly sensitive to noise in the data because the prediction is based on very few neighbors. This can lead to **overfitting**, where the model fits the training data too closely but fails to generalize well to new data.

2. **Large k**: When k is large, the model becomes more robust to noise, as it averages over more neighbors. However, if k is too large, the model may become too simplistic, leading to **underfitting** because it considers neighbors that are farther away and less relevant to the new data point.

A common approach to choosing k is to experiment with different values and use cross-validation to find the value that gives the best performance. Typically, an odd value of k is chosen for binary classification to avoid ties.

Classification with k-NN

In classification tasks, k-NN assigns a class label to a new data point based on the **majority class** of its k nearest neighbors. If most of the nearest neighbors belong to class A, the new data point will be classified as class A.

For example, if k = 3 and the three nearest neighbors are labeled as **A**, **A**, and **B**, then the algorithm will classify the new point as **A** because the majority class is **A**.

Regression with k-NN

In regression tasks, k-NN predicts the outcome for a new data point by calculating the **average value** of the k nearest neighbors. The algorithm takes the numerical target values of the neighbors and computes their mean to predict the output for the new data point.

For example, if k = 3 and the nearest neighbors have target values of 10, 15, and 20, the predicted value for the new point will be:

Prediction = (10 + 15 + 20) / 3 = 15

Advantages of k-Nearest Neighbors

1. **Simplicity**: k-NN is intuitive and easy to understand, requiring no explicit training phase. The algorithm simply stores the training data and makes predictions based on similarity.

2. **Flexibility**: k-NN can handle both classification and regression tasks, making it a versatile algorithm.

3. **No Training Time**: Unlike other algorithms that require a training phase, k-NN has no explicit training time. The algorithm starts making predictions as soon as the dataset is loaded.

4. **Non-parametric**: k-NN is a non-parametric algorithm, meaning it doesn't make assumptions about the underlying distribution of the data. This makes it useful for problems where the relationship between features and target is complex.

5. **Handles Non-Linear Relationships**: Since k-NN is based on proximity in feature space, it naturally captures non-linear relationships between the input features and the target variable.

Disadvantages of k-Nearest Neighbors

1. **Computationally Expensive**: Since k-NN involves calculating the distance between the new data point and all points in the training data, it can be computationally expensive, especially for large datasets. The time complexity grows linearly with the number of data points.

2. **Memory-Intensive**: k-NN requires storing the entire training dataset, which can be memory-intensive for large datasets.

3. **Sensitive to Feature Scaling**: k-NN is sensitive to the scale of the input features because distance metrics like Euclidean distance rely on the absolute values of features. If the features are on different scales, it can lead to poor performance. Therefore, it is essential to standardize or normalize the features before applying k-NN.

4. **Curse of Dimensionality**: As the number of features (dimensions) increases, the distances between points become less informative, making it harder for the algorithm to find meaningful nearest neighbors. This is known as the **curse of dimensionality**, and it can

degrade the performance of k-NN in high-dimensional datasets.

5. **Imbalanced Data**: k-NN struggles with imbalanced datasets where one class is much larger than the other. In such cases, the algorithm may be biased towards the majority class.

Applications of k-Nearest Neighbors

1. **Recommendation Systems**: k-NN is often used in recommendation systems to suggest products or content based on the similarity between users' preferences or behaviors.

2. **Pattern Recognition**: k-NN is applied in image and speech recognition tasks where the goal is to classify patterns based on their similarity to known examples.

3. **Anomaly Detection**: k-NN can be used to detect anomalies in data by identifying points that are far away from the majority of other points, making them potential outliers.

4. **Medical Diagnosis**: k-NN is used in medical applications to classify diseases or predict patient outcomes based on past medical data, comparing new patients to similar past cases.

5. **Text Classification**: In natural language processing, k-NN is used to classify documents or pieces of text into categories based on their similarity to previously classified texts.

Improving k-Nearest Neighbors Performance

There are several ways to improve the performance of the k-NN algorithm:

1. **Feature Scaling**: Since k-NN relies on distance metrics, it is important to standardize or normalize the input features so that they are on a comparable scale. Without scaling, features with larger ranges can dominate the distance calculation.

2. **Dimensionality Reduction**: To address the curse of dimensionality, techniques like **Principal Component Analysis (PCA)** or **feature selection** can be used to reduce the number of input features while preserving the most important information.

3. **Distance Metrics**: While Euclidean distance is commonly used, different distance metrics may work better for different types of data. Alternatives include **Manhattan distance** (absolute distance) and **Minkowski distance** (a generalization of Euclidean and Manhattan distances). Experimenting with different metrics can improve performance.

4. **Weighted k-NN**: In some cases, it's beneficial to give more weight to closer neighbors when making predictions. **Weighted k-NN** assigns higher weights to closer neighbors, making their influence stronger on the final prediction.

5. **Cross-Validation**: Using cross-validation to tune the value of **k** helps ensure that the model generalizes well to new data and avoids overfitting or underfitting.

k-Nearest Neighbors (k-NN) is a simple, intuitive algorithm that works well for both classification and regression tasks. Despite its simplicity, k-NN can be highly effective in a variety of applications, including recommendation systems, pattern recognition, and medical diagnosis. The algorithm's non-parametric nature allows it to handle complex data relationships without making assumptions about the underlying distribution.

However, k-NN has limitations, particularly when dealing with large, high-dimensional datasets or imbalanced classes. It is also sensitive to feature scaling and can be computationally expensive since it requires calculating distances between points at prediction time.

Despite these challenges, k-NN remains a powerful tool for many machine learning tasks, and with appropriate tuning and preprocessing, it can deliver accurate and reliable predictions. Its ease of use and versatility make it a valuable algorithm for beginners and experienced practitioners alike.

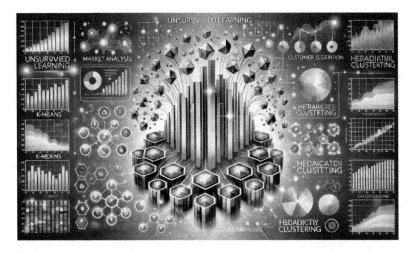

Chapter 4: Unsupervised Learning Algorithms

4.1 Clustering: k-Means and Hierarchical Clustering

Clustering is a fundamental **unsupervised learning** technique used to group similar data points together. Unlike supervised learning methods like classification, clustering does not rely on labeled data. Instead, it identifies patterns and structures within the data to divide it into groups, or **clusters**, based on similarities between data points. Clustering is widely used in areas such as customer segmentation, market analysis, image compression, document classification, and biology.

Two of the most commonly used clustering methods are **k-Means Clustering** and **Hierarchical Clustering**. While both methods aim to partition the data into meaningful groups, they approach the problem in different ways.

k-Means Clustering

k-Means Clustering is a straightforward and widely used algorithm for partitioning a dataset into **k** distinct clusters. The number of clusters, **k**, is predefined by the user. The goal of k-

Means is to group data points into clusters such that points within the same cluster are as similar as possible, while points in different clusters are as dissimilar as possible.

How k-Means Clustering Works

The k-Means algorithm follows a simple, iterative process:

1. **Initialize Centroids**: The algorithm starts by selecting **k** random points from the data as the initial centroids. These centroids represent the center of each cluster.

2. **Assign Points to Clusters**: Each data point is assigned to the cluster with the nearest centroid. The distance between each point and the centroids is typically calculated using **Euclidean distance**, but other distance measures (e.g., Manhattan distance) can be used.

3. **Update Centroids**: After assigning all points to clusters, the algorithm recalculates the centroids by averaging the positions of all points in each cluster. The centroid is now the mean of the points in the cluster.

4. **Repeat**: The assignment and update steps are repeated until the centroids no longer change, meaning the clusters are stable. This indicates that the algorithm has converged.

Example of k-Means Clustering

Imagine you are tasked with segmenting customers based on their spending habits. You decide to use k-Means clustering with **k = 3**, representing three customer segments. After running the algorithm, the customers are divided into three clusters based on how similar their spending patterns are. This allows you to target each group with tailored marketing strategies.

Advantages of k-Means Clustering

1. **Simplicity**: k-Means is easy to understand and implement.

2. **Scalability**: It works efficiently on large datasets, especially with relatively small values of **k**.

3. **Speed**: k-Means is computationally fast, making it suitable for real-time applications.

4. **Interpretability**: The clusters formed by k-Means are easy to interpret because each cluster is represented by a centroid.

Disadvantages of k-Means Clustering

1. **Predefined k**: The number of clusters (**k**) must be specified before running the algorithm, and choosing the correct value can be challenging.

2. **Sensitivity to Initialization**: The initial choice of centroids can significantly affect the final clusters. Poor initialization can lead to suboptimal solutions, but techniques like **k-Means++** can help improve the initial selection.

3. **Assumes Spherical Clusters**: k-Means assumes that the clusters are spherical and of equal size, which may not hold true for all datasets.

4. **Sensitive to Outliers**: Outliers can distort the cluster centroids, as k-Means minimizes the squared error, making it sensitive to extreme values.

How to Choose the Right k

Choosing the right value of **k** is crucial to obtaining meaningful clusters. One common method for selecting **k** is the **elbow method**. In this method, the sum of squared distances between data points and their corresponding centroids is plotted against different values of **k**. The point where the curve forms an "elbow" (where the rate of decrease sharply slows down) is considered a good choice for **k**.

Hierarchical Clustering

Hierarchical Clustering is another popular clustering method that builds a hierarchy of clusters. It does not require specifying the number of clusters beforehand, unlike k-Means. Hierarchical clustering creates a tree-like structure called a **dendrogram**, where each level represents a possible grouping of the data points.

There are two main types of hierarchical clustering:

1. **Agglomerative (Bottom-Up) Clustering**: This is the most common approach. It starts with each data point as its own cluster and then merges the closest clusters at each step, continuing until all points are grouped into one cluster.

2. **Divisive (Top-Down) Clustering**: This approach starts with all points in a single cluster and recursively splits them into smaller clusters.

How Agglomerative Hierarchical Clustering Works

1. **Initialize Clusters**: Start with each data point as its own cluster.

2. **Compute Proximity Matrix**: Compute the distance (proximity) between each pair of clusters. The distance can be calculated using different methods, such as **single**

linkage (minimum distance between points in two clusters) or **complete linkage** (maximum distance between points in two clusters).

3. **Merge Clusters**: At each step, merge the two closest clusters based on the proximity matrix.

4. **Repeat**: Continue merging clusters until all data points are combined into a single cluster or until the desired number of clusters is reached.

5. **Dendrogram**: The result of hierarchical clustering can be visualized as a **dendrogram**, a tree-like diagram that shows how clusters are merged at each step. The height of the branches represents the distance or dissimilarity between clusters.

Example of Hierarchical Clustering

Suppose you are grouping species based on genetic similarities. Hierarchical clustering can be used to build a dendrogram that illustrates the relationships between different species. Species that are more genetically similar will be merged into clusters earlier in the process, while more distant species will be merged later.

Advantages of Hierarchical Clustering

1. **No Need to Predefine k**: Unlike k-Means, hierarchical clustering does not require specifying the number of clusters in advance.

2. **Produces a Dendrogram**: The dendrogram provides a visual representation of the clustering process and allows you to see the entire hierarchy of clusters.

3. **Works for Any Shape:** Hierarchical clustering can create clusters of different shapes and sizes, making it more flexible than k-Means.

Disadvantages of Hierarchical Clustering

1. **Computationally Expensive:** Hierarchical clustering is computationally intensive, especially for large datasets, because it requires calculating and updating the proximity matrix at each step.

2. **No Reassignment:** Once a data point is assigned to a cluster, it cannot be reassigned, which can lead to suboptimal clustering.

3. **Sensitive to Noise:** Like k-Means, hierarchical clustering can be sensitive to outliers and noisy data points, which may distort the resulting clusters.

k-Means vs. Hierarchical Clustering

1. **Speed:** k-Means is faster and more scalable than hierarchical clustering, making it more suitable for large datasets. Hierarchical clustering is computationally expensive and is generally used for smaller datasets.

2. **Interpretability:** k-Means provides centroids for each cluster, which can be interpreted as the "average" data point of the cluster. Hierarchical clustering offers a dendrogram, which provides a more detailed hierarchical structure but may be harder to interpret in terms of centroids.

3. **Flexibility:** Hierarchical clustering is more flexible in capturing clusters of varying shapes and sizes, whereas k-Means assumes that clusters are spherical and of similar size.

4. **Reassignment of Points**: In k-Means, data points can be reassigned to different clusters during the iterative process, while in hierarchical clustering, once a data point is assigned to a cluster, it cannot be reassigned.

Applications of Clustering

1. **Customer Segmentation**: Clustering is used to group customers based on purchasing behavior, demographics, or other factors to create targeted marketing strategies.

2. **Document Classification**: In text mining, clustering is applied to organize documents into topics or categories based on similarities in word usage.

3. **Image Compression**: Clustering can be used to reduce the number of colors in an image by grouping similar pixels, making the image easier to compress.

4. **Anomaly Detection**: Clustering algorithms can identify outliers or anomalies in the data by grouping together normal data points and flagging those that do not belong to any cluster.

5. **Biological Data**: In genomics and bioinformatics, clustering is used to group genes or proteins with similar characteristics to better understand biological functions and relationships.

Clustering is an essential tool in unsupervised learning that helps uncover hidden patterns and structures in data. **k-Means** is simple and efficient, making it a great choice for partitioning large datasets into distinct groups when you have a predefined number of clusters in mind.

Hierarchical Clustering, on the other hand, offers a more detailed view of the data's structure, allowing you to explore the relationships between data points at different levels of granularity.

Both methods have their strengths and weaknesses, and the choice between them depends on the specific problem, the nature of the data, and the desired output. While k-Means is well-suited for speed and scalability, hierarchical clustering provides a richer and more flexible representation of the data, especially when the number of clusters is not known in advance.

By applying the right clustering technique to your dataset, you can gain valuable insights and make data-driven decisions in a variety of domains, from marketing to biology to computer vision.

4.2 Dimensionality Reduction with PCA (Principal Component Analysis)

Dimensionality reduction is a key concept in data analysis and machine learning, especially when dealing with high-dimensional datasets. High-dimensional data (with many features) can be challenging to work with due to issues like increased computational complexity, overfitting, and the **curse of dimensionality**. One of the most popular techniques for reducing dimensionality while preserving important information is **Principal Component Analysis (PCA)**. PCA is widely used to simplify datasets, making them easier to analyze and visualize, while maintaining the essential structure and relationships within the data.

What is Principal Component Analysis (PCA)?

Principal Component Analysis (PCA) is an unsupervised learning technique used to reduce the dimensionality of a dataset. It does this by transforming the original features into a new set of features called **principal components**. These components are linear combinations of the original features and are designed to capture as much variance in the data as possible. The first principal component captures the most variance, the second principal component captures the next highest variance, and so on. By focusing on the most significant components, PCA allows you to reduce the number of features while retaining the most important information in the data.

The main objectives of PCA are:

1. **Reduce Dimensionality**: Simplify the dataset by reducing the number of features.

2. **Preserve Variance**: Retain the most important variance in the data, so the reduced dataset still captures the key patterns.

3. **Improve Efficiency**: By reducing the number of features, PCA helps speed up computation and makes models less prone to overfitting.

How PCA Works

PCA works by transforming the dataset into a new coordinate system where the axes (principal components) represent directions of maximum variance in the data. The steps involved in PCA are as follows:

1. **Standardize the Data**: Before applying PCA, the data is often standardized (scaled) so that each feature has a mean of zero and a standard deviation of one. This step ensures that all features contribute equally to the analysis, as PCA is sensitive to the scale of the data.

2. **Compute the Covariance Matrix:** The next step is to compute the **covariance matrix**, which measures the pairwise relationships between the features. The covariance matrix shows how much two variables vary together. If the variables are correlated, PCA will find directions (principal components) along which they vary the most.

3. **Compute Eigenvectors and Eigenvalues:** Eigenvectors and eigenvalues are calculated from the covariance matrix. The **eigenvectors** represent the directions (or principal components) of maximum variance, and the **eigenvalues** represent the magnitude of the variance along each eigenvector. The eigenvectors with the largest eigenvalues correspond to the directions that capture the most variance in the data.

4. **Select the Principal Components:** The principal components are the eigenvectors that correspond to the largest eigenvalues. These components form a new basis for the data, and the original dataset is projected onto these components. The number of components chosen depends on how much variance you want to preserve. Often, a small number of components can capture most of the variance, allowing for significant dimensionality reduction.

5. **Transform the Data:** Finally, the original data is transformed into the new space defined by the principal components. The transformed data has fewer dimensions but retains most of the important information from the original dataset.

Geometric Interpretation of PCA

In a geometric sense, PCA can be viewed as rotating the coordinate axes so that the new axes (the principal components) point in the direction of maximum variance. The first principal component is the direction along which the data varies the most, and the second principal component is orthogonal to the first and captures the next most variance. This continues until all the components have been calculated.

By projecting the data onto the first few principal components, you can reduce the number of features while preserving as much of the data's structure as possible.

Example of PCA

Imagine you have a dataset with multiple features, such as the height, weight, and age of individuals. While each feature provides some information, they may also be correlated. For instance, height and weight might be correlated because taller people tend to weigh more. PCA would find the directions in which the data varies the most (e.g., a combination of height and weight) and allow you to reduce the dataset to the most important features while discarding redundant information.

In this case, you could reduce the dataset from three dimensions (height, weight, and age) to two dimensions by keeping the first two principal components. These components capture most of the variance in the original data, enabling you to work with a simpler dataset without losing significant information.

Choosing the Number of Principal Components

One of the key decisions in PCA is selecting how many principal components to keep. The goal is to reduce the number of dimensions while preserving as much variance as possible. To help with this decision, several techniques are used:

1. **Explained Variance Ratio**: This metric tells you how much of the total variance is captured by each principal component. By plotting the explained variance ratio for each component (known as a **scree plot**), you can visually determine the point at which adding more components has diminishing returns. Typically, you aim to keep enough components to capture around 90-95% of the variance.

2. **Cumulative Explained Variance**: The cumulative explained variance shows the total variance captured by the first n principal components. This is often used to decide how many components to retain. For example, if the first three components capture 95% of the variance, you might decide to reduce the dataset to three dimensions.

3. **Elbow Method**: Similar to the elbow method in k-Means clustering, this method looks for an "elbow" in the scree plot, where the explained variance stops increasing significantly with each additional component. This is a good point to stop adding components.

Advantages of PCA

1. **Dimensionality Reduction**: PCA reduces the number of features while retaining the most important information, making the data easier to work with and visualize.

2. **Prevents Overfitting**: By reducing the number of dimensions, PCA helps prevent models from overfitting

the training data, leading to better generalization on new data.

3. **Improves Computational Efficiency**: With fewer features, machine learning algorithms can run faster and more efficiently, particularly on large datasets.

4. **Removes Multicollinearity**: PCA can help eliminate multicollinearity (when features are highly correlated), which can cause problems in models like linear regression.

5. **Improves Data Visualization**: For datasets with many dimensions, PCA makes it possible to visualize the data in two or three dimensions, making it easier to identify patterns or clusters.

Disadvantages of PCA

1. **Loss of Interpretability**: While PCA reduces dimensionality, the new principal components are linear combinations of the original features, making them harder to interpret in a meaningful way.

2. **Assumes Linearity**: PCA assumes that the relationships between features are linear, which may not always be the case. Non-linear relationships cannot be captured effectively with PCA.

3. **Sensitive to Scaling**: PCA is sensitive to the scale of the data. If the features are on different scales (e.g., income in thousands vs. age in years), the principal components may be dominated by features with larger ranges. To avoid this, it's important to standardize the data before applying PCA.

4. **Requires Numeric Data**: PCA only works with numeric data, so categorical features must be converted to numerical form (e.g., using one-hot encoding) before applying PCA.

Applications of PCA

1. **Image Compression**: PCA is commonly used in image compression to reduce the size of images by keeping only the most important information. This allows for significant reductions in file size while retaining the overall structure of the image.

2. **Data Visualization**: In high-dimensional datasets, PCA can be used to reduce the data to two or three dimensions, making it easier to visualize clusters or patterns. This is particularly useful in exploratory data analysis.

3. **Noise Reduction**: PCA can help reduce noise in the data by discarding the components that capture little variance (often representing noise) and retaining only the most important components.

4. **Genomics and Bioinformatics**: PCA is used in fields like genomics to reduce the dimensionality of gene expression data, allowing researchers to focus on the most important genes while simplifying the analysis.

5. **Finance**: In finance, PCA is used to reduce the complexity of portfolios by identifying the underlying factors (principal components) that drive asset prices, enabling better risk management and portfolio optimization.

Principal Component Analysis (PCA) is a powerful technique for reducing the dimensionality of large datasets while retaining the most important information. By transforming the data into a new set of features (principal components) that capture the maximum variance, PCA simplifies the dataset, making it easier to work with, visualize, and analyze.

Despite its advantages, PCA does have some limitations, particularly in terms of interpretability and its assumption of linear relationships. However, when used appropriately, PCA can significantly improve the performance of machine learning algorithms, reduce overfitting, and enhance computational efficiency.

Whether you're working with high-dimensional data in image processing, genomics, or finance, PCA is an essential tool for making complex datasets more manageable and insightful.

4.3 Association Rule Mining: Apriori and Market Basket Analysis

Association rule mining is a popular data mining technique used to uncover interesting relationships, correlations, or patterns between items in large datasets. It is commonly applied in transactional databases to find associations between items purchased together, often referred to as **Market Basket Analysis**. The goal of association rule mining is to discover **if-then** relationships, such as "if a customer buys product A, they are likely to also buy product B." These patterns can be used to improve sales strategies, product placement, and recommendations.

Two important concepts in association rule mining are **support** and **confidence**:

- **Support**: The proportion of transactions that contain a specific itemset (group of items). It indicates how frequently an item or itemset appears in the dataset.

- **Confidence**: The conditional probability that a customer will buy item B, given that they have already bought item A. It measures the strength of the association between items.

One of the most well-known algorithms for discovering association rules is the **Apriori Algorithm.**

What is Market Basket Analysis?

Market Basket Analysis is a data mining technique that analyzes the relationships between different items purchased by customers in a transactional setting, such as in a supermarket or online store. The goal is to find patterns in customer behavior by examining which products are often bought together.

For example, if customers who buy bread frequently also purchase butter, the retailer can use this information to place these items closer together or offer discounts on combined purchases. These insights can be valuable for cross-selling, product bundling, and improving customer experience.

Association Rules

Association rules are typically written in the form:

If {A}, then {B}

Where:

- **{A}** is the antecedent (the item or itemset that triggers the rule),

- **{B}** is the consequent (the item or itemset that is predicted).

For example, the rule "if {milk}, then {bread}" means that customers who buy milk are likely to also buy bread.

The effectiveness of association rules is measured using the following metrics:

- **Support**: Measures the proportion of transactions that contain both the antecedent and the consequent.

Formula: **Support(A → B) = (Number of transactions containing both A and B) / (Total number of transactions)**

- **Confidence**: Measures the probability that a customer who buys the antecedent will also buy the consequent.

Formula: **Confidence(A → B) = (Number of transactions containing both A and B) / (Number of transactions containing A)**

- **Lift**: Measures the strength of the rule relative to the overall occurrence of the consequent. Lift greater than 1 suggests that the occurrence of the antecedent increases the likelihood of the consequent.

Formula: **Lift(A → B) = Confidence(A → B) / Support(B)**

A high lift indicates a strong positive association between the antecedent and the consequent.

The Apriori Algorithm

The **Apriori Algorithm** is one of the most widely used algorithms for mining frequent itemsets and generating association rules. It is based on the **apriori principle**, which states that "if an itemset is frequent, then all of its subsets must also be frequent." This means that if an itemset doesn't meet a minimum support threshold, none of its supersets will either, allowing the algorithm to efficiently prune the search space.

How the Apriori Algorithm Works

The Apriori algorithm works in two main steps:

1. **Frequent Itemset Generation**: The algorithm identifies all itemsets that have support greater than a user-defined threshold (known as **minimum support**). This step is important because only itemsets that appear frequently in the data are considered for rule generation.

2. **Association Rule Generation**: Once frequent itemsets are identified, the algorithm generates association rules by calculating the confidence for each possible rule. Only rules that meet a minimum confidence threshold are retained.

Steps of the Apriori Algorithm

1. **Set a Minimum Support and Confidence**: The user defines the minimum support and confidence thresholds to filter out uninteresting or irrelevant rules.

2. **Generate Candidate Itemsets**: The algorithm starts by identifying all individual items that meet the minimum support threshold. Then, it generates combinations of these items (itemsets) and counts their occurrences in the dataset.

3. **Prune Infrequent Itemsets**: Itemsets that do not meet the minimum support threshold are discarded. The

algorithm only keeps frequent itemsets for further processing.

4. **Repeat**: The process is repeated by generating larger itemsets (combinations of more items) from the frequent itemsets of the previous iteration. This continues until no more frequent itemsets can be generated.

5. **Generate Rules**: For each frequent itemset, association rules are generated by calculating the confidence for each possible rule. Only rules with confidence above the minimum threshold are retained.

Example of Apriori Algorithm

Suppose a supermarket wants to analyze transactions to find associations between items. The transactions are:

1. {bread, milk, butter}

2. {bread, milk}

3. {bread, butter}

4. {milk, butter}

5. {bread, milk, butter, cheese}

Using the Apriori algorithm with a minimum support threshold of 0.4 (40% of the transactions), the algorithm first identifies frequent individual items, such as {bread}, {milk}, and {butter}. Then, it generates combinations of these items and calculates their support. Finally, it generates rules like "if {bread}, then {butter}" and evaluates their confidence and lift.

Advantages of Apriori Algorithm

1. **Simplicity**: The algorithm is easy to understand and implement.

2. **Pruning**: By using the apriori principle, the algorithm efficiently reduces the search space, making it feasible to analyze large datasets.

3. **Versatility**: Apriori can be applied to a wide range of applications, including market basket analysis, web usage mining, and bioinformatics.

Disadvantages of Apriori Algorithm

1. **Computational Complexity**: Apriori can be slow, especially with large datasets, because it requires multiple passes over the data and generates a large number of candidate itemsets.

2. **Requires User-Defined Thresholds**: The effectiveness of Apriori depends on setting appropriate minimum support and confidence values, which can be challenging without domain knowledge.

Market Basket Analysis with Apriori

Market Basket Analysis is one of the most common applications of the Apriori algorithm. It involves analyzing customer transactions to find which items are frequently bought together. Retailers use this information to optimize product placement, promotions, and cross-selling strategies.

For example:

- A grocery store might discover that customers who buy bread are also likely to buy butter. This insight could lead to placing bread and butter near each other in the store or offering discounts on butter when customers buy bread.

- An online retailer could use market basket analysis to recommend additional items to customers during the checkout process based on items they have added to their cart.

Hierarchical Association Rules

In addition to simple association rules, more complex rules can be generated using **hierarchical association rule mining**, which allows the discovery of patterns at multiple levels of abstraction. For instance, in a supermarket dataset, a hierarchical rule might be "if {fruit}, then {dairy products}" at a higher level and "if {apples}, then {milk}" at a more specific level.

Hierarchical association rules can provide more comprehensive insights by analyzing relationships between broader categories and specific items.

Applications of Association Rule Mining

1. **Retail and E-commerce**: Association rule mining is widely used in retail and e-commerce to discover product combinations frequently bought together. These insights help with store layout optimization, cross-selling, and product recommendations.

2. **Recommender Systems**: E-commerce platforms, streaming services, and other digital platforms use association rules to recommend related products or content to users.

3. **Healthcare:** Association rule mining can be used in healthcare to identify relationships between different treatments, symptoms, and diagnoses. For example, discovering which medications are frequently prescribed together.

4. **Fraud Detection:** In financial services, association rules can help detect unusual patterns of transactions, which may indicate fraudulent activity.

5. **Web Usage Mining:** Association rule mining is applied to analyze web usage patterns. By finding frequent patterns in user navigation, websites can improve content recommendations and optimize user experience.

6. **Bioinformatics:** In bioinformatics, association rule mining is used to find relationships between genes, proteins, or biological pathways, helping researchers discover patterns in complex biological data.

Association rule mining, particularly with the **Apriori Algorithm**, is a powerful tool for uncovering hidden patterns and relationships in large datasets. It is most commonly associated with **Market Basket Analysis**, where retailers use it to find product combinations frequently purchased together. The discovered patterns are then used to improve business strategies, product recommendations, and customer satisfaction.

By identifying the most relevant associations based on support, confidence, and lift, association rule mining helps businesses understand customer behavior, optimize inventory, and increase sales. While Apriori is simple and effective, it can become computationally expensive for very large datasets. Nonetheless, its versatility makes it a valuable tool for various domains beyond retail, including healthcare, fraud detection, and web usage mining.

4.4 Anomaly Detection Techniques

Anomaly detection is a crucial technique in data mining and machine learning, used to identify unusual patterns, outliers, or unexpected observations that deviate significantly from the majority of the data. These **anomalies** (also known as outliers) could indicate critical events, errors, or rare occurrences, such as fraudulent transactions, network intrusions, equipment failures, or unusual customer behavior. Detecting such anomalies can prevent serious problems or uncover hidden insights in various fields like cybersecurity, finance, manufacturing, and healthcare.

Anomaly detection techniques can be broadly categorized into **supervised**, **unsupervised**, and **semi-supervised** methods, depending on the availability of labeled data. In this section, we'll explore several widely-used anomaly detection techniques, their applications, and the strengths and limitations of each approach.

Types of Anomalies

Before diving into the techniques, it's important to understand the types of anomalies typically encountered:

1. **Point Anomalies**: A single data point that significantly deviates from the rest of the data. For example, a bank transaction of an unusually large amount compared to the customer's typical spending.

2. **Contextual Anomalies**: Anomalies that are context-dependent, meaning they are unusual only in a specific context. For instance, a high temperature might be normal in the summer but anomalous in the winter.

3. **Collective Anomalies**: A set of data points that, when taken together, exhibit abnormal behavior. Individually, these points may not be anomalous, but as a group, they deviate from the norm. An example could be a sequence of network traffic that signals an ongoing cyber attack.

Techniques for Anomaly Detection

1. Statistical Methods

Statistical methods are among the oldest and simplest approaches for anomaly detection. These methods assume that normal data follows a known distribution (e.g., Gaussian or normal distribution), and any data point that deviates significantly from this distribution is considered an anomaly.

- **Z-Score (Standard Score)**: The Z-score is a simple method used to measure how far a data point is from the mean in terms of standard deviations. A Z-score that is significantly greater or smaller than 0 indicates an anomaly.

Formula: $Z = (X - \mu) / \sigma$

Where:

  o **X** is the data point,

  o μ is the mean of the data,

  o σ is the standard deviation.

- **Grubbs' Test**: This is a statistical hypothesis test that identifies whether the highest or lowest value in a dataset is an outlier. It works by calculating a test statistic based on the difference between the extreme value and the mean of the data.

- **Box Plot Method**: A box plot visually displays the distribution of data. Outliers are typically defined as points that fall outside 1.5 times the interquartile range (IQR), which is the distance between the 25th and 75th percentiles.

Advantages:

- Simple and interpretable.

- Works well with normally distributed data.

Disadvantages:

- Assumes a predefined distribution (e.g., normal distribution), which may not hold for all datasets.

- Sensitive to the choice of thresholds (e.g., Z-score cutoffs).

2. Distance-Based Methods

Distance-based methods rely on calculating the distance between data points. If a point is far from its neighbors, it is considered an anomaly.

- **k-Nearest Neighbors (k-NN) for Anomaly Detection**: In this approach, the distance between a data point and its **k** nearest neighbors is calculated. If the average distance is large compared to other points, the data point is considered an anomaly.

A variation of this is **local outlier factor (LOF)**, which measures the density of a point relative to its neighbors. Points in regions of lower density are more likely to be anomalies.

- **Mahalanobis Distance**: This distance measure accounts for the correlation between variables. It calculates the distance between a point and the mean of the dataset, considering the covariance of the data. Points that have a large Mahalanobis distance are flagged as anomalies.

Advantages:

- Does not assume a specific distribution of the data.

- Effective when normal and anomalous data points are separated by distance.

Disadvantages:

- Sensitive to the choice of distance metric.

- Computationally expensive for large datasets.

- Performs poorly when normal and anomalous data overlap.

3. Clustering-Based Methods

Clustering methods can also be used for anomaly detection by identifying data points that do not belong to any cluster or that belong to small, sparse clusters.

- **k-Means Clustering**: k-Means can be used for anomaly detection by treating data points that are far from the cluster centroids as anomalies. These points have a higher **distance to the nearest centroid** compared to other points.

- **DBSCAN (Density-Based Spatial Clustering of Applications with Noise)**: DBSCAN is a density-based clustering method that defines clusters as regions of high density. Points that are not part of any cluster are considered outliers.

Advantages:

- Can detect anomalies in clusters with varying densities.

- DBSCAN is particularly good at detecting collective anomalies.

Disadvantages:

- Clustering algorithms require setting parameters like the number of clusters (for k-Means) or the minimum number of points (for DBSCAN).

- May struggle with high-dimensional data or datasets where clusters overlap.

4. Machine Learning-Based Methods

Machine learning approaches for anomaly detection can be either **supervised** or **unsupervised**. Supervised methods require labeled data, where the model is trained on both normal and anomalous data points. In practice, most anomaly detection tasks are unsupervised due to the scarcity of labeled anomalous data.

- **Isolation Forest**: This is an unsupervised anomaly detection method that works by randomly partitioning the data using decision trees. The idea is that anomalies are easier to isolate (i.e., require fewer splits) because they lie in low-density regions of the data. Anomalous points have shorter paths in the tree structure.

- **One-Class SVM (Support Vector Machines)**: A variation of SVM, one-class SVM finds a boundary that separates normal data from the rest of the feature space. Points that fall outside this boundary are considered anomalies.

- **Autoencoders**: Autoencoders are neural networks used for unsupervised learning. In anomaly detection, an autoencoder learns to compress and reconstruct normal data. Anomalous data points will have higher reconstruction errors because they do not conform to the normal patterns.

Advantages:

- Can model complex relationships between variables.

- Suitable for high-dimensional datasets.

- Can detect both point and collective anomalies.

Disadvantages:

- Supervised methods require labeled data, which is often unavailable for anomalies.

- Unsupervised methods may struggle if anomalies resemble normal data.

5. Time-Series Anomaly Detection

When dealing with time-series data, anomalies are often context-dependent. Detecting anomalies in time-series data requires considering both the temporal patterns and the contextual information.

- **Moving Average**: A simple technique where the average of a sliding window of previous values is calculated. Deviations from this moving average are considered anomalies.

- **Seasonal Hybrid Extreme Studentized Deviate (S-H-ESD)**: This method detects anomalies in time-series data that exhibit seasonality. It adjusts for both global trends and seasonal patterns, making it effective for real-world time-series anomalies like equipment failures.

- **Recurrent Neural Networks (RNNs) and LSTMs**: These neural network architectures are designed to handle sequential data. For anomaly detection, an RNN or LSTM can learn the normal patterns in time-series data. Anomalies are identified when the model's predictions deviate significantly from the actual observations.

Advantages:

- Effective for detecting contextual and collective anomalies in time-series data.

- Can capture temporal dependencies and seasonal patterns.

Disadvantages:

- Sensitive to parameter settings (e.g., window size for moving averages).

- Complex models like RNNs and LSTMs require significant training time and computational resources.

Applications of Anomaly Detection

1. **Fraud Detection**: In financial systems, anomaly detection is widely used to identify fraudulent transactions. Unusual patterns in transaction data, such as unexpectedly large withdrawals or purchases in different locations, can signal fraud.

2. **Network Intrusion Detection**: In cybersecurity, detecting network intrusions involves identifying

abnormal network traffic or behavior. Anomalies could indicate unauthorized access, denial-of-service attacks, or malware infections.

3. **Healthcare**: Anomaly detection is applied to monitor patients' vital signs. Deviations from normal patterns in heart rate, blood pressure, or oxygen levels can signal medical emergencies.

4. **Manufacturing and Equipment Monitoring**: Anomaly detection is used in predictive maintenance to identify equipment failures. By monitoring sensor data from machines, sudden changes in temperature, vibration, or pressure can be flagged as anomalies, helping to prevent equipment breakdowns.

5. **Credit Scoring**: Financial institutions use anomaly detection techniques to identify unusual credit behavior, such as excessive borrowing or payment delays, which may indicate credit risk.

6. **Social Media and Web Analytics**: Anomalies in web traffic or social media activity can signal events such as viral content, website issues, or unusual user behavior.

Challenges in Anomaly Detection

1. **Imbalanced Data**: Anomalies are typically rare events, meaning that the dataset is highly imbalanced, with far more normal data points than anomalous ones. This can make it difficult for models to learn and accurately detect anomalies.

2. **Evolving Data**: In many real-world scenarios, the data distribution evolves over time. A pattern that is normal today might become anomalous in the future, and vice

versa. This makes detecting anomalies in dynamic environments challenging.

3. **High Dimensionality**: Many anomaly detection techniques struggle with high-dimensional data, where the concept of "distance" becomes less meaningful, and the relationship between features becomes complex.

4. **Interpretability**: In many cases, it is important to not only detect anomalies but also explain why a data point is considered anomalous. Techniques like neural networks or ensemble methods may have high predictive power but can be difficult to interpret.

Anomaly detection is an essential tool in various domains, from fraud detection and cybersecurity to healthcare and industrial monitoring. Different techniques, such as **statistical methods**, **distance-based approaches**, **clustering algorithms**, and **machine learning models**, each have their strengths and are suited to different types of anomalies and datasets. Choosing the right technique depends on the nature of the data, the problem being solved, and the computational resources available.

While detecting anomalies can be challenging due to the imbalanced nature of the data, the evolving nature of many real-world systems, and the complexity of high-dimensional data, advances in machine learning have made anomaly detection more robust and scalable.

By leveraging the appropriate techniques, businesses and organizations can detect anomalies early and take action to prevent fraud, improve system reliability, and enhance operational efficiency.

Chapter 5: Neural Networks and Deep Learning

5.1 Introduction to Neural Networks

Neural networks are one of the core concepts in machine learning and artificial intelligence (AI). Inspired by the structure and functioning of the human brain, neural networks are designed to recognize patterns in data through layers of interconnected nodes, known as **neurons**. These networks have the ability to model complex relationships between inputs and outputs, and they are widely used in tasks such as image classification, natural language processing, speech recognition, and autonomous systems.

Neural networks have gained tremendous popularity due to their ability to perform well on a wide range of problems, particularly those involving large amounts of data and complex patterns. One of the most significant advances in AI, **deep learning**, is based on neural networks with many layers, called **deep neural networks**.

What is a Neural Network?

A neural network is a collection of **neurons** (or nodes) arranged in **layers**. Each neuron performs a simple mathematical operation and passes the result to other neurons in the network. A typical neural network consists of three types of layers:

1. **Input Layer:** This is the first layer in the network and receives the raw input data. Each neuron in this layer corresponds to one feature of the input data (e.g., pixel values in an image or words in a sentence).

2. **Hidden Layer(s):** These are the intermediate layers where most of the computation takes place. Hidden layers apply various transformations to the input data to capture patterns and features that help in making predictions. A neural network can have one or more hidden layers, depending on its complexity.

3. **Output Layer:** The final layer of the network provides the output, which can be a predicted label for classification problems, a numerical value for regression tasks, or a set of probabilities for multiple classes.

Each connection between neurons has an associated **weight**, which determines the strength of the connection. The network adjusts these weights during training to minimize the error between its predictions and the actual outcomes.

How Neural Networks Work

Neural networks work by passing the input data through the layers of neurons, with each layer transforming the data to make it more useful for solving the task at hand. This process, called **forward propagation**, involves the following steps:

1. **Input Processing**: The input data is fed into the neurons of the input layer. Each neuron passes the input to the next layer after performing a weighted sum of its inputs.

2. **Activation Function**: After calculating the weighted sum, each neuron applies an **activation function** to introduce non-linearity into the network. Non-linearity is important because it allows the network to learn complex relationships. Common activation functions include:

   o **Sigmoid**: Maps the input to a value between 0 and 1.

   o **ReLU (Rectified Linear Unit)**: Sets all negative values to zero and keeps positive values unchanged.

   o **Tanh**: Similar to sigmoid but outputs values between -1 and 1.

3. **Output Generation**: The transformed data is passed through the layers, ultimately reaching the output layer. The output layer produces the final prediction, which could be a classification, a numerical value, or probabilities for multiple classes.

4. **Loss Function**: The network's prediction is compared to the actual target value using a **loss function**. The loss function measures how far the predicted output is from the true value. Common loss functions include:

   o **Mean Squared Error (MSE)**: Used in regression tasks.

   o **Cross-Entropy Loss**: Used in classification tasks.

5. **Backpropagation and Optimization:** Once the loss is calculated, the network adjusts the weights to reduce the error. This process is known as **backpropagation**. During backpropagation, the error is propagated backward through the network, and the weights are updated using an optimization algorithm like **gradient descent**.

Training a Neural Network

The process of training a neural network involves two key phases: **forward propagation** and **backpropagation**. These steps are repeated multiple times over the training data, with each iteration referred to as an **epoch**.

1. **Forward Propagation:** In this phase, the input data is passed through the network layer by layer. The network computes its predictions based on the current weights and biases. This is called the forward pass.

2. **Backpropagation:** After the forward pass, the error (the difference between the predicted and actual values) is calculated. The network then adjusts its weights to minimize this error. Backpropagation is the process of calculating the gradient of the loss function with respect to each weight and updating the weights in the direction that minimizes the loss. This update is performed using an optimization algorithm like **stochastic gradient descent (SGD)** or **Adam**.

The combination of forward propagation and backpropagation allows the network to iteratively learn the optimal weights that minimize the prediction error.

Key Components of Neural Networks

1. **Weights**: Each connection between neurons has a weight that influences the strength of the signal being passed. The goal of training is to adjust these weights to minimize the prediction error.

2. **Bias**: A bias term is added to each neuron to allow the network to model patterns that are not centered around the origin (zero point). Biases provide additional flexibility in the model's predictions.

3. **Activation Functions**: Activation functions introduce non-linearity into the network, enabling it to learn complex patterns. Without activation functions, the neural network would behave like a simple linear model and be unable to capture intricate relationships between features.

4. **Loss Function**: The loss function measures the performance of the network by comparing the predicted output to the actual target. The objective is to minimize the loss function during training.

5. **Learning Rate**: The **learning rate** is a hyperparameter that controls the size of the weight updates during backpropagation. If the learning rate is too high, the network may converge too quickly and miss the optimal solution. If it's too low, the training process will be slow.

Types of Neural Networks

There are several types of neural networks, each designed for specific tasks and use cases:

1. **Feedforward Neural Networks (FNNs):** These are the simplest type of neural networks where the data flows in one direction—from the input layer to the output layer. There are no feedback loops, and each neuron is connected only to the next layer. FNNs are commonly used for tasks like image classification and regression.

2. **Convolutional Neural Networks (CNNs):** CNNs are specifically designed for processing grid-like data such as images. They use **convolutional layers** to capture spatial relationships in the data. CNNs are widely used in image recognition, object detection, and video analysis.

3. **Recurrent Neural Networks (RNNs):** RNNs are designed to handle sequential data, such as time series or text. Unlike feedforward networks, RNNs have feedback loops that allow information to persist across time steps, making them ideal for tasks like speech recognition and language translation.

4. **Generative Adversarial Networks (GANs):** GANs consist of two neural networks—a generator and a discriminator—that work together to generate realistic data, such as images or text. GANs have been used in applications like image synthesis, style transfer, and data augmentation.

5. **Autoencoders:** These networks are used for unsupervised learning, particularly for dimensionality reduction and anomaly detection. Autoencoders learn to compress the input data into a smaller representation and then reconstruct it back to its original form.

Applications of Neural Networks

Neural networks are applied across various industries and fields due to their ability to model complex relationships in data. Some notable applications include:

1. **Image and Video Recognition:** Neural networks, particularly CNNs, are widely used in image classification tasks, such as facial recognition, object detection, and medical image analysis.

2. **Natural Language Processing (NLP):** Neural networks power many NLP tasks, including language translation, sentiment analysis, and text generation. Models like **transformers** and **LSTMs** are commonly used in this domain.

3. **Speech Recognition:** Neural networks are used to convert speech into text by recognizing patterns in audio signals. This is the foundation of technologies like virtual assistants (e.g., Siri, Alexa).

4. **Autonomous Systems:** Neural networks are critical in autonomous vehicles, drones, and robots, where they help machines perceive and interact with their environment through sensors and cameras.

5. **Recommendation Systems:** Neural networks are used in e-commerce and streaming platforms to recommend products, movies, or songs to users based on their past behavior and preferences.

6. **Healthcare:** In healthcare, neural networks are used for diagnosing diseases, analyzing medical images, predicting patient outcomes, and even discovering new drugs.

Advantages of Neural Networks

1. **Ability to Learn Complex Patterns:** Neural networks excel at capturing intricate, non-linear relationships

between features, making them suitable for a wide range of tasks.

2. **Adaptability:** Neural networks can be applied to various domains, including vision, language, and speech. They can be tailored to different problem types, such as classification, regression, and generation.

3. **Scalability:** With advancements in hardware (such as GPUs) and techniques like **parallelization**, neural networks can be scaled to handle massive datasets and deep architectures.

4. **Automated Feature Engineering:** Neural networks can automatically learn the most relevant features from raw data, reducing the need for manual feature engineering.

Disadvantages of Neural Networks

1. **Computationally Intensive:** Training deep neural networks requires significant computational resources, including specialized hardware like GPUs.

2. **Large Amounts of Data Required:** Neural networks typically perform best when trained on large datasets. In scenarios where data is limited, other algorithms may be more suitable.

3. **Black-Box Nature:** Neural networks are often criticized for being difficult to interpret. While they can achieve high accuracy, understanding the reasoning behind their decisions is challenging.

4. **Overfitting:** Neural networks are prone to overfitting, especially if the network is too complex or trained for too long on small datasets.

Neural networks are a foundational technology in modern machine learning and artificial intelligence. They are capable of solving complex tasks that were once thought to be beyond the reach of machines, such as recognizing faces, understanding natural language, and driving autonomous vehicles.

their complexity, the underlying principles of neural networks—forward propagation, backpropagation, and optimization—are relatively simple.

As data continues to grow in volume and complexity, neural networks will remain a key tool for extracting meaningful insights and building intelligent systems. Their ability to model non-linear relationships, adapt to various domains, and process vast amounts of data make them indispensable in the age of AI.

5.2 Deep Learning Architectures: CNNs, RNNs, and LSTMs

Deep learning has revolutionized the field of machine learning, making it possible to tackle complex tasks like image recognition, natural language processing, and time-series prediction with high accuracy. Three key architectures that have emerged as the backbone of many deep learning applications are **Convolutional Neural Networks (CNNs)**, **Recurrent Neural Networks (RNNs)**, and **Long Short-Term Memory networks (LSTMs)**. Each of these architectures is designed to address specific types of data and tasks, from image processing to sequential data analysis.

1. Convolutional Neural Networks (CNNs)

Convolutional Neural Networks (CNNs) are specialized neural networks designed to process grid-like data structures, such as images. CNNs are highly effective in tasks that involve spatial data because they can automatically capture patterns, edges, textures, and hierarchical features within images. CNNs have become the go-to architecture for tasks like image classification, object detection, and even video analysis.

How CNNs Work

CNNs consist of several types of layers, each serving a specific purpose in processing the data:

1. **Convolutional Layer**: The convolutional layer is the core building block of a CNN. It applies **filters** (also called kernels) to the input image to extract features such as edges, corners, and textures. The filter slides over the image, performing a convolution operation at each position, which results in a **feature map**. The goal is to detect various features across the image that are important for the task at hand.

2. **Pooling Layer**: After convolution, a **pooling layer** is typically applied to reduce the spatial dimensions of the feature map while retaining the most important information. This layer helps in reducing the number of parameters, which in turn reduces computational cost and prevents overfitting. **Max pooling** is the most common pooling technique, where the maximum value from each region of the feature map is retained.

3. **Fully Connected Layer**: After several convolutional and pooling layers, the high-level features are flattened and passed through one or more **fully connected layers**. These layers perform the final classification or regression task based on the learned features.

4. **Activation Functions**: Activation functions such as **ReLU (Rectified Linear Unit)** are used to introduce

non-linearity into the network. ReLU is particularly popular in CNNs because it allows the network to learn complex patterns more effectively by applying non-linear transformations to the feature maps.

Example of CNN Usage

Consider a task like classifying images of cats and dogs. A CNN would first apply convolutional layers to detect low-level features like edges and corners. As the network deepens, it would capture more abstract patterns, such as the shape of an ear or the texture of fur. By the time the data reaches the fully connected layers, the CNN would have learned to distinguish between the images of cats and dogs with high accuracy.

Applications of CNNs

1. **Image Classification**: CNNs are widely used in image classification tasks, such as recognizing objects in photos or medical images (e.g., detecting tumors in X-rays).

2. **Object Detection**: CNN-based models are used for detecting and localizing objects in images. This is useful in applications like self-driving cars and security systems.

3. **Facial Recognition**: CNNs are used in facial recognition systems, which identify individuals based on their facial features.

4. **Video Processing**: CNNs can be extended to handle video data by applying convolutions over time, making them suitable for tasks like action recognition and video summarization.

Advantages of CNNs

1. **Feature Learning**: CNNs automatically learn relevant features from raw data, reducing the need for manual feature engineering.

2. **Spatial Awareness**: CNNs maintain the spatial relationships between pixels, making them highly effective for image and video tasks.

3. **Efficient with Large Datasets**: CNNs can handle large datasets effectively, making them suitable for tasks like medical image analysis, satellite imagery, and autonomous driving.

Disadvantages of CNNs

1. **Computationally Intensive**: CNNs require significant computational resources, especially for deep architectures with many layers and large datasets.

2. **Lack of Interpretability**: While CNNs are highly accurate, they are often viewed as "black boxes," meaning it can be difficult to interpret exactly how the network makes its decisions.

2. Recurrent Neural Networks (RNNs)

Recurrent Neural Networks (RNNs) are designed to handle **sequential data,** such as time-series data, text, or speech. Unlike traditional feedforward networks, RNNs have **loops** that allow information to persist over time, enabling them to remember previous inputs and use this information to make predictions. This makes RNNs particularly effective for tasks where the order of the data is important, such as predicting the next word in a sentence or forecasting future stock prices.

How RNNs Work

In an RNN, each neuron not only receives input from the previous layer but also has a connection to itself from the previous time step. This creates a form of memory that allows the network to take into account past inputs when making predictions.

1. **Hidden State**: At each time step, the RNN maintains a **hidden state** that captures information from previous time steps. This hidden state is updated at each time step based on the current input and the previous hidden state.

2. **Looping Mechanism**: The looping mechanism allows the RNN to pass information forward through time, making it suitable for tasks involving sequences.

3. **Backpropagation Through Time (BPTT)**: RNNs are trained using a variation of the backpropagation algorithm known as **Backpropagation Through Time (BPTT)**. In BPTT, the error is propagated back through time, allowing the network to learn the influence of previous time steps on the current prediction.

Example of RNN Usage

A common application of RNNs is **language modeling**, where the task is to predict the next word in a sequence. For example, given the input "I am going to the," the RNN would use the context from previous words to predict that the next word might be "store," "gym," or "park."

Applications of RNNs

1. **Natural Language Processing (NLP)**: RNNs are widely used in NLP tasks such as machine translation, text generation, and sentiment analysis.

2. **Speech Recognition**: RNNs are used to transcribe spoken words into text by processing sequential audio data.

3. **Time-Series Forecasting**: RNNs are used for predicting future values in time-series data, such as stock prices or weather conditions.

4. **Sequential Data Analysis**: RNNs are applied to tasks that require understanding the order of events, such as video analysis or gesture recognition.

Advantages of RNNs

1. **Captures Temporal Dependencies**: RNNs are specifically designed to capture temporal dependencies in sequential data, making them highly effective for time-series and language data.

2. **Flexible with Input Lengths**: RNNs can handle variable-length input sequences, such as sentences of different lengths, which is important for NLP tasks.

Disadvantages of RNNs

1. **Vanishing Gradient Problem**: RNNs suffer from the **vanishing gradient problem**, where the gradients used for weight updates become extremely small as they are propagated back through time. This makes it difficult for RNNs to learn long-term dependencies.

2. **Computational Complexity**: RNNs can be slow to train, especially for long sequences, due to the complexity of Backpropagation Through Time.

3. Long Short-Term Memory Networks (LSTMs)

Long Short-Term Memory (LSTM) networks are a specialized type of RNN designed to overcome the vanishing gradient problem and capture long-term dependencies in sequential data. LSTMs are capable of learning patterns over much longer time horizons compared to standard RNNs, making them highly effective for tasks that require understanding long sequences of data.

How LSTMs Work

LSTMs introduce a special architecture with **gates** that control the flow of information, allowing the network to maintain long-term memory.

1. **Forget Gate**: The forget gate determines which information from the previous hidden state should be discarded. It uses a sigmoid function to decide how much information to retain or forget.

2. **Input Gate**: The input gate controls what new information should be added to the cell state. This helps the network update its memory with relevant new inputs.

3. **Output Gate**: The output gate controls the final output of the LSTM, determining which parts of the cell state should be passed to the next layer or used for the final prediction.

4. **Cell State**: The cell state is the key to LSTMs' ability to retain long-term memory. It acts as a conveyor belt that

runs through the network, allowing information to flow unchanged, or with minor modifications, through time steps.

These gates make LSTMs robust against the vanishing gradient problem, enabling them to learn dependencies that span many time steps.

Example of LSTM Usage

LSTMs are commonly used in **speech recognition**. When transcribing spoken words into text, LSTMs can capture long-term dependencies in the audio signal, allowing them to recognize entire phrases or sentences accurately.

Applications of LSTMs

1. **Text Generation**: LSTMs are used to generate coherent text by predicting the next word or character based on previous context.

2. **Machine Translation**: LSTMs power translation systems that convert text from one language to another by retaining long-term dependencies in sentences.

3. **Time-Series Forecasting**: LSTMs are highly effective in predicting future values in time-series data, such as energy consumption or stock market prices.

4. **Speech Recognition and Generation**: LSTMs are used to recognize spoken language or generate natural-sounding speech.

Advantages of LSTMs

1. **Handles Long-Term Dependencies**: LSTMs are specifically designed to capture long-term dependencies,

making them superior to standard RNNs for tasks involving long sequences.

2. **Resilient to Vanishing Gradient Problem**: LSTMs solve the vanishing gradient problem that plagues traditional RNNs, enabling them to retain information over longer periods.

Disadvantages of LSTMs

1. **Computationally Expensive**: LSTMs are more complex than standard RNNs, making them slower to train and more computationally expensive.

2. **Requires Large Datasets**: LSTMs often require large amounts of data to train effectively, which can be a limitation for certain tasks.

CNNs, RNNs, and LSTMs are three of the most powerful deep learning architectures, each tailored to specific types of data and tasks.

CNNs excel at processing spatial data like images and videos, making them ideal for tasks such as image classification, object detection, and facial recognition.

RNNs, on the other hand, are built to handle sequential data like text and time-series, allowing them to model temporal dependencies.

LSTMs extend RNNs by enabling the network to capture long-term dependencies, overcoming the limitations of standard RNNs in tasks such as language modeling, speech recognition, and time-series forecasting.

By understanding the strengths and limitations of each architecture, data scientists and machine learning engineers can choose the most appropriate model for their specific tasks.

These architectures continue to drive advancements in AI, enabling machines to understand images, language, and sequential data with remarkable accuracy.

5.3 Backpropagation and Gradient Descent

Backpropagation and **Gradient Descent** are two foundational concepts in training neural networks. Together, they enable a neural network to learn from data by adjusting its parameters (weights and biases) to minimize prediction errors. These two concepts work hand in hand: **Gradient Descent** is the optimization algorithm that updates the model's weights, and **Backpropagation** calculates the gradients needed for those updates.

Understanding these techniques is crucial for anyone looking to grasp how deep learning models, including neural networks, improve their performance over time.

1. What is Backpropagation?

Backpropagation (short for **backward propagation of errors**) is an algorithm used to compute the gradients of the loss function with respect to the weights in a neural network. It allows the network to adjust its parameters to reduce errors over time by passing error information backward through the network, layer by layer.

In a neural network, each neuron is connected to others through **weights**. These weights are the parameters the network learns during training, and backpropagation helps update them to minimize the **loss** (error between predicted and actual output).

How Backpropagation Works

Backpropagation works in two main steps:

1. **Forward Pass**: In the forward pass, the input data is passed through the network layer by layer. Each neuron applies its weighted sum of inputs and passes the result to the next layer. The final layer produces an output, which is compared to the true target to compute the **loss**. The commonly used loss functions include **mean squared error (MSE)** for regression tasks and **cross-entropy loss** for classification tasks.

2. **Backward Pass**: After computing the loss, backpropagation calculates how much each weight contributed to the error. This is done by applying the **chain rule** of calculus to compute the gradient of the loss function with respect to each weight. Starting from the output layer, the algorithm works backward through the network, layer by layer, calculating gradients and updating the weights accordingly.

The key steps in the backward pass are:

- **Calculate the Error at the Output Layer**: The difference between the predicted output and the actual target is calculated to find the error in the output layer.

- **Propagate the Error Backward**: The error is propagated back through the hidden layers of the network, using the chain rule to calculate the contribution of each neuron and weight to the overall error.

- **Update the Weights**: The gradients calculated during backpropagation are used to update the weights. This update is done using an optimization algorithm like **Gradient Descent**, which we'll discuss next.

Example of Backpropagation

Imagine a neural network designed to classify handwritten digits. In the forward pass, an input image of a digit (e.g., a "5") is passed through the network, which produces a prediction (e.g., the digit "3"). The error is computed by comparing the predicted output with the true label ("5"). In the backward pass, this error is propagated back through the network to calculate how much each weight contributed to the wrong prediction. Based on these calculations, the weights are adjusted to reduce the error for future predictions.

2. What is Gradient Descent?

Gradient Descent is an optimization algorithm used to minimize a function by iteratively moving toward the direction of the steepest descent, as defined by the negative gradient of the function. In the context of neural networks, Gradient Descent is used to minimize the **loss function** by updating the model's weights in the direction that reduces the error.

In simpler terms, Gradient Descent adjusts the weights in the neural network so that the output of the network gets closer to the desired target.

How Gradient Descent Works

Gradient Descent works by taking small steps in the direction of the negative gradient of the loss function. The gradient tells us the direction in which the loss increases most rapidly. By moving in the opposite direction of the gradient, the algorithm ensures that the loss decreases at each step.

The weight update rule in Gradient Descent is given by:

$$w = w - \alpha * \nabla L(w)$$

Where:

- w is the current weight,

- α is the **learning rate**, a hyperparameter that controls the size of the step taken in the direction of the negative gradient,

- $\nabla L(w)$ is the gradient of the loss function with respect to the weight w.

The key idea is to keep adjusting the weights until the loss function reaches a minimum, meaning that the network has learned to make accurate predictions.

Types of Gradient Descent

There are three main types of Gradient Descent, depending on how much data is used to compute the gradient:

1. **Batch Gradient Descent: In batch gradient descent,** the gradients are computed using the entire training dataset in one go. This can lead to more stable weight updates, but it is computationally expensive for large datasets. One weight update is made per epoch (pass over the entire dataset).

2. **Stochastic Gradient Descent (SGD): In SGD,** the gradient is computed using a single random data point from the dataset, and the weights are updated after every single data point. This makes the algorithm faster and allows it to escape local minima, but it introduces more variance, leading to noisier updates.

3. **Mini-batch Gradient Descent: Mini-batch gradient descent** is a compromise between batch gradient descent and SGD. The gradients are computed using a small batch of data points (typically between 32 and 256), which balances the computational efficiency of SGD with the stability of batch gradient descent.

Learning Rate in Gradient Descent

The **learning rate** is a critical hyperparameter in Gradient Descent. It controls the size of the step taken in the direction of the gradient during each update. Choosing the right learning rate is essential:

- **Too small:** The algorithm converges slowly, requiring more iterations to find the minimum.

- **Too large:** The algorithm may overshoot the minimum, failing to converge, or may even cause the loss to diverge.

A common strategy is to start with a moderate learning rate and adjust it during training using techniques like **learning rate schedules** or **adaptive learning rate methods**.

Combining Backpropagation and Gradient Descent

In a neural network, **backpropagation** calculates the gradients of the loss function with respect to each weight, and **Gradient Descent** uses these gradients to update the weights in a way that minimizes the loss.

The combination of these two techniques works as follows:

1. During the forward pass, the input data is passed through the network, and the loss is calculated based on the network's prediction.

2. In the backward pass, backpropagation computes the gradients of the loss function with respect to each weight using the chain rule.

3. Gradient Descent updates the weights by taking small steps in the direction that minimizes the loss, as determined by the gradients.

This process is repeated iteratively for many epochs until the model converges, meaning the loss function reaches a minimum and the network's predictions are sufficiently accurate.

Challenges in Gradient Descent and Backpropagation

While Gradient Descent and Backpropagation are powerful tools for training neural networks, they come with some challenges:

1. **Vanishing Gradient Problem**: In deep networks, the gradients of the loss function can become extremely small as they are propagated back through many layers. This is called the **vanishing gradient problem** and makes it difficult for the network to learn. This issue is particularly common in neural networks with **sigmoid** or **tanh** activation functions.

2. **Exploding Gradient Problem**: The opposite of vanishing gradients, exploding gradients occur when the gradients become excessively large, causing the weights to change dramatically and destabilizing the training process. This can happen in very deep networks with long sequences of backpropagation.

3. **Local Minima**: Gradient Descent can sometimes get stuck in **local minima**, where the loss function is minimized for a small region of the parameter space but not for the overall global minimum. Stochastic Gradient

Descent (SGD) helps overcome this by introducing noise, which can help the algorithm escape local minima.

4. **Choosing the Learning Rate**: Selecting an appropriate learning rate is crucial for effective training. Too high, and the model may not converge. Too low, and the model may take too long to converge or get stuck in a suboptimal solution.

Optimizations to Gradient Descent

Several variants of Gradient Descent have been developed to address its limitations and improve convergence:

1. **Momentum**: Momentum adds a fraction of the previous weight update to the current update, which helps accelerate the convergence, especially in cases of high curvature or small but consistent gradients.

2. **RMSProp (Root Mean Square Propagation)**: RMSProp divides the learning rate by a running average of recent gradient magnitudes, allowing the algorithm to adapt the learning rate based on the frequency of updates for each weight. This helps in smoothing the updates and improving convergence.

3. **Adam (Adaptive Moment Estimation)**: Adam combines the benefits of both momentum and RMSProp. It computes adaptive learning rates for each parameter and uses moving averages of both the gradient and the squared gradient. Adam is one of the most popular optimization algorithms for training neural networks.

Applications of Backpropagation and Gradient Descent

Backpropagation and Gradient Descent are fundamental components of many machine learning models, particularly in deep learning:

1. **Image Classification**: Neural networks trained using backpropagation and gradient descent are commonly used for tasks like identifying objects in images or recognizing handwritten digits.

2. **Natural Language Processing (NLP)**: Recurrent neural networks (RNNs) and transformers, trained using these techniques, are applied in NLP tasks such as language translation, sentiment analysis, and question answering.

3. **Speech Recognition**: Neural networks trained with these methods are used to transcribe spoken language into text.

4. **Time-Series Forecasting**: Models like LSTMs, trained using backpropagation and gradient descent, are used to predict future values in time-series data, such as stock prices or weather conditions.

Backpropagation and **Gradient Descent** are the driving forces behind neural network training. Backpropagation enables the efficient calculation of gradients, while Gradient Descent updates the network's weights to minimize the loss.

Together, they form the backbone of modern machine learning, allowing neural networks to learn from data and make accurate predictions.

Despite challenges like the vanishing gradient problem and the need to carefully select learning rates, backpropagation and gradient descent have proven to be highly effective for training deep learning models.

These techniques continue to be refined and optimized, making them more efficient and capable of solving increasingly complex problems in fields such as computer vision, natural language processing, and beyond.

5.4 Transfer Learning and Pre-trained Models

Transfer Learning is a machine learning technique that leverages knowledge learned from one task and applies it to another, often related, task. This approach is especially useful when the target task has limited data, but a similar source task has abundant data.

Transfer learning significantly reduces the time and resources needed to train models, enabling faster development and higher accuracy, especially for complex tasks like image classification, natural language processing, and speech recognition.

At the heart of transfer learning are **pre-trained models**— models that have been trained on large, general-purpose datasets, and whose learned weights and features can be transferred to solve new, specific tasks.

These pre-trained models allow us to bypass the need to train from scratch, making it possible to achieve high performance with less computational effort and fewer labeled data points.

What is Transfer Learning?

Transfer learning focuses on storing knowledge gained while solving one problem and applying it to a different but related problem. It is particularly useful in situations where the dataset for the new task is too small to train a model effectively from scratch.

Instead of training a neural network from the ground up, transfer learning involves taking a **pre-trained model** (which has learned general features from a large dataset) and fine-tuning it for a new, specific task.

How Transfer Learning Works

1. **Pre-trained Model**: Start with a neural network that has already been trained on a large dataset for a similar task. For instance, a convolutional neural network (CNN) trained on the ImageNet dataset (which contains millions of images) can be used to classify new images.

2. **Fine-tuning**: Modify the pre-trained model by fine-tuning it for the specific task you want to solve. This often involves:

   o **Freezing earlier layers**: Early layers of the network, which have learned general features (like edges, textures, and shapes in the case of images), are usually frozen so their weights don't change during training.

   o **Training later layers**: The later layers, which are more task-specific, are retrained or replaced with new layers to adapt the model to the specific task.

3. **Transfer Knowledge**: The knowledge learned from the source task (e.g., ImageNet classification) is transferred to the target task (e.g., classifying a small dataset of medical images).

Types of Transfer Learning

1. **Fine-Tuning**: Fine-tuning involves taking a pre-trained model and adapting it to a new task by training its later layers while keeping earlier layers frozen. This approach works well when the target task is similar to the source task.

2. **Feature Extraction**: In this approach, a pre-trained model is used as a **feature extractor**. The model's early layers, which capture generic patterns and features, are kept unchanged. Only the final classification layer is replaced to fit the new task.

3. **Domain Adaptation**: Domain adaptation focuses on transferring knowledge across different but related domains (e.g., applying a model trained on satellite images to drone images). It is useful when the source and target data come from slightly different distributions.

4. **Cross-Task Transfer**: Here, the knowledge gained from one task is transferred to a completely different task. For example, transferring features learned from an image classification model to a video processing task.

Pre-trained Models

Pre-trained models are neural networks that have been trained on large benchmark datasets and can be reused to solve new tasks. These models are commonly used in transfer learning as they save time and computational resources. Pre-trained models are particularly helpful in deep learning, where training large models from scratch requires massive amounts of data and computational power.

Several pre-trained models are available for tasks such as image recognition, object detection, language modeling, and more. Below are some widely used pre-trained models for different domains.

1. Pre-trained Models for Image Processing

- **VGG16 and VGG19**: These are deep CNN architectures pre-trained on the ImageNet dataset. They have proven effective in tasks like image classification and feature extraction. VGG models are popular because of their simplicity and effectiveness in a variety of tasks.

- **ResNet**: ResNet (Residual Networks) introduced the concept of **skip connections**, which allow layers to learn residual mappings instead of direct mappings, addressing the vanishing gradient problem in deep networks. ResNet models (e.g., ResNet-50, ResNet-101) are pre-trained on ImageNet and are widely used for transfer learning in tasks like object detection and image segmentation.

- **Inception**: The Inception architecture (e.g., Inception-v3) was designed to be computationally efficient while maintaining high accuracy. It is pre-trained on ImageNet and is often used for transfer learning in tasks such as medical image analysis.

- **EfficientNet**: EfficientNet models are known for their high accuracy and efficiency. They are pre-trained on ImageNet and are scalable, meaning you can adjust the size of the model based on your computational resources.

- **MobileNet**: Designed for mobile and edge devices, MobileNet is lightweight and computationally efficient. It is pre-trained on ImageNet and is commonly used for applications requiring real-time processing, such as mobile image recognition and augmented reality.

2. Pre-trained Models for Natural Language Processing (NLP)

- **BERT (Bidirectional Encoder Representations from Transformers)**: BERT is a transformer-based model pre-trained on large text corpora. It learns contextual relationships between words in a sentence and is widely used for NLP tasks like sentiment analysis, text classification, and question answering. BERT is available in several versions, such as BERT-Base and BERT-Large.

- **GPT (Generative Pretrained Transformer)**: GPT models, including GPT-2 and GPT-3, are transformer-based models pre-trained to generate text. They can be fine-tuned for a variety of NLP tasks, such as text summarization, translation, and dialogue generation.

- **RoBERTa**: A variant of BERT, RoBERTa (Robustly Optimized BERT Pretraining Approach) improves upon BERT by tweaking hyperparameters and training on more data. It has become popular for NLP tasks requiring high performance, such as language translation and text generation.

- **T5 (Text-to-Text Transfer Transformer)**: T5 treats every NLP task as a text-to-text task, converting inputs and outputs into text strings. It is pre-trained on a massive dataset and can be fine-tuned for tasks like machine translation, summarization, and question answering.

- **XLNet**: XLNet is another transformer-based model that improves upon BERT by incorporating autoregressive training techniques. It achieves state-of-the-art performance on various NLP tasks, including text generation and language modeling.

3. Pre-trained Models for Speech Recognition and Audio Processing

- **DeepSpeech**: DeepSpeech is an open-source speech recognition model trained on large audio datasets. It can be used for speech-to-text conversion and is particularly useful for applications like virtual assistants and voice-controlled systems.

- **Wave2Vec**: Wave2Vec is a model designed for self-supervised learning of speech representations. Pre-trained on large audio corpora, Wave2Vec can be fine-tuned for speech recognition, speaker identification, and audio classification.

- **Wav2Vec 2.0**: An improved version of Wave2Vec, this model uses transformers to model speech representations and has been shown to achieve state-of-the-art performance on automatic speech recognition (ASR) tasks.

Benefits of Transfer Learning and Pre-trained Models

1. **Reduced Training Time**: Training a neural network from scratch can take days or weeks, especially for large models. Transfer learning drastically reduces the time needed to train a model by reusing pre-trained weights.

2. **Higher Accuracy**: Pre-trained models have already learned general features from massive datasets, so fine-

tuning them for a specific task often leads to better performance, especially when the target dataset is small.

3. **Works Well with Limited Data**: Many machine learning tasks suffer from limited labeled data. Transfer learning allows you to leverage knowledge from large, well-labeled datasets to improve performance on tasks where you have only a small amount of data.

4. **Efficient Resource Utilization**: Training deep neural networks from scratch requires significant computational resources. By using pre-trained models, you can achieve state-of-the-art performance without the need for powerful hardware.

5. **Versatility Across Domains**: Transfer learning is highly flexible and can be applied to various domains, from computer vision to NLP and beyond. Pre-trained models provide a starting point for a wide range of tasks, from image classification to text translation and speech recognition.

6. **Reduced Risk of Overfitting**: When training on small datasets, models are prone to overfitting (i.e., learning patterns that don't generalize to new data). Transfer learning helps mitigate this risk by starting with a model that has already learned useful features.

Challenges and Considerations in Transfer Learning

1. **Task Similarity**: Transfer learning works best when the source task (for which the model was pre-trained) is similar to the target task. If the tasks are too different, the transferred features may not be useful, leading to poor performance.

2. **Fine-Tuning Complexity**: Fine-tuning pre-trained models requires careful hyperparameter tuning. Overfitting can occur if too many layers are retrained, while freezing too many layers may prevent the model from adapting well to the new task.

3. **Computational Resources**: While transfer learning reduces the training time, fine-tuning large models (e.g., BERT, GPT-3) still requires significant computational power, especially if dealing with large datasets.

4. **Data Privacy and Domain Differences**: In some cases, the source data used to pre-train the model may differ significantly from the target data. For example, models trained on public datasets may not perform as well on private, domain-specific data without careful fine-tuning.

5. **Availability of Pre-trained Models**: Transfer learning requires access to pre-trained models, and for some specific tasks or industries, such models may not be readily available.

Applications of Transfer Learning

1. **Image Recognition**: Transfer learning is widely used in image classification and object detection tasks, where pre-trained models like ResNet or EfficientNet, trained on large datasets like ImageNet, are fine-tuned to recognize specific objects in smaller datasets.

2. **Natural Language Processing**: In NLP, transfer learning has revolutionized tasks like text classification, language translation, sentiment analysis, and question answering. Models like BERT, GPT, and T5 are pre-trained on massive text corpora and then fine-tuned for specific tasks.

3. **Speech Recognition**: Transfer learning is used in speech-to-text systems, where pre-trained models like DeepSpeech are adapted for different languages or domains (e.g., medical transcription, customer service).

4. **Medical Imaging**: In healthcare, transfer learning is applied to medical image analysis, such as detecting tumors in X-rays or MRI scans. Pre-trained models like VGG or ResNet are fine-tuned to classify medical images with high accuracy.

5. **Autonomous Vehicles**: Transfer learning is used in autonomous systems, where pre-trained models are adapted for tasks like object detection, lane detection, and pedestrian recognition in self-driving cars.

6. **Robotics**: Transfer learning allows robots to adapt to new environments by fine-tuning pre-trained models that recognize objects, actions, or spatial layouts.

Transfer Learning and **pre-trained models** have transformed the landscape of machine learning and deep learning, offering a powerful way to leverage knowledge from large datasets and apply it to new tasks with minimal data and computational resources.

By fine-tuning pre-trained models, we can achieve state-of-the-art performance in tasks ranging from image classification and natural language processing to speech recognition and medical imaging.

The use of pre-trained models saves time, reduces overfitting, and enables machine learning practitioners to solve problems efficiently, even when data is scarce. As new models and architectures emerge, transfer learning will continue to play a key role in advancing AI across various domains and applications.

5.5 Implementing Deep Learning Models with TensorFlow and Keras

When implementing deep learning models, **TensorFlow** and **Keras** are two popular tools that make the process easier and more effective. TensorFlow is an open-source platform developed by Google for machine learning, while Keras is a high-level API that runs on top of TensorFlow. Using these tools together provides an accessible way to design, train, and deploy neural networks.

With TensorFlow's powerful backend and Keras's easy-to-use interface, you can build complex models efficiently, whether for image recognition, natural language processing, or time-series forecasting.

Why Use TensorFlow and Keras?

There are several reasons why TensorFlow and Keras are highly recommended for implementing deep learning models:

1. **Ease of Use**: Keras provides a high-level API that simplifies the process of building and experimenting with neural networks. This is perfect for beginners and experts alike because it abstracts much of the complexity of neural network architectures.

2. **Flexibility**: TensorFlow offers low-level control for designing custom deep learning models while maintaining the flexibility needed for research and production environments.

3. **Scalability**: TensorFlow can scale across CPUs, GPUs, and even TPUs (Tensor Processing Units), making it efficient for training models on large datasets and for deployment in real-world scenarios.

4. **Extensive Ecosystem**: TensorFlow's ecosystem supports a wide range of tools for model deployment (such as TensorFlow Lite for mobile devices and TensorFlow Serving for web services), making it easier to bring models into production.

Key Steps in Building a Deep Learning Model

The process of building a deep learning model with TensorFlow and Keras can be summarized in six main steps:

1. **Loading and Preprocessing the Data**

2. **Defining the Model Architecture**

3. **Compiling the Model**

4. **Training the Model**

5. **Evaluating the Model**

6. **Making Predictions**

1. Loading and Preprocessing the Data

The first step is to load the dataset and prepare it for training. For image classification, for example, the data might need to be reshaped into a suitable format for neural networks, and the pixel values might need to be normalized so that they lie between 0 and 1. Labels (e.g., class names for classification) are often converted into categorical or one-hot encoded formats.

When working with Keras, datasets such as MNIST (a dataset of handwritten digits) are available directly through its dataset utilities. Once loaded, the data can be split into training and testing sets. Preprocessing techniques are applied to ensure the data is in a suitable format for the neural network to process efficiently.

2. Defining the Model Architecture

The next step involves defining the architecture of the neural network. In Keras, this is done by specifying layers that transform the input data into the desired output. For example, in a convolutional neural network (CNN) used for image classification, you might define several convolutional layers to detect patterns in the images, followed by pooling layers to reduce the spatial dimensions.

A typical CNN for image classification might include:

- **Convolutional layers** to extract features such as edges, shapes, and textures from images.

- **Pooling layers** to reduce the size of the feature maps and retain only the most important information.

- **Fully connected (dense) layers** to make predictions based on the extracted features.

- A **softmax activation function** in the output layer to provide probabilities for each class.

Similarly, for other types of data such as text or time-series data, you might use recurrent neural networks (RNNs) or long short-term memory networks (LSTMs) to capture sequential dependencies.

3. Compiling the Model

Once the architecture is defined, the model needs to be compiled. This step involves specifying:

- An **optimizer**: The optimizer controls how the model's parameters (weights) are updated based on the error (or loss). Common optimizers include Adam and Stochastic Gradient Descent (SGD).

- **A loss function**: The loss function measures how well the model's predictions match the true labels. For classification tasks, the cross-entropy loss is often used, while for regression tasks, mean squared error is a common choice.

- **Evaluation metrics**: These metrics (such as accuracy) are used to monitor the model's performance during training and testing.

Compiling the model brings all these components together so that it's ready for training.

4. Training the Model

After compiling the model, it is trained on the dataset. During training, the model adjusts its weights to minimize the error based on the training data. The model is trained over several **epochs** (passes over the entire training dataset), and the data is typically processed in **batches** to make the computation more manageable.

Training also involves monitoring the model's performance on both the training data and validation data (a portion of the data set aside to test the model during training). This helps ensure that the model is not overfitting to the training data and can generalize well to new, unseen data.

Common parameters in this step include:

- **Epochs**: The number of times the entire dataset is passed through the network during training.

- **Batch size:** The number of samples processed before the model's weights are updated.

During training, you might also use **callbacks**, such as early stopping (which halts training if the model's performance on the validation set stops improving) or model checkpointing (which saves the model's weights after each epoch).

5. Evaluating the Model

Once training is complete, the model needs to be evaluated on the **test set**—data it has never seen before—to assess its generalization performance. The model is tested on its ability to make predictions on new data, and metrics such as accuracy or loss are calculated to determine how well the model performs.

In classification tasks, accuracy is a common metric, while for regression, mean squared error or root mean squared error might be used.

6. Making Predictions

After evaluating the model, it can be used to make predictions on new or unseen data. For example, in a classification task, the model will output probabilities for each class, and the class with the highest probability is selected as the prediction.

The model can be deployed in various ways, such as serving it in a web application, running it on mobile devices using TensorFlow Lite, or using it in batch processing systems.

Model Saving and Loading

One of the useful features of TensorFlow and Keras is the ability to save a trained model and reload it later for further training or making predictions. This is particularly useful for long-running models that you want to resume training or for deploying models into production environments.

Saving a model includes both the model architecture and the learned weights. The saved model can be easily reloaded and used without needing to retrain it from scratch.

Advanced Concepts in TensorFlow and Keras

As you become more comfortable with implementing basic models, TensorFlow and Keras offer more advanced features to help you experiment and refine your models:

1. **Custom Layers and Models**: You can create custom neural network layers and models, allowing for more flexibility in the architecture and behavior of the network.

2. **Transfer Learning**: Pre-trained models, such as VGG16 or ResNet, can be fine-tuned for new tasks using transfer learning. This technique allows you to leverage knowledge gained from large-scale datasets to improve performance on tasks with smaller datasets.

3. **Callbacks**: Keras offers callbacks, which allow you to execute certain actions at different stages of training, such as saving the model's weights or adjusting the learning rate based on training progress.

4. **Handling Imbalanced Datasets**: When working with imbalanced datasets (where some classes are underrepresented), you can use techniques such as class weighting to ensure the model gives equal importance to all classes.

5. **Custom Loss Functions**: You can define custom loss functions that tailor the model's training process to the specific needs of your task.

6. **Distributed Training**: TensorFlow supports distributed training across multiple GPUs or even across clusters, making it possible to train very large models on massive datasets.

Implementing deep learning models using **TensorFlow** and **Keras** is a highly efficient and scalable approach to solving complex machine learning problems.

With Keras' high-level API, building, training, and evaluating models is streamlined, while TensorFlow provides the flexibility needed for custom architectures and large-scale deployment.

By following the steps outlined above—loading data, defining the model architecture, compiling, training, evaluating, and making predictions—you can quickly build and deploy high-performance deep learning models.

These tools are versatile enough to handle tasks ranging from image classification to natural language processing, making them essential in modern machine learning workflows.

Chapter 6: Model Evaluation and Optimization

6.1 Evaluation Metrics: Accuracy, Precision, Recall, and F1 Score

When building machine learning models, it is essential to evaluate their performance using suitable metrics. These evaluation metrics help determine how well a model is performing, how accurately it is making predictions, and whether it is effectively handling both correct and incorrect predictions. The most commonly used metrics in classification tasks are **Accuracy**, **Precision**, **Recall**, and **F1 Score**. Each metric focuses on a specific aspect of the model's performance and can give different insights depending on the problem at hand.

Some models may perform well in terms of accuracy but perform poorly in terms of precision or recall, especially in imbalanced datasets. Hence, choosing the right evaluation metric is crucial, depending on the nature of the problem and the data you are working with. Below, we will explore these metrics in detail, understand how they are calculated, and examine when to use each one.

Accuracy

Accuracy is probably the most commonly used metric for evaluating machine learning models. It tells us what proportion of all predictions made by the model are correct. In other words, accuracy measures how many predictions (both positive and negative) the model got right out of the total number of predictions it made.

The formula for accuracy is simple:

Accuracy = (True Positives + True Negatives) / Total Predictions

Where:

- **True Positives (TP)**: These are the instances where the model correctly predicted the positive class.

- **True Negatives (TN)**: These are the instances where the model correctly predicted the negative class.

- **Total Predictions**: This is the total number of instances the model made predictions for, including both correct and incorrect predictions.

For example, in a binary classification task such as predicting whether an email is spam or not, if the model correctly classifies 900 out of 1000 emails, the accuracy would be:

Accuracy = 900 / 1000 = 90%

While accuracy seems to provide a straightforward measure of model performance, it can be misleading, particularly in cases where the dataset is **imbalanced**. An imbalanced dataset is one where one class dominates the other. For example, in a fraud detection task, if only 1% of transactions are fraudulent, a model that always predicts "not fraudulent" would have 99% accuracy, even though it is not detecting any fraudulent transactions. Therefore, while accuracy is easy to calculate and interpret, it may not be the best metric in all cases.

Precision

Precision focuses on the quality of the model's positive predictions. It answers the question: "Of all the instances the model predicted as positive, how many were actually positive?" In other words, precision measures how good the model is at avoiding false positives.

The formula for precision is:

Precision = True Positives / (True Positives + False Positives)

Where:

- **False Positives (FP)**: These are instances where the model incorrectly predicted the positive class (i.e., it predicted positive when the actual class was negative).

Let's revisit the spam email example. If your model identifies 200 emails as spam, but only 150 of those are actually spam, the precision of the model would be:

Precision = 150 / (150 + 50) = 0.75 or 75%

This means that 75% of the emails that the model flagged as spam were correct. A high precision score indicates that the model makes few false positive errors. Precision is a useful metric in situations where **false positives** are costly or undesirable. For instance, in medical diagnostics, predicting that a patient has a disease when they do not (a false positive) could lead to unnecessary medical tests and treatments, which can be costly, invasive, and anxiety-inducing for the patient. In such cases, a high precision score is important because it minimizes the number of incorrect positive predictions.

Recall (Sensitivity)

Recall focuses on the model's ability to detect positive instances correctly. It answers the question: "Of all the actual positive instances, how many did the model correctly identify?" This metric measures how good the model is at avoiding **false negatives** (when it fails to predict a positive instance).

The formula for recall is:

Recall = True Positives / (True Positives + False Negatives)

Where:

- **False Negatives (FN)**: These are instances where the model incorrectly predicted the negative class (i.e., it predicted negative when the actual class was positive).

For example, in a medical test for cancer, if there are 100 patients with cancer and the model correctly identifies 80 of them but misses 20, the recall would be:

Recall = 80 / (80 + 20) = 0.80 or 80%

This means that 80% of the actual positive cases (patients with cancer) were correctly identified by the model. A high recall score indicates that the model is good at detecting most positive instances, even if it means making more false positive errors.

Recall is particularly important when **false negatives** are costly or dangerous. In the case of disease detection, failing to identify a patient who has a disease (false negative) could have severe consequences, such as delaying necessary treatment. Similarly, in fraud detection, missing fraudulent transactions can lead to significant financial losses. Therefore, recall becomes a crucial metric in scenarios where it is important to catch all positive cases, even at the expense of a few false alarms.

F1 Score

The **F1 Score** is a metric that combines both precision and recall into a single number, providing a balanced measure of a model's performance. It is the harmonic mean of precision and recall, which gives a single score that accounts for both types of errors (false positives and false negatives).

The formula for the F1 score is:

F1 Score = 2 * (Precision * Recall) / (Precision + Recall)

The F1 score ranges between 0 and 1, where 1 represents perfect precision and recall, and 0 represents the worst possible performance. The harmonic mean used in the F1 score ensures that both precision and recall are given equal importance. If a model has high precision but low recall, or vice versa, the F1 score will reflect this imbalance.

For example, if a model has a precision of 0.75 and a recall of 0.60, the F1 score would be:

F1 Score = 2 * (0.75 * 0.60) / (0.75 + 0.60) = 0.67

This means that the model's F1 score is 0.67, indicating that it has a moderate balance between precision and recall. The F1 score is particularly useful when you need a single metric that accounts for both false positives and false negatives, and it is especially valuable in situations where the dataset is imbalanced.

When to Use Each Metric

Each of these evaluation metrics serves a specific purpose, and the choice of which one to use depends on the problem you are solving and the nature of your dataset.

- **Accuracy** is a good metric when the dataset is balanced and you care equally about both classes. It gives a general sense of how well the model is performing overall. However, in imbalanced datasets, accuracy can be misleading, as it may give a false sense of good performance by simply predicting the majority class most of the time.

- **Precision** is important when the cost of a **false positive** is high. If you want to be more confident that the positive predictions your model makes are actually correct, precision is the metric to focus on. Precision is crucial in applications like email spam detection, where false positives (legitimate emails marked as spam) can cause users to miss important communications.

- **Recall** is important when the cost of a **false negative** is high. If your primary goal is to identify all positive cases, recall should be prioritized. Recall is critical in applications like medical diagnosis, where missing a positive case (false negative) could lead to serious health consequences.

- **F1 Score** is best used when you need to balance both precision and recall, especially in situations where there is a trade-off between the two. It is particularly useful for imbalanced datasets, where you want a single metric to give you a sense of overall performance.

Practical Example: Using Metrics in Fraud Detection

Consider a credit card fraud detection system. Fraudulent transactions are relatively rare compared to legitimate transactions, so the dataset is highly imbalanced. In this case:

- **Accuracy** might give an overly optimistic view of the model's performance because a model that always predicts "not fraudulent" could have high accuracy due to the dominance of legitimate transactions.

- **Precision** would be important because you don't want to incorrectly classify too many legitimate transactions as fraudulent, which could annoy customers and cause financial disruption.

- **Recall** would be equally important because you want to catch as many fraudulent transactions as possible to prevent financial loss.

- The **F1 score** would be a good way to balance precision and recall, ensuring that the model identifies as much fraud as possible without flagging too many legitimate transactions as fraud.

Understanding and choosing the right evaluation metrics is a crucial part of building machine learning models, particularly in classification tasks. While **accuracy** is a simple and commonly used metric, it can be misleading in cases of imbalanced datasets.

Metrics like **precision, recall**, and the **F1 score** provide deeper insights into a model's performance, especially when certain types of errors are more costly than others.

The choice of evaluation metric depends on the nature of your data and the specific goals of your machine learning project. Whether you're working in fraud detection, medical diagnosis, or spam filtering, selecting the right metric will help you build a more effective and reliable model.

6.2 Cross-Validation Techniques

Cross-validation is a vital technique in machine learning for assessing how well a model will generalize to unseen data. It helps you understand whether your model is overfitting, underfitting, or performing well on the available data. By splitting the dataset into different subsets, cross-validation provides a reliable way to estimate how well a model will perform on new data, preventing common pitfalls such as overfitting to the training set.

In this section, we'll discuss various **cross-validation techniques**, their importance, how they work, and when to use each technique. These techniques ensure that your machine learning models are evaluated correctly, improving their robustness and helping you make more informed decisions.

What is Cross-Validation?

At its core, cross-validation involves splitting the available dataset into several smaller parts, or **folds**, where different parts of the data are used for training and testing. This allows for a better estimation of a model's performance compared to using a single train-test split.

The idea is to repeatedly train the model on different subsets of the data and test it on the remaining parts, obtaining a more comprehensive view of the model's generalization capability.

One of the primary goals of cross-validation is to avoid

overfitting—a situation where a model performs well on training data but poorly on new, unseen data. By evaluating the model on different data splits, cross-validation gives you a more accurate indication of how the model will perform on real-world data.

Why Cross-Validation is Important

Cross-validation is important because it:

1. **Reduces Overfitting**: By training the model on different portions of the data, cross-validation reduces the risk of overfitting to a specific subset of data, leading to a more generalized model.

2. **Improves Model Selection**: Cross-validation helps in selecting the best model by comparing how different models perform across various data splits.

3. **Optimizes Hyperparameters**: In machine learning, hyperparameters (such as learning rates or the depth of decision trees) need to be tuned. Cross-validation provides a systematic way to choose the best hyperparameters.

4. **Estimates Performance**: It provides a better estimate of the model's real-world performance compared to a single train-test split.

Cross-Validation Techniques

Several cross-validation techniques can be used depending on the size of the dataset, the computational resources available, and the specific requirements of the model or task. Let's explore the most widely used cross-validation techniques:

1. K-Fold Cross-Validation

K-Fold Cross-Validation is one of the most popular cross-validation techniques. In K-fold cross-validation, the dataset is split into **K equal-sized folds** (or subsets). The model is trained **K times**, each time using K-1 folds for training and the remaining fold for testing. This process is repeated K times, and the overall performance of the model is the average performance across all K folds.

For example, if you use 5-fold cross-validation (K=5), the dataset is split into 5 parts:

- In the first iteration, folds 1-4 are used for training, and fold 5 is used for testing.

- In the second iteration, folds 1-3 and 5 are used for training, and fold 4 is used for testing.

- This process is repeated until all folds have been used as the test set once.

Finally, the results from all folds are averaged to give a final performance score.

Advantages:

- **Better Performance Estimate**: It provides a more accurate estimate of model performance compared to a single train-test split.

- **Efficient Use of Data**: All data is used for both training and testing, leading to better generalization and a robust performance estimate.

Disadvantages:

- **Computation Time:** K-fold cross-validation can be computationally expensive, especially for large datasets or complex models, as the model needs to be trained K times.

- **K Selection:** The choice of K can affect the performance estimate. Common choices are K=5 or K=10.

When to Use: K-Fold cross-validation is ideal when you want a reliable performance estimate and have sufficient computational resources to train the model multiple times.

2. Stratified K-Fold Cross-Validation

Stratified K-Fold Cross-Validation is a variation of K-fold cross-validation, where each fold is created in such a way that it maintains the **class distribution** of the data. This is particularly important for classification tasks with **imbalanced datasets.**

For example, if 90% of the data belongs to class A and 10% belongs to class B, regular K-fold cross-validation might randomly split the data, resulting in some folds that are imbalanced (e.g., some folds might contain mostly class A). **Stratified K-fold** ensures that each fold maintains the same ratio of class A to class B as the original dataset.

Advantages:

- **Handles Imbalanced Data:** It works well for classification problems where the dataset is imbalanced, ensuring that each fold has a representative distribution of classes.

- **Reduces Variance:** By preserving the class distribution, stratified K-fold reduces the variance in performance estimates, making them more reliable.

Disadvantages:

- **Computational Overhead:** Like K-fold, it is computationally expensive for large datasets.

When to Use: Use stratified K-fold cross-validation when working with imbalanced datasets, particularly in classification tasks where maintaining the class ratio across folds is important.

3. Leave-One-Out Cross-Validation (LOOCV)

In **Leave-One-Out Cross-Validation (LOOCV)**, the dataset is split into N folds, where N is the total number of instances in the dataset. The model is trained N times, each time using N-1 instances for training and the remaining single instance for testing. This process is repeated for every data point.

Advantages:

- **Maximizes Training Data:** Since all data except one point is used for training in each iteration, LOOCV makes full use of the available data for training.

- **Minimal Bias:** LOOCV provides a nearly unbiased estimate of model performance, as each data point gets tested independently.

Disadvantages:

- **Computationally Expensive:** LOOCV requires training the model N times, which can be highly resource-intensive for large datasets.

- **High Variance:** Since only one data point is used for testing in each iteration, LOOCV can have high variance, meaning that the performance might vary significantly across iterations.

When to Use: LOOCV is ideal when you have a small dataset and want to maximize the training data available, but it's not practical for large datasets due to its high computational cost.

4. Hold-Out Method

The **Hold-Out Method** is the simplest form of cross-validation. In this technique, the dataset is randomly split into two parts:

- **Training set:** Used to train the model.

- **Testing set:** Used to evaluate the model's performance.

Typically, the data is split in a ratio like 70% for training and 30% for testing, or 80-20.

Advantages:

- **Simple and Fast:** The hold-out method is quick and easy to implement since the data is split once, and the model is trained only once.

- **Less Computationally Intensive:** It requires less computational power compared to K-fold or LOOCV, making it a good choice for large datasets.

Disadvantages:

- **Potential Overfitting:** Since the model is trained only on a portion of the data, there's a risk of overfitting to the training set.

- **Less Reliable:** The performance estimate may be less reliable compared to techniques like K-fold cross-validation because the evaluation is based on a single train-test split.

When to Use: The hold-out method is suitable when you have a very large dataset and computational efficiency is important. However, it should be avoided with small datasets, where more advanced techniques like K-fold provide a more robust evaluation.

5. Time-Series Cross-Validation

Time-series data presents unique challenges because the data is ordered by time, and splitting it randomly (as in K-fold) would break the temporal structure. In **time-series cross-validation**, the splits are made respecting the temporal order of the data.

One common method is the **sliding window approach**, where:

- The model is trained on data from the first window of time and tested on the next time window.

- The window then "slides" forward, and the process is repeated with different training and testing periods, always maintaining the temporal order.

Another approach is the **expanding window method**, where the training set grows with each iteration. The model starts by training on the first part of the data, and in each subsequent iteration, more historical data is included in the training set.

Advantages:

- **Respects Time Dependencies:** It ensures that the temporal structure of the data is maintained, making it suitable for time-series forecasting or sequential tasks.

- **Accurate Performance Estimate**: Time-series cross-validation provides a more realistic estimate of the model's ability to predict future data based on past information.

Disadvantages:

- **Less Training Data per Iteration**: Since you are training on earlier time windows, the amount of training data in the early iterations can be small, potentially reducing the model's ability to learn effectively.

When to Use: Time-series cross-validation is essential when working with time-dependent data, such as stock prices, weather data, or any other task where the temporal order matters.

6. Nested Cross-Validation

Nested Cross-Validation is a technique used for model selection and hyperparameter tuning, especially when you want to prevent overfitting during the tuning process. It involves two levels of cross-validation:

- **Outer loop**: Used to assess the performance of the model.

- **Inner loop**: Used for hyperparameter tuning (e.g., choosing the best parameters for a model).

In nested cross-validation, the outer loop splits the data into training and testing sets, while the inner loop performs cross-validation on the training set to tune hyperparameters. The result is a more robust evaluation of the model, as it avoids "data leakage" between the training and testing phases.

Advantages:

- **Prevents Overfitting in Hyperparameter Tuning**: By separating the tuning and evaluation processes, nested cross-validation ensures that the model is not overfitted to the test set.

- **Reliable Performance Estimate**: It provides a more reliable estimate of model performance when hyperparameters need to be tuned.

Disadvantages:

- **Computationally Expensive**: Nested cross-validation can be very slow, especially for large datasets or complex models, as it involves multiple levels of cross-validation.

When to Use: Use nested cross-validation when you need to perform hyperparameter tuning and want a robust evaluation of the model without overfitting to the test data.

Which Cross-Validation Technique Should You Use?

The choice of cross-validation technique depends on several factors, such as the size of the dataset, the task at hand, the computational resources available, and the balance between precision and computational cost. Here's a quick summary of when to use each technique:

- **K-Fold Cross-Validation**: Use this when you have a reasonably large dataset and want a robust estimate of model performance.

- **Stratified K-Fold Cross-Validation**: Use this when dealing with imbalanced datasets in classification tasks to ensure each fold has a representative distribution of classes.

- **Leave-One-Out Cross-Validation (LOOCV)**: Ideal for small datasets where maximizing the use of data is critical, but it's computationally expensive.

- **Hold-Out Method**: Use this for very large datasets where computational efficiency is important, though it's less reliable for small datasets.

- **Time-Series Cross-Validation**: Essential for time-series data to maintain temporal order and ensure accurate forecasting.

- **Nested Cross-Validation**: Best for hyperparameter tuning when you want to avoid overfitting and obtain a reliable performance estimate.

Cross-validation is a critical tool in machine learning that helps evaluate how well a model generalizes to unseen data. By applying different cross-validation techniques, you can gain a more accurate understanding of your model's performance, select the best model, and tune hyperparameters in a way that avoids overfitting.

Understanding when and how to use each cross-validation method allows you to build more robust and reliable models, ensuring they perform well in real-world scenarios.

6.3 Hyperparameter Tuning: Grid Search and Random Search

In machine learning, **hyperparameter tuning** plays a critical role in building models that perform optimally. Hyperparameters are the external configurations of a model that are set before the learning process begins. They control aspects like learning rate, the depth of a decision tree, the number of layers in a neural network, or the number of clusters in a clustering algorithm.

Unlike model parameters (which are learned during training), hyperparameters are not learned and need to be carefully selected to improve a model's performance.

Selecting the right hyperparameters is essential because the wrong choices can lead to underfitting (where the model is too simple to capture the underlying patterns in the data) or overfitting (where the model becomes too complex and captures noise in the data instead of general trends). Two of the most popular techniques for hyperparameter tuning are **Grid Search** and **Random Search**. Both are designed to help find the best combination of hyperparameters for a given model.

This section explores these two techniques, their advantages and disadvantages, and how to use them effectively.

What is Hyperparameter Tuning?

Hyperparameter tuning is the process of optimizing the hyperparameters of a machine learning model to improve its performance. Since hyperparameters are not learned during the training process, you need to try different combinations of them, train the model, and evaluate the model's performance to find the best set.

For example, in a decision tree model, key hyperparameters might include:

- **Max depth**: The maximum depth of the tree.

- **Min samples split**: The minimum number of samples required to split an internal node.

- **Criterion**: The function used to measure the quality of a split (e.g., "gini" or "entropy").

In a neural network, hyperparameters could include:

- **Learning rate**: Controls how quickly the model learns.

- **Batch size**: The number of training samples used to update the model parameters.

- **Number of layers**: Determines the complexity of the neural network.

Since manually testing different combinations of hyperparameters is impractical, especially for large models, we use systematic techniques like Grid Search and Random Search to automate the process.

Grid Search

Grid Search is an exhaustive search method for hyperparameter tuning. It works by specifying a set of possible hyperparameter values for each hyperparameter, creating a grid of all possible combinations, and then evaluating the model's performance for each combination. The combination that gives the best performance (according to a chosen evaluation metric, such as accuracy or F1 score) is selected as the optimal set of hyperparameters.

How Grid Search Works

The process of Grid Search involves the following steps:

1. **Define the Hyperparameter Grid**: Specify a range of values for each hyperparameter you want to tune. For example, if tuning a support vector machine (SVM), you might define:

   o **C**: The penalty parameter, with possible values [0.1, 1, 10, 100].

- o **Kernel**: The kernel type, with possible values ["linear", "rbf"].

- o **Gamma**: The kernel coefficient, with possible values [0.001, 0.01, 0.1, 1].

The hyperparameter grid would include all possible combinations of these values.

2. **Train the Model for Each Combination**: For each combination of hyperparameters in the grid, the model is trained on the training data and evaluated on the validation set. If K-fold cross-validation is used, the model will be trained and tested multiple times for each combination.

3. **Evaluate Performance**: For each combination, calculate the performance metric (such as accuracy, precision, or recall). The combination with the best performance is selected as the optimal set of hyperparameters.

4. **Select the Best Hyperparameters**: The combination of hyperparameters that yields the best performance is returned as the final set of hyperparameters.

Example of Grid Search

Suppose you are building a **Random Forest** classifier, and you want to tune the following hyperparameters:

- **Number of trees** (n_estimators): [50, 100, 150]

- **Max depth** (max_depth): [5, 10, 15]

- **Minimum samples to split** (min_samples_split): [2, 4]

The grid search would try all possible combinations of these hyperparameters. For example:

- Combination 1: n_estimators=50, max_depth=5, min_samples_split=2

- Combination 2: n_estimators=50, max_depth=5, min_samples_split=4

- Combination 3: n_estimators=50, max_depth=10, min_samples_split=2

- And so on, until all combinations have been tested.

The model is trained for each combination, and the performance is evaluated on a validation set or using cross-validation. The hyperparameter combination that gives the highest performance is selected as the final model.

Advantages of Grid Search

1. **Exhaustive**: Grid Search evaluates all possible combinations of hyperparameters, ensuring that the best combination is found.

2. **Easy to Implement**: Grid Search is straightforward and can be easily applied to a wide range of machine learning algorithms.

Disadvantages of Grid Search

1. **Computationally Expensive**: Since Grid Search tries every possible combination of hyperparameters, it becomes computationally expensive, especially when there are many hyperparameters and a large number of possible values for each.

2. **Time-Consuming**: The time required to evaluate all combinations grows exponentially with the number of

hyperparameters, making Grid Search impractical for very large datasets or complex models.

When to Use Grid Search

Grid Search is best used when:

- You have a small number of hyperparameters and a relatively small range of possible values for each.

- You want to guarantee that you find the best combination of hyperparameters.

- You have access to sufficient computational resources to perform an exhaustive search.

Random Search

Random Search is an alternative to Grid Search that randomly samples combinations of hyperparameters from the search space instead of exhaustively trying every possible combination. This approach can be more efficient because it explores the hyperparameter space in a less structured but often more effective way.

Rather than evaluating every combination in a grid, Random Search selects random combinations of hyperparameters and evaluates the model's performance for each. It may not guarantee that the absolute best hyperparameter combination is found, but it often finds a near-optimal combination more quickly than Grid Search.

How Random Search Works

The process of Random Search is similar to Grid Search, with one key difference: instead of trying every combination of hyperparameters, it randomly selects a fixed number of combinations from the search space and evaluates the model for each.

1. **Define the Search Space**: Specify the range of possible values for each hyperparameter. The same ranges you would use in Grid Search can be used here.

2. **Random Sampling**: Instead of testing every combination, the algorithm randomly selects a fixed number of hyperparameter combinations. You can specify how many random samples to evaluate.

3. **Train and Evaluate**: For each randomly selected combination, the model is trained and evaluated using a validation set or cross-validation.

4. **Select the Best Hyperparameters**: After testing the specified number of random combinations, the combination with the best performance is chosen as the final set of hyperparameters.

Example of Random Search

Let's consider the same Random Forest example from Grid Search, with the following hyperparameters:

- **Number of trees** (n_estimators): [50, 100, 150]

- **Max depth** (max_depth): [5, 10, 15]

- **Minimum samples to split** (min_samples_split): [2, 4]

Rather than testing all combinations (as in Grid Search), Random Search would randomly pick a set number of combinations from this space. For example, if you set the number of random samples to 5, Random Search might evaluate the following combinations:

- Combination 1: n_estimators=150, max_depth=10, min_samples_split=4

- Combination 2: n_estimators=50, max_depth=5, min_samples_split=2

- Combination 3: n_estimators=100, max_depth=15, min_samples_split=4

- And so on for 5 random samples.

After evaluating the performance of these 5 random combinations, the combination with the best performance is selected.

Advantages of Random Search

1. **More Efficient**: Random Search is often faster than Grid Search because it evaluates fewer combinations while still exploring the hyperparameter space effectively.

2. **Handles High-Dimensional Search Spaces**: In cases where there are many hyperparameters or the search space is large, Random Search is more practical, as it does not suffer from the exponential growth in combinations that Grid Search does.

3. **Better Exploration**: Random Search can find good combinations more quickly because it samples the search space in a less rigid manner, potentially exploring areas of the hyperparameter space that Grid Search might miss.

Disadvantages of Random Search

1. **No Guarantee of Optimal Solution**: Random Search may not find the absolute best combination of

hyperparameters, as it does not evaluate all possible combinations.

2. **Still Computationally Intensive**: While more efficient than Grid Search, Random Search can still be computationally expensive for large datasets or complex models, depending on the number of random samples chosen.

When to Use Random Search

Random Search is a good choice when:

- You have a large number of hyperparameters or a large search space.

- You want to quickly find a good (though not necessarily the best) set of hyperparameters.

- You have limited computational resources and cannot afford to run exhaustive Grid Search.

- You're willing to sacrifice exhaustive searching for faster performance, especially when you expect diminishing returns from evaluating additional hyperparameter combinations.

Comparing Grid Search and Random Search

Both Grid Search and Random Search have their advantages and disadvantages, and the choice between them depends on your specific use case, the complexity of your model, the size of your dataset, and the available computational resources.

Grid Search is ideal when:

- You need to perform an exhaustive search of a small hyperparameter space.

- You want to ensure that you find the best combination of hyperparameters.

- You have sufficient computational resources and time to evaluate all combinations.

Random Search is ideal when:

- You have a large hyperparameter space and exhaustive search is impractical.

- You need a faster, more efficient way to find a good set of hyperparameters.

- You want to explore more diverse regions of the hyperparameter space in less time.

- You're willing to trade off the certainty of finding the absolute best parameters for speed.

Practical Tips for Hyperparameter Tuning

1. **Start with Random Search**: When you're not sure which hyperparameters are most important or which ranges to use, Random Search is a good starting point. It helps you quickly identify promising regions in the hyperparameter space.

2. **Use Grid Search for Fine-Tuning**: Once you've identified a promising set of hyperparameter ranges using Random Search, you can use Grid Search to fine-tune the model further, narrowing the search space to focus on the most promising areas.

3. **Combine with Cross-Validation**: Always combine hyperparameter tuning with cross-validation to get a more reliable estimate of model performance and avoid overfitting to a single validation set.

4. **Don't Overcomplicate**: Only tune hyperparameters that are likely to have a significant impact on model performance. For many models, not all hyperparameters are equally important.

5. **Monitor Computational Costs**: Hyperparameter tuning can be computationally expensive. Use tools like parallel computing (if available) or cloud resources to speed up the search process.

Hyperparameter tuning is an essential part of building effective machine learning models. **Grid Search** and **Random Search** are two of the most widely used techniques for this task, each with its own strengths and weaknesses.

While **Grid Search** provides a more thorough, exhaustive search of the hyperparameter space, **Random Search** offers a more efficient alternative by exploring random combinations.

Choosing the right tuning method depends on your dataset, model complexity, and available computational resources. By understanding the benefits and trade-offs of each method, you can make more informed decisions and build models that perform well on unseen data, while optimizing time and computational costs.

6.4 Avoiding Overfitting: Regularization and Dropout

Overfitting is one of the most common challenges when training machine learning models. It occurs when a model performs well on the training data but fails to generalize to new, unseen data. This happens when the model becomes too complex and starts memorizing the noise or irrelevant patterns in the training data rather than learning the true underlying structure.

There are several techniques to combat overfitting, with

regularization and **dropout** being two of the most effective methods. These techniques help simplify the model and improve its generalization ability, allowing it to perform better on unseen data.

In this section, we will explore the causes of overfitting, how regularization and dropout work, and when to use each technique to improve your model's performance.

What is Overfitting?

Overfitting happens when a machine learning model learns to perform exceptionally well on the training data but struggles when it encounters new data. This usually means the model has become too complex, capturing details that are not relevant for generalization.

Overfitting typically occurs when:

- **The model is too complex**: Models with too many parameters or layers (in the case of deep learning) are more prone to overfitting because they have the capacity to memorize the data rather than learn useful patterns.

- **Not enough training data**: When the amount of training data is small, it is easier for the model to memorize the specifics of the data rather than learn general patterns that apply more broadly.

- **Noise in the data**: If the data contains a lot of noise or outliers, the model may mistakenly learn these irrelevant features, resulting in poor performance on unseen data.

The goal of machine learning is to build a model that can generalize well, meaning it can make accurate predictions on new, unseen data. To achieve this, techniques like regularization and dropout are commonly used.

Regularization: L1 and L2

Regularization is a technique used to prevent overfitting by adding a penalty to the model's complexity. This is done by introducing an additional term to the loss function that discourages the model from learning overly complex patterns. There are two common types of regularization: **L1** and **L2**.

L2 Regularization (Ridge Regression)

L2 regularization, also known as **ridge regression**, works by adding a penalty equal to the square of the magnitude of the model's coefficients (weights) to the loss function. This encourages the model to keep the weights small, preventing it from fitting to the noise in the training data.

The loss function with L2 regularization is modified as follows:

Loss = Original Loss + $\lambda * \Sigma w^2$

Where:

- λ (lambda) is the regularization parameter that controls the strength of the penalty. A larger value of λ increases the regularization strength.

- Σw^2 is the sum of the squared weights of the model.

By penalizing large weights, L2 regularization forces the model to focus on simpler patterns that generalize better to new data. It doesn't eliminate any weights completely, but it reduces them, making the model less sensitive to individual data points.

L1 Regularization (Lasso Regression)

L1 regularization, also known as **lasso regression**, works similarly to L2 regularization but penalizes the absolute values of the weights rather than their squares. The loss function with L1 regularization is modified as follows:

Loss = Original Loss + $\lambda * \Sigma\ |w|$

Where:

- λ (lambda) is the regularization parameter, controlling the strength of the regularization.

- $\Sigma\ |w|$ is the sum of the absolute values of the weights.

The key difference between L1 and L2 regularization is that L1 can lead to **sparse models**, where some weights are driven to zero, effectively performing **feature selection**. This makes L1 regularization particularly useful when dealing with high-dimensional data, as it helps reduce the number of features used by the model.

Elastic Net Regularization

Elastic Net regularization combines the strengths of both L1 and L2 regularization by adding penalties for both the absolute values of the weights (L1) and the squared values of the weights (L2). The loss function for Elastic Net is:

Loss = Original Loss + $\lambda_1 * \Sigma\ |w| + \lambda_2 * \Sigma\ w^2$

Elastic Net is useful when you want to benefit from the sparsity-inducing properties of L1 regularization while also maintaining the shrinkage properties of L2 regularization. It is particularly effective in scenarios where the data contains a large number of features that are highly correlated.

Choosing Between L1, L2, and Elastic Net

- **L2 regularization** is ideal when you expect all features to contribute somewhat to the model, but you want to prevent any one feature from dominating the learning process.

- **L1 regularization** is suitable when you expect many irrelevant or redundant features, as it can lead to sparse solutions by driving some weights to zero.

- **Elastic Net** is useful when there is a mix of highly correlated features and irrelevant features, as it provides the benefits of both L1 and L2 regularization.

Dropout

Dropout is another highly effective technique for preventing overfitting, particularly in deep learning models. It works by randomly "dropping out" (i.e., setting to zero) a fraction of the neurons in the network during training. This prevents the model from becoming overly reliant on any particular neuron or set of neurons, encouraging it to learn more robust and generalizable patterns.

How Dropout Works

Dropout is applied during training, where, in each forward pass, a random subset of neurons is ignored or "dropped out." This means that during training, the model is essentially training on a slightly different architecture in each pass. This forces the network to learn redundant representations of the data, making it more robust and reducing the likelihood of overfitting.

Dropout is controlled by a hyperparameter **p**, which represents the probability of a neuron being dropped out. For example, a dropout rate of 0.5 means that 50% of the neurons will be randomly dropped during each forward pass.

During testing or inference, dropout is not applied. Instead, the weights are scaled by the dropout rate so that the total contribution of the neurons remains consistent with what was learned during training.

Why Dropout Works

Dropout works by introducing randomness into the learning process, making the model less dependent on any specific subset of neurons. This prevents the model from overfitting to the training data, as no single neuron can become too influential.

Dropout is particularly effective in deep neural networks, where the risk of overfitting is high due to the large number of parameters involved.

By randomly dropping neurons, dropout achieves the following:

- **Reduces co-adaptation**: Dropout prevents neurons from co-adapting too much, meaning they cannot rely on each other too heavily to make predictions. This encourages the network to learn more distributed representations.

- **Encourages redundancy**: Since neurons are randomly dropped during training, the network learns to rely on multiple redundant pathways, making it more resilient to noise and variations in the data.

Dropout in Practice

Dropout is commonly used in **deep learning architectures** such as convolutional neural networks (CNNs) and recurrent neural networks (RNNs). It is often applied to the fully connected layers near the end of the network, where overfitting is most likely to occur due to the large number of parameters.

A typical dropout rate ranges between **0.2 and 0.5**, with 0.5 being a common choice for fully connected layers. The exact dropout rate depends on the complexity of the model and the size of the dataset—higher dropout rates are generally used in more complex models to reduce overfitting.

Other Techniques to Prevent Overfitting

In addition to regularization and dropout, there are several other techniques you can use to avoid overfitting:

1. **Early Stopping**: Early stopping monitors the model's performance on a validation set during training and stops training when the performance on the validation set starts to degrade. This prevents the model from continuing to learn and overfitting to the training data.

2. **Data Augmentation**: Data augmentation artificially increases the size of the training dataset by applying random transformations (such as rotations, scaling, or flipping) to the input data. This is particularly useful in computer vision tasks, where augmenting the data can help the model learn more general patterns.

3. **Cross-Validation**: Using cross-validation helps in evaluating model performance across different subsets of data, ensuring that the model does not overfit to a specific train-test split.

4. **Reduce Model Complexity**: Simplifying the model by reducing the number of layers or parameters can also

help prevent overfitting. A less complex model is less likely to memorize the training data.

5. **Ensemble Learning**: Combining the predictions of multiple models (e.g., using bagging or boosting) can help improve generalization by averaging out the biases of individual models.

When to Use Regularization and Dropout

- **Regularization** (L1, L2, or Elastic Net) is suitable for models like linear regression, logistic regression, support vector machines, and neural networks when you want to penalize large weights and improve generalization. It is particularly useful when dealing with high-dimensional data or when you suspect that some features may be irrelevant or redundant.

- **Dropout** is especially effective in deep learning models with many parameters, such as deep neural networks, where the risk of overfitting is high. It works well in fully connected layers and can be applied to convolutional or recurrent layers in deep learning architectures.

Overfitting is a significant challenge in machine learning, but techniques like **regularization** and **dropout** provide powerful tools to combat it. Regularization (L1, L2, or Elastic Net) adds a penalty to the model's complexity by controlling the size of the weights, preventing the model from fitting the noise in the data.

Dropout, on the other hand, introduces randomness during training, forcing the model to learn more robust and generalizable patterns by randomly deactivating neurons.

By using these techniques, along with other methods like early stopping, data augmentation, and cross-validation, you can significantly improve your model's ability to generalize and reduce the risk of overfitting. This ensures that your model not only performs well on the training data but also on new, unseen data in real-world applications.

6.5 Model Interpretability and Explainability

As machine learning models become more complex, achieving high predictive performance often comes at the cost of interpretability. In many real-world applications, it's not enough for a model to produce accurate predictions—stakeholders often need to understand **why** a model made a particular decision. This is where the concepts of **model interpretability** and **explainability** come into play.

In fields such as healthcare, finance, and law, model decisions can have serious consequences, and understanding the reasoning behind these decisions is crucial for trust, transparency, and regulatory compliance. This section will explore the importance of model interpretability, the differences between interpretability and explainability, and various techniques for interpreting and explaining machine learning models.

What is Model Interpretability?

Model interpretability refers to the ability to understand and reason about the internal workings of a machine learning model. A model is considered interpretable if its decision-making process is transparent, and a human can easily grasp how it arrived at a specific output based on the input data.

Interpretability is especially important when the model's predictions impact decisions that require accountability and justification, such as approving loans, diagnosing diseases, or assessing risk in criminal justice.

Interpretable models are often simpler models, like linear regression or decision trees, where the relationship between inputs and outputs is clear and understandable. However, more complex models like deep neural networks, random forests, and ensemble methods—often referred to as **black-box models**—are much harder to interpret, as they involve numerous parameters and intricate relationships between features.

What is Model Explainability?

Model explainability goes a step beyond interpretability. It involves providing insights into **why** a model made a specific prediction or how a model behaves in response to different inputs. Explainability focuses on explaining the behavior of complex models (e.g., deep neural networks) by using post-hoc methods—techniques that generate explanations after the model has made predictions.

Explainability is important for:

- **Trust**: Users are more likely to trust a model if they understand how it works and why it made certain decisions.

- **Accountability**: In regulated industries, like finance and healthcare, explanations are often required by law to ensure decisions are fair, transparent, and non-discriminatory.

- **Debugging**: Explainability helps identify model biases or errors, which can improve model performance.

- **Ethical AI**: Ensuring that models make ethical and fair decisions is becoming increasingly important, and explainability is essential for identifying potential biases in the model.

While interpretability and explainability are closely related, **interpretability** refers to how understandable a model is on its own, while **explainability** refers to the tools and methods used to understand and communicate the decisions of potentially complex models.

The Importance of Model Interpretability and Explainability

Model interpretability and explainability are crucial for several reasons:

1. **Regulatory Compliance**: In industries like banking, healthcare, and insurance, regulations often require models to be interpretable. For example, the General Data Protection Regulation (GDPR) in the European Union includes the "right to explanation," where individuals can ask for an explanation of decisions made by automated systems.

2. **Trust and Transparency**: In critical applications, users need to trust the model's predictions. A model that makes inexplicable predictions is less likely to be trusted, regardless of its accuracy. Explainability builds trust by showing how the model arrived at its decisions.

3. **Bias Detection and Fairness**: Machine learning models can sometimes exhibit bias, especially when trained on biased data. Interpretable and explainable models allow data scientists to detect and address these biases to ensure fairness in decision-making.

4. **Debugging and Model Improvement**: Understanding the decision-making process helps data scientists diagnose problems in the model, such as overfitting, underfitting, or inappropriate feature weighting.

Interpretability provides insights into how the model can be improved.

5. **Ethical Considerations**: In applications where decisions have moral or societal implications (e.g., hiring, criminal justice), explainability is necessary to ensure that the model is making decisions ethically and fairly.

Types of Models: Interpretable vs. Black-Box

Machine learning models can be categorized as **interpretable** or **black-box** based on their transparency.

Interpretable Models

Interpretable models are inherently easy to understand because their structure or decision-making process is simple. Examples of interpretable models include:

1. **Linear Regression**: A linear model that assumes a linear relationship between the input features and the target variable. The coefficients of the model can be easily interpreted to understand the effect of each feature on the output.

2. **Logistic Regression**: Similar to linear regression but used for binary classification tasks. The coefficients indicate how each feature affects the probability of belonging to a particular class.

3. **Decision Trees**: A tree-based model where decisions are made by following paths from the root to the leaf nodes based on feature values. Each node represents a decision rule, making it easy to interpret how the model makes predictions.

4. **K-Nearest Neighbors (k-NN)**: A simple algorithm that classifies new data points based on the majority class of their nearest neighbors in the training data. Its predictions can be explained by looking at the neighbors that influenced the decision.

Black-Box Models

Black-box models are complex models where the internal decision-making process is not easily understood by humans. These models often achieve higher accuracy but at the expense of interpretability. Examples include:

1. **Neural Networks**: Deep learning models with multiple layers of neurons are highly flexible but notoriously difficult to interpret. It's challenging to understand how each neuron's activation leads to the final output.

2. **Random Forests**: An ensemble of decision trees where the final prediction is based on the majority vote or averaging of the predictions from multiple trees. While individual decision trees are interpretable, the combined output of a large forest of trees becomes opaque.

3. **Gradient Boosting Machines (GBM)**: A model that builds a series of decision trees sequentially, with each tree correcting the errors of the previous one. GBMs, like random forests, are difficult to interpret due to their complexity.

4. **Support Vector Machines (SVM)**: While the concept of finding a hyperplane to separate data is understandable, the influence of individual features on the decision boundary is not easily interpretable in high-dimensional spaces.

Techniques for Model Interpretability and Explainability

There are several techniques for improving the interpretability and explainability of machine learning models, especially when dealing with black-box models.

1. Feature Importance

Feature importance is a method that ranks the importance of each feature in making predictions. For decision trees and ensemble models like random forests, feature importance scores indicate how much each feature contributed to reducing the overall impurity in the model.

- **Tree-based models**: In models like random forests and gradient boosting, the importance of a feature is often determined by how much it improves the model's performance when it is used to split the data. Features that lead to large reductions in impurity are considered more important.

- **Permutation Importance**: This method works by randomly permuting the values of each feature and measuring how much the model's performance decreases. A large drop in performance indicates that the feature is important.

Feature importance provides a simple way to interpret models by identifying which features have the most significant impact on predictions.

2. Partial Dependence Plots (PDP)

Partial Dependence Plots (PDPs) show how the predicted outcome changes as one or two features change, holding all other features constant. This helps in understanding the relationship between individual features and the target variable, even in complex models.

For example, a partial dependence plot could show how the probability of loan approval increases or decreases as a customer's income changes, holding other factors like age and credit score constant.

3. SHAP (SHapley Additive exPlanations)

SHAP is a popular method for explaining the output of machine learning models. It is based on cooperative game theory and calculates the contribution of each feature to the final prediction. SHAP values show how much each feature contributes positively or negatively to the prediction for a specific instance.

The key advantages of SHAP:

- **Global and local explanations**: SHAP provides both global explanations (how the model behaves overall) and local explanations (why the model made a specific prediction for a given instance).

- **Fair and consistent**: SHAP values satisfy important mathematical properties, ensuring that the contributions of features are fairly distributed.

4. LIME (Local Interpretable Model-Agnostic Explanations)

LIME is a technique used to explain individual predictions of any machine learning model. It works by generating a local surrogate model (usually a simpler, interpretable model like linear regression) around the specific instance being explained. This surrogate model is then used to approximate the behavior of the more complex black-box model locally, allowing for a clear explanation of why the model made a particular prediction.

LIME is model-agnostic, meaning it can be used with any machine learning model. It is particularly useful when you need to explain predictions for individual cases rather than understanding the overall model behavior.

5. Surrogate Models

A **surrogate model** is a simpler, interpretable model trained to mimic the behavior of a more complex black-box model. For example, a decision tree might be trained to approximate the predictions of a neural network. While the surrogate model might not be as accurate as the original model, it provides an interpretable approximation that can help explain how the original model works.

Surrogate models are useful for gaining insights into the decision-making process of complex models, even if they don't capture every detail of the original model's predictions.

6. Counterfactual Explanations

Counterfactual explanations focus on providing answers to "what-if" questions. They show how an input could be modified to change the outcome. For example, in a loan approval scenario, a counterfactual explanation might show that if a customer's income were $5,000 higher, their loan would have been approved.

These explanations are particularly helpful in high-stakes decision-making processes, where individuals may want to know how they can change their situation to get a different outcome.

Balancing Interpretability and Accuracy

There is often a trade-off between **interpretability** and **accuracy** in machine learning. Simple models like decision trees or linear regression are highly interpretable but may not capture complex patterns in the data as well as more advanced models like neural networks or random forests.

On the other hand, complex models often provide higher accuracy but are harder to interpret. In many cases, choosing between interpretability and accuracy depends on the specific application:

- In high-stakes decision-making, such as healthcare or finance, interpretability is crucial because decisions must be explained and justified.

- In applications like image recognition or natural language processing, where accuracy is paramount and interpretability is less important, black-box models may be preferable.

The challenge is to strike the right balance, depending on the needs of the project.

Model interpretability and explainability are essential for ensuring transparency, trust, and accountability in machine learning applications. While simple models like linear regression and decision trees are inherently interpretable, more complex models like neural networks and random forests require additional techniques to explain their behavior.

Methods like **SHAP**, **LIME**, **feature importance**, and **partial dependence plots** provide powerful tools for understanding and communicating the decisions made by black-box models. By making models more interpretable and explainable, we can build more trustworthy, transparent, and fair machine learning systems that can be confidently used in critical applications like healthcare, finance, and criminal justice.

Chapter 7: Deployment of Machine Learning Models

7.1 Building a Machine Learning Pipeline

A **machine learning pipeline** is a systematic, organized workflow that automates the process of data preparation, model training, evaluation, and deployment in a structured manner. It ensures that all the necessary steps in the machine learning process are executed in the correct sequence and are reproducible. Pipelines are vital because they help streamline the machine learning workflow, making it efficient, scalable, and more maintainable, especially in production environments.

Building a machine learning pipeline is essential for ensuring that all components—from data preprocessing to model deployment—work smoothly together. This section covers the key stages of constructing a machine learning pipeline, its importance, and the tools and techniques used to automate the process.

What is a Machine Learning Pipeline?

A machine learning pipeline is essentially a series of steps involved in the end-to-end process of training and deploying a machine learning model. It involves a collection of components that transform raw data into a model capable of making predictions. Each component in the pipeline performs a specific task, and the output of one component serves as the input for the next.

The key steps in a machine learning pipeline typically include:

1. **Data Collection and Ingestion**

2. **Data Preprocessing**

3. **Feature Engineering**

4. **Model Training**

5. **Model Evaluation**

6. **Model Deployment**

A well-structured machine learning pipeline allows for automation of repetitive tasks and ensures that the machine learning workflow is efficient and reliable.

Why Are Pipelines Important?

Building a machine learning pipeline offers several advantages:

1. **Automation:** By automating repetitive tasks, such as data preprocessing and model training, pipelines reduce the

need for manual intervention, speeding up the process and minimizing errors.

2. **Reproducibility**: Pipelines ensure that experiments are reproducible, meaning the same steps can be executed in the same order to achieve consistent results.

3. **Scalability**: Pipelines can handle large volumes of data and scale efficiently when deployed in production environments.

4. **Maintenance**: By structuring the machine learning workflow into separate components, pipelines make it easier to modify, update, or troubleshoot individual steps.

5. **Collaboration**: Teams can collaborate more effectively by working on different components of the pipeline independently, without disrupting the overall workflow.

Key Stages of a Machine Learning Pipeline

Let's explore each stage of a machine learning pipeline in detail, understanding the tasks performed at each step.

1. Data Collection and Ingestion

The first step in any machine learning pipeline is collecting and ingesting data. Data can come from multiple sources, such as databases, APIs, data streams, or files (e.g., CSV, JSON). The process of data ingestion ensures that the raw data is properly loaded and available for the next steps in the pipeline.

Key considerations for data collection:

- Data sources: Data might come from structured databases (SQL, NoSQL), unstructured sources (web scraping, text), or streaming data (IoT sensors, social media feeds).

- Data formats: You need to handle various formats, including CSV, JSON, XML, and database records.

- Automation: Data ingestion should be automated to handle data updates and new data entries continuously.

Tools:

- **SQL:** For extracting data from relational databases.

- **Apache Kafka:** For ingesting streaming data.

- **Pandas:** For reading data from CSV or Excel files.

- **APIs:** For ingesting data from external services.

2. Data Preprocessing

Once the data is collected, it needs to be preprocessed to clean and format it properly before training the machine learning model. Data preprocessing ensures that the raw data is transformed into a suitable format for the model to process. This step includes several key tasks:

- **Handling missing data:** Filling missing values using imputation techniques or removing records with missing values.

- **Dealing with outliers:** Identifying and treating outliers that might distort the model's performance.

- **Data normalization and scaling:** Rescaling features to standard ranges (e.g., 0 to 1) so that no single feature dominates the learning process.

- **Encoding categorical variables:** Converting categorical variables into numerical form (e.g., one-hot encoding) so that machine learning algorithms can process them.

- **Splitting the data:** Dividing the data into training, validation, and test sets to evaluate the model's performance.

Tools:

- **Scikit-learn:** For preprocessing tasks such as scaling, normalization, and encoding.

- **Pandas:** For data manipulation, handling missing values, and splitting data.

3. Feature Engineering

Feature engineering is the process of transforming raw data into features that better represent the underlying patterns in the data. This is a crucial step because the quality of the features directly impacts the performance of the model. Feature engineering involves creating new features, selecting the most important ones, and transforming features to better suit the model's needs.

Common feature engineering tasks include:

- **Creating new features:** Deriving new variables from existing ones (e.g., calculating the age from a birthdate).

- **Feature selection:** Identifying the most relevant features that contribute to the model's performance and removing irrelevant or redundant features.

- **Dimensionality reduction**: Techniques like Principal Component Analysis (PCA) can be used to reduce the number of features while retaining as much information as possible.

Tools:

- **Scikit-learn**: For feature selection and dimensionality reduction.

- **Featuretools**: A library for automated feature engineering.

4. Model Training

Once the data is preprocessed and engineered, the next step is **model training**. This involves selecting a suitable machine learning algorithm, training the model on the training data, and tuning the hyperparameters to improve performance.

During model training, the pipeline automatically feeds the preprocessed data into the chosen model. The model learns from the training data by optimizing the weights (for deep learning models) or fitting the parameters (for classical machine learning models).

Steps in model training:

- **Choosing the model**: Selecting a machine learning algorithm (e.g., linear regression, random forests, or neural networks) based on the problem.

- **Hyperparameter tuning**: Using techniques such as grid search or random search to find the optimal hyperparameters for the model.

- **Training the model**: Fitting the model to the training data and optimizing the model parameters.

- **Cross-validation**: Splitting the training data into K folds to validate the model's performance and prevent overfitting.

Tools:

- **Scikit-learn**: For classical machine learning models such as logistic regression, decision trees, and SVMs.

- **TensorFlow/Keras**: For training deep learning models.

- **XGBoost**: For gradient boosting algorithms.

- **GridSearchCV**: For hyperparameter tuning.

5. Model Evaluation

Once the model is trained, it must be evaluated to measure its performance. Model evaluation involves assessing how well the model generalizes to unseen data by testing it on the validation and test sets. Common evaluation metrics depend on the type of problem (classification or regression) and include:

- **Accuracy**: The percentage of correct predictions in a classification task.

- **Precision and Recall**: Metrics that evaluate the performance of classification models, especially in imbalanced datasets.

- **F1 Score**: The harmonic mean of precision and recall, useful when you want a balance between the two.

- **Mean Squared Error (MSE)**: Used for regression tasks to measure the difference between predicted and actual values.

- **ROC-AUC**: The area under the receiver operating characteristic curve, used to evaluate the performance of classification models.

The evaluation step helps identify overfitting or underfitting and provides insights into how well the model is expected to perform on new data.

Tools:

- **Scikit-learn**: For calculating evaluation metrics such as accuracy, precision, recall, and MSE.

- **Matplotlib**: For visualizing the model's performance with plots like ROC curves.

6. Model Deployment

After the model has been trained and evaluated, the final step is to **deploy** it into a production environment where it can be used to make predictions on new data in real-time or batch mode. Model deployment ensures that the model is integrated into business processes or applications.

Steps in model deployment:

- **Exporting the model**: Saving the trained model (e.g., using joblib for scikit-learn models or saving a Keras model as a .h5 file) so that it can be loaded later for inference.

- **Serving the model**: Setting up an API or service that allows other systems to interact with the model and request predictions. Common deployment platforms include cloud services like AWS, Google Cloud, or Azure.

- **Monitoring and maintenance**: Continuously monitoring the model's performance in production to ensure that it performs well on new data. If the model's performance degrades (e.g., due to changes in data distribution), it may need to be retrained or updated.

Tools:

- **Flask/FastAPI**: For creating APIs to serve machine learning models.

- **TensorFlow Serving**: For deploying TensorFlow models.

- **AWS SageMaker**: A cloud platform for deploying machine learning models at scale.

- **Docker**: For containerizing the model to ensure consistency across different environments.

Tools and Libraries for Building Machine Learning Pipelines

There are several tools and libraries available to build and automate machine learning pipelines. Some of the most popular include:

1. **Scikit-learn Pipelines**: Scikit-learn provides a built-in pipeline class that allows you to sequentially apply transformations and train a model. It automates data preprocessing, feature engineering, and model training in a single object.

2. **TensorFlow Extended (TFX):** TFX is an end-to-end platform for deploying production machine learning pipelines. It includes tools for data validation, preprocessing, model analysis, and serving.

3. **Kubeflow:** Kubeflow is a Kubernetes-based platform for orchestrating machine learning workflows. It automates the deployment and management of machine learning models in distributed environments.

4. **Apache Airflow:** Airflow is an open-source workflow automation tool that can be used to orchestrate machine learning pipelines. It schedules and monitors workflows, ensuring that different tasks in the pipeline are executed in the correct order.

5. **MLflow:** MLflow is an open-source platform for managing the complete machine learning lifecycle. It tracks experiments, manages models, and supports model deployment.

Building a machine learning pipeline is essential for automating and structuring the end-to-end process of data preparation, model training, evaluation, and deployment. A well-designed pipeline ensures that the entire workflow is efficient, scalable, and reproducible, making it easier to handle large datasets and complex models.

By breaking down the pipeline into key stages—data ingestion, preprocessing, feature engineering, model training, evaluation, and deployment—you can ensure that each step is optimized and executed in the correct sequence. Tools like **scikit-learn pipelines, TensorFlow Extended**, and **MLflow** help automate and manage the pipeline, making machine learning workflows more robust and easier to maintain in production environments.

Building a well-structured pipeline not only speeds up the machine learning process but also ensures that your models perform consistently and reliably, from the development phase to deployment.

7.2 Model Export and Serialization: Saving and Loading Models

In the machine learning lifecycle, training a model is only one part of the process. Once a model has been trained and validated, it needs to be **exported** and **serialized** so that it can be used again without retraining it from scratch. Model export and serialization are essential for deploying models in production environments, sharing them with other teams, or simply saving the model's state for future predictions.

Exporting a model allows you to save it to disk, making it easy to load and reuse in production, even if you close your environment or move your code to another machine. Serialization converts the model's internal state, including its parameters and structure, into a format that can be stored, and then reloaded later. This helps to maintain consistency and reproducibility in machine learning workflows.

Why is Model Export and Serialization Important?

Model export and serialization play a crucial role in ensuring that a trained model can be reused efficiently without the need for retraining. Here are some key reasons why this step is important:

1. **Saving Time and Resources**: Retraining a model from scratch every time it is needed can be time-consuming, especially with large datasets or complex models. Exporting a model allows you to save its learned

parameters so it can be reloaded and used directly for predictions or further analysis.

2. **Deployment in Production:** In real-world applications, machine learning models need to be deployed in production environments where they can make real-time or batch predictions. Exporting and serializing the model ensures that it can be loaded into production systems seamlessly.

3. **Reproducibility:** Once a model is trained, it's important to ensure that the exact same model can be used for future predictions or testing. Saving the model ensures that you can reproduce the same results later, even if the environment or data has changed.

4. **Model Sharing:** When working in collaborative teams, it's useful to share trained models with other team members or departments. By exporting a model, you can send it to others who can load and use it without needing access to the training process.

5. **Version Control:** Saving different versions of a model can help track improvements or changes over time. Each version can be saved with specific parameters, hyperparameters, and performance metrics for future reference.

Common Formats for Model Serialization

Various formats are available for model export and serialization, depending on the machine learning library or framework you are using. Each format has its advantages and is suited to different scenarios.

1. Pickle (Python)

Pickle is a Python-specific format that allows you to serialize and deserialize Python objects, including machine learning models. It is a simple and widely used method for saving models built with Python libraries like scikit-learn.

Advantages:

- Easy to use with Python-based machine learning libraries.

- Supports a wide range of machine learning models and data structures.

However, Pickle is specific to Python and may not be suitable if the model needs to be deployed in non-Python environments. Additionally, it is not the most secure option, as it can execute arbitrary code when loading the model.

2. Joblib

Joblib is another popular serialization library in Python, optimized for efficiently saving and loading large machine learning models, particularly those that involve large numpy arrays or data structures. It is often preferred over Pickle when working with large datasets.

Advantages:

- More efficient for models involving large arrays or complex data structures.

- Well-suited for models built using libraries like scikit-learn.

Like Pickle, Joblib is Python-specific, so it is primarily used within Python environments.

3. HDF5 (Hierarchical Data Format)

HDF5 is a widely used format for storing large amounts of data, particularly in deep learning frameworks like TensorFlow and Keras. HDF5 is well-suited for saving models with many layers and parameters, such as deep neural networks.

Advantages:

- Efficient for storing large-scale models, especially in deep learning.

- Allows for hierarchical data structures, making it suitable for complex models with many components.

HDF5 is primarily used in deep learning contexts and is supported by TensorFlow and Keras for saving and loading models.

4. ONNX (Open Neural Network Exchange)

ONNX is an open-source format designed to promote interoperability between different machine learning frameworks. It allows models trained in one framework, such as PyTorch or TensorFlow, to be exported and used in another environment.

Advantages:

- Enables models to be shared and deployed across multiple frameworks.

- Useful for production environments where models need to be run in different infrastructures.

ONNX is becoming increasingly popular for cross-platform model deployment, especially in production settings where flexibility and compatibility are important.

5. PMML (Predictive Model Markup Language)

PMML is a standardized language for describing predictive models, allowing them to be shared across various systems without needing to retrain or rebuild them. PMML is often used in business environments where models need to be exchanged between different software systems.

Advantages:

- A widely accepted standard for sharing machine learning models across different platforms.

- Supports many types of models, including regression, decision trees, and clustering algorithms.

While PMML is supported by several tools and frameworks, it may not be as widely adopted in deep learning as formats like ONNX or HDF5.

Saving and Loading Models in Different Frameworks

Different machine learning frameworks offer their own built-in functions for saving and loading models. Here's how model export and serialization are typically handled in popular frameworks:

Scikit-learn

Scikit-learn provides a straightforward way to export models using libraries like Pickle or Joblib. Both methods allow you to save trained models to disk and reload them later.

- Pickle is commonly used for simpler models.

- Joblib is preferred when working with models involving large datasets or arrays due to its better performance with large objects.

TensorFlow and Keras

TensorFlow and Keras offer multiple options for saving models, including the **HDF5** format and the **SavedModel** format, which is the default for TensorFlow.

- HDF5 is useful when working with Keras models and for saving the entire model, including its architecture, weights, and optimizer state.

- The TensorFlow **SavedModel** format is more versatile, storing the model structure, training configuration, and weights separately, allowing the model to be used across various platforms and devices.

PyTorch

In PyTorch, models are typically saved by exporting their **state_dict**, which contains all the model parameters (weights and biases). This approach is more flexible and allows for loading the model into different versions of the code or environments.

XGBoost and LightGBM

Both XGBoost and LightGBM provide built-in functions to save and load models in binary formats. These formats are optimized for speed and performance, especially when working with large-scale datasets and models.

Best Practices for Model Export and Serialization

To ensure efficient and safe model export, follow these best practices:

1. **Save Model Metadata**: In addition to saving the model itself, it's essential to save metadata, such as feature names, data preprocessing steps, and hyperparameters. This ensures that the same data transformations and settings can be applied when the model is loaded and used for prediction.

2. **Version Control for Models**: Keep track of different versions of your models by adding version numbers to filenames or using a model versioning tool. This allows you to go back to previous versions of the model and ensures that you can reproduce the same results later.

3. **Model Security**: Be cautious when loading models from untrusted sources. Formats like Pickle can execute arbitrary code during loading, which may pose a security risk. Ensure that models are only loaded from trusted locations or use more secure formats for model deployment.

4. **Document Preprocessing Steps**: When exporting a model, document the data preprocessing steps that were applied during training. This ensures that the same transformations can be applied when the model is used for predictions, avoiding discrepancies in performance.

5. **Monitor and Update Models**: After a model is deployed, it is essential to monitor its performance and retrain or update it as new data becomes available. Storing multiple versions of a model allows you to compare performance over time and implement changes if the model's predictions start to degrade.

Model export and serialization are critical steps in the machine learning process, enabling you to save, load, and deploy models efficiently. Whether you are working with classical machine learning libraries like scikit-learn, deep learning frameworks like TensorFlow, or advanced platforms like ONNX for cross-platform interoperability, knowing how to save and load models is essential for ensuring that your models are ready for production.

By carefully choosing the right format, documenting your preprocessing steps, and following best practices, you can make sure that your machine learning models are not only accurate but also scalable, shareable, and ready for real-world deployment.

7.3 Integrating Machine Learning Models into Web Applications

Integrating machine learning models into web applications is a critical step in bringing the power of machine learning to end-users. While building and training machine learning models is a key part of any data-driven project, the real value often comes when these models are deployed in applications where they can make real-time predictions or provide insights for decision-making.

This integration allows users to interact with the models via a familiar web interface, whether it's to make predictions, classify inputs, or recommend products. In this section, we will explore the steps and best practices involved in deploying machine learning models into web applications, the tools and frameworks that make it easier, and common challenges to watch out for.

Why Integrate Machine Learning Models into Web Applications?

Integrating machine learning into web applications bridges the gap between technical machine learning models and everyday business use. Here are a few key reasons why integrating machine learning models into web applications is essential:

1. **Real-time Predictions**: Web applications allow users to interact with models in real-time. For example, in a recommendation system for an e-commerce site, users can receive personalized product suggestions immediately based on their browsing history and preferences.

2. **Accessibility**: Web applications make machine learning accessible to non-technical users. By deploying a model through a user-friendly web interface, users can benefit from the underlying machine learning capabilities without needing to understand how the model works.

3. **Scalability**: Once a machine learning model is integrated into a web application, it can handle multiple users at once and scale to meet the needs of large numbers of users. This is especially useful in high-traffic environments like e-commerce websites, where models need to handle many predictions simultaneously.

4. **Automation**: Integrating machine learning models into web applications allows for automated decision-making processes. For instance, a web app can automatically approve or deny loan applications based on a machine learning model, without manual intervention.

5. **Improved Business Outcomes**: By providing real-time insights and predictions, machine learning-enhanced web applications can improve decision-making, customer experiences, and business operations, leading to increased revenue and efficiency.

Key Steps to Integrating Machine Learning Models into Web Applications

Integrating a machine learning model into a web application involves several steps, from model training and deployment to creating a user interface that communicates with the model. Below, we'll outline these key steps and explain how they fit together to create an end-to-end solution.

1. Train and Export the Model

Before you can integrate a model into a web application, the first step is to train the model on your data and export it. This involves building and evaluating the model using a machine learning framework, such as scikit-learn, TensorFlow, PyTorch, or others.

- **Train the Model**: The model is trained on historical data, tuned for accuracy, and validated for performance. The goal is to ensure that the model can make predictions or classifications based on new data.

- **Export the Model**: Once the model is trained and validated, it needs to be saved (serialized) in a format that can be loaded into the web application. Formats such as Pickle, Joblib, or TensorFlow's SavedModel are commonly used to save the trained model. This ensures the model can be reused without needing to be retrained from scratch.

2. Set Up a Backend for Model Inference

The next step is to set up a backend server that will host the machine learning model and handle requests from the web application. This backend performs the role of running the machine learning model, receiving input data from the web application, and returning predictions.

Here's how the backend typically works:

- **Load the Model**: The saved model (from the export step) is loaded into the backend server.

- **Receive Input**: When the web application sends input data (e.g., user data, images, or text), the backend receives this input and prepares it for the model.

- **Run the Model**: The backend runs the input data through the model to make a prediction or classification.

- **Return the Output**: The backend returns the result (e.g., a prediction, classification label, or probability score) back to the web application for display or further processing.

Popular frameworks for creating backends include:

- **Flask**: A lightweight web framework for Python that is easy to use and ideal for creating simple APIs to serve machine learning models.

- **Django**: A full-stack Python web framework that includes built-in features for database management, security, and authentication, making it a great choice for more complex applications.

- **FastAPI**: A modern, high-performance web framework for building APIs. It's ideal for applications that require high-speed processing and asynchronous operations, making it suitable for serving machine learning models that need to handle multiple requests at once.

3. Create an API for Model Access

To allow the web application to communicate with the machine learning model hosted on the backend, you need to set up an **API** (Application Programming Interface). An API serves as the communication bridge between the frontend (the web application) and the backend (the machine learning model).

Here's what an API does:

- **Endpoint Creation**: The API defines one or more endpoints where the web application can send data for predictions. For example, an endpoint might be /predict, where user input is sent as a POST request, and the prediction is returned as a response.

- **Data Formatting**: The API receives input data in formats such as JSON, processes it to match the model's input requirements (e.g., converting JSON data into a numpy array or tensor), and sends it to the model for inference.

- **Return Predictions**: After the model processes the input data, the API sends the output (e.g., a predicted class or probability) back to the web application in a readable format (often JSON).

Using Flask or FastAPI, you can quickly set up a simple API that allows users to send requests to the model and receive predictions in return.

4. Build the Frontend User Interface (UI)

The frontend is the part of the web application that the end-users interact with. It provides a user interface (UI) for inputting data, such as filling out forms, uploading files (like images or documents), or selecting options. The frontend is responsible for collecting this input from users and sending it to the backend API, where the machine learning model processes it.

Key components of the frontend UI:

- **Input Forms**: Allow users to input data that will be sent to the machine learning model for prediction. For example, a text field where a user enters loan application details, or an image upload button for submitting an image to a classification model.

- **Submit Button**: Once the user provides the input, the frontend includes a submit button that sends the data to the backend API via an HTTP request.

- **Display Results**: After the backend processes the data and the model makes a prediction, the result is sent back to the frontend. The UI should display the prediction or result in a user-friendly manner. For example, if the model is a sentiment analysis classifier, the frontend might display whether the input text is classified as positive or negative sentiment.

Frontend frameworks like **React**, **Vue.js**, or **Angular** can be used to build dynamic, interactive web interfaces that work well with APIs for real-time machine learning predictions.

5. Deploy the Application

Once the model, backend, and frontend are working together, the final step is to deploy the web application so it can be accessed by users.

Steps in deployment:

- **Choose a Hosting Platform**: There are many platforms where you can deploy your machine learning-powered web applications, including cloud services like **AWS**,

Google Cloud, and **Microsoft Azure**, or platforms like **Heroku** for simpler deployments.

- **Deploy the Backend and API**: The backend server (where the model is hosted) needs to be deployed to a platform that can handle HTTP requests. Cloud services like AWS or Google Cloud can provide the infrastructure for handling model inference at scale.

- **Deploy the Frontend**: The frontend UI can be hosted on a web server or cloud platform. It should be accessible via a URL, where users can interact with the web application and send requests to the machine learning model.

- **Scaling and Monitoring**: Once deployed, it's essential to monitor the application's performance. As user traffic increases, the backend needs to scale to handle multiple requests efficiently. Cloud services often provide autoscaling features that automatically adjust resources based on traffic demand.

6. Handling Real-Time and Batch Predictions

Depending on the use case, the web application may need to handle real-time predictions (where the model provides immediate feedback) or batch predictions (where large datasets are processed in bulk).

- **Real-Time Predictions**: In this scenario, the application sends individual user inputs to the backend API, and the model processes them and returns predictions instantly. This is commonly used in applications like chatbots, recommendation systems, and fraud detection.

- **Batch Predictions**: In some cases, the web application may upload a file containing large amounts of data (e.g., a CSV file with multiple rows) for batch processing. The backend processes the data in bulk, and the results are returned to the user after the batch inference is complete.

7. Securing the Application

Security is an important consideration when integrating machine learning models into web applications. Since sensitive data may be involved, such as personal information or financial records, it's important to secure both the API and the web application.

Key security measures:

- **Data Encryption**: Ensure that all communication between the frontend and backend is encrypted using HTTPS. This protects data from being intercepted during transmission.

- **Authentication and Authorization**: Implement user authentication to restrict access to the API. Only authorized users should be able to send data to the model for predictions. Techniques like API tokens or OAuth can be used to authenticate users.

- **Rate Limiting**: Set rate limits on API requests to prevent abuse or overloading of the backend server. This is especially important for public-facing applications that may experience high traffic.

Tools and Frameworks for Integrating Machine Learning into Web Applications

Several tools and frameworks make it easier to integrate machine learning models into web applications:

- **Flask and Django**: Python web frameworks that allow you to easily set up APIs for serving machine learning models.

- **FastAPI**: A high-performance API framework, ideal for machine learning models that need to handle high volumes of traffic.

- **TensorFlow Serving**: A flexible and high-performance system for serving machine learning models in production environments.

- **Heroku and AWS**: Cloud platforms that provide easy deployment solutions for both the backend and frontend of machine learning-powered web applications.

Challenges in Integrating Machine Learning Models into Web Applications

Integrating machine learning models into web applications presents several challenges:

1. **Latency**: Machine learning models, especially deep learning models, can be computationally expensive to run. Ensuring that the model delivers real-time predictions without introducing delays requires careful optimization.

2. **Scaling**: As traffic to the web application increases, the backend needs to scale to handle multiple requests. Load balancing, autoscaling, and caching strategies can help ensure the application remains responsive.

3. **Model Updates**: When a model needs to be updated or retrained with new data, the transition should be seamless. Versioning models and deploying updates without disrupting the user experience is critical.

4. **Data Privacy**: Handling sensitive user data securely is crucial, especially when working in industries like healthcare or finance. Ensuring that data is anonymized and securely transmitted is necessary to maintain user trust.

Integrating machine learning models into web applications opens up many possibilities for real-time decision-making, personalized experiences, and automation. By following a systematic process that includes training the model, setting up a backend server, building an API, creating a frontend interface, and deploying the application, you can bring the power of machine learning to end-users through a simple web interface.

Whether you are building an application that recommends products, detects fraudulent transactions, or classifies images, the integration of machine learning into web applications transforms data into actionable insights and provides immense value to businesses and users alike.

7.4 Monitoring and Maintaining Deployed Models

Once a machine learning model has been deployed in production, the journey is far from over. While deployment is a critical milestone, ensuring the ongoing reliability, accuracy, and performance of the model requires continuous monitoring and maintenance.

Deployed models are subject to changing data distributions, shifts in business goals, and evolving user requirements, all of which can degrade model performance over time. This is where **model monitoring** and **maintenance** become essential.

In this section, we will explore the importance of monitoring and maintaining deployed machine learning models, the common challenges that arise post-deployment, and best practices to ensure models remain effective in real-world environments.

Why Monitoring and Maintenance Are Crucial

When a machine learning model is deployed into production, its environment becomes dynamic and unpredictable. The data that the model sees in production may differ from the training data, and changes in this data can lead to performance degradation, bias, or incorrect predictions. Thus, monitoring and maintaining models is essential for the following reasons:

1. **Model Drift**: Over time, the underlying data that the model was trained on may change. This phenomenon, known as **data drift** or **concept drift**, can lead to a situation where the model no longer accurately reflects current patterns. Monitoring is necessary to detect when the model's accuracy starts to decline due to these changes.

2. **Model Performance**: Machine learning models need to maintain a high level of performance to remain useful. Regular monitoring ensures that the model continues to make accurate predictions, and alerts can be set up to notify data scientists or engineers if the model's performance falls below a certain threshold.

3. **Bias and Fairness**: Deployed models can sometimes introduce or exacerbate biases, especially if they are making predictions about human behavior or sensitive attributes (e.g., gender, race, income). Monitoring for fairness ensures that the model is not making biased decisions that could have legal or ethical implications.

4. **Scalability and Latency**: In production environments, the model needs to handle a large number of requests

efficiently. Monitoring helps track the system's ability to scale, ensuring that the model can handle increased traffic without causing delays in predictions.

5. **Security**: Deployed models can be targets for malicious attacks, such as adversarial inputs designed to deceive the model. Monitoring helps detect any unusual patterns in the data that may indicate an attack and ensures that the model is secure.

6. **Retraining and Updates**: As data evolves, the model may need to be retrained periodically to incorporate new trends or patterns. Monitoring helps identify when a model should be retrained to maintain its relevance and accuracy.

Key Components of Model Monitoring

Effective model monitoring requires tracking several key aspects of the model's performance, as well as the broader system within which it operates. Here are the main components that should be monitored:

1. Data Drift and Concept Drift

Data drift occurs when the statistical properties of the input data change over time. This can happen for various reasons, such as changes in user behavior, market dynamics, or seasonal trends. **Concept drift** refers to changes in the relationship between the input data and the target variable.

For example, in an e-commerce recommendation system, user preferences may evolve over time. The model may have been trained on historical data that reflects older trends, but user behavior could shift due to new products or marketing campaigns, leading to concept drift.

Detecting drift involves monitoring the distribution of the input data and the model's predictions over time. Techniques like **population stability index (PSI)** or **Kullback-Leibler divergence** can be used to measure how much the current data distribution deviates from the training distribution.

2. Model Performance Metrics

To ensure the model is performing well in production, it's important to monitor key performance metrics continuously.

These include:

- **Accuracy**: For classification models, accuracy measures the proportion of correct predictions. Monitoring accuracy over time helps ensure that the model maintains its predictive power.

- **Precision, Recall, and F1 Score**: These metrics are especially important in cases where false positives or false negatives are costly (e.g., fraud detection, medical diagnoses).

- **Mean Squared Error (MSE)**: For regression models, MSE measures the average squared difference between the predicted and actual values. Regularly tracking MSE ensures the model remains accurate over time.

- **Area Under the ROC Curve (AUC-ROC)**: In binary classification problems, this metric helps evaluate the trade-offs between true positive and false positive rates, ensuring the model continues to balance these well.

By monitoring these metrics in real-time, any significant drop in performance can trigger an alert, prompting further investigation or model retraining.

3. Latency and Scalability

In production, the speed at which the model delivers predictions is critical, especially for real-time applications such as recommendation systems, fraud detection, or chatbots. Monitoring the model's **latency**—the time it takes to process a request and return a prediction—is important to ensure that the model operates within acceptable performance limits.

Similarly, monitoring the system's ability to **scale** as the number of users or requests increases is essential to prevent bottlenecks. Metrics like request per second (RPS) and CPU or memory usage help assess whether the model can handle the workload efficiently.

4. Fairness and Bias Detection

Ensuring fairness in machine learning models is becoming increasingly important, especially in domains like finance, healthcare, hiring, and criminal justice. Deployed models need to be monitored for any signs of **bias** that could disadvantage certain groups of people.

For example, a credit scoring model might show bias by consistently giving lower scores to people from a particular demographic. Monitoring tools can track model decisions across different user segments to identify and address any patterns of discrimination. Techniques such as **demographic parity** or **equal opportunity difference** can help evaluate fairness in the model.

5. Security and Adversarial Threats

Deployed machine learning models can be vulnerable to adversarial attacks, where malicious actors provide carefully crafted inputs designed to deceive the model. For example, in image classification, subtle alterations to an image might cause the model to misclassify it.

Monitoring for unusual input patterns or unexpected outputs can help detect adversarial activity. It's also important to implement security protocols, such as **input validation** and **rate limiting**, to reduce the risk of attacks.

Tools for Monitoring Deployed Models

Several tools and platforms can assist in monitoring machine learning models in production. These tools help automate the monitoring process, provide real-time insights, and generate alerts when the model's performance or behavior changes unexpectedly.

1. Prometheus

Prometheus is an open-source monitoring and alerting toolkit commonly used to monitor system metrics, including those related to machine learning models. It allows you to define thresholds for performance metrics (e.g., latency, CPU usage) and sends alerts when those thresholds are crossed.

2. Grafana

Grafana is a visualization tool that integrates with Prometheus and other data sources to create real-time dashboards. You can use Grafana to monitor the performance of your machine learning model visually, tracking metrics like accuracy, request volumes, latency, and more.

3. Seldon Core

Seldon Core is an open-source platform for deploying and

monitoring machine learning models on Kubernetes. It provides advanced features such as A/B testing, canary deployments, and real-time model performance monitoring, making it suitable for large-scale production environments.

4. Evidently AI

Evidently AI is a tool designed specifically for monitoring data drift and model performance in production. It tracks changes in data distributions and model predictions, alerting users to potential issues like data drift or concept drift. Evidently AI can also monitor key performance metrics and generate visual reports.

5. AWS SageMaker Model Monitor

AWS SageMaker offers built-in tools for monitoring models deployed on its platform. SageMaker Model Monitor can automatically detect data drift, bias, and performance degradation in deployed models. It allows for automated retraining based on predefined triggers and is ideal for users already using the AWS ecosystem for their machine learning workflows.

6. MLflow

MLflow is an open-source platform for managing the machine learning lifecycle, including experimentation, model tracking, and deployment. MLflow provides built-in tools for monitoring model performance and can be integrated with other monitoring solutions for real-time insights into production models.

Best Practices for Maintaining Deployed Models

Monitoring is essential, but it's also important to establish a plan for maintaining deployed models over time. As data and business needs evolve, models may need to be updated, retrained, or replaced. Below are some best practices for maintaining deployed machine learning models:

1. Schedule Regular Retraining

As data evolves, models may become less effective over time. Regularly retraining the model on fresh data can help it stay up-to-date with the latest trends. Retraining can be done periodically (e.g., weekly, monthly) or triggered by performance degradation detected through monitoring.

2. Version Control

Maintaining different versions of a model is essential for tracking changes and ensuring reproducibility. When retraining or updating a model, create a new version and keep track of its performance against the previous version. Tools like **MLflow** and **DVC** (Data Version Control) can help manage versioning.

3. A/B Testing and Canary Deployments

Before fully replacing a model in production, it's important to test the new version against the current one to ensure it performs better. **A/B testing** involves serving the current and updated models to different subsets of users and comparing their performance.

Canary deployments gradually roll out the new model to a small portion of users to monitor its performance in production before fully replacing the old model.

4. Model Audits

Perform periodic audits of the model to check for biases, data drift, or performance issues that may have gone undetected.

Model audits are especially important for ensuring fairness and compliance with regulatory requirements, such as GDPR or fairness guidelines in financial or healthcare applications.

5. Automated Retraining Pipelines

Automating the retraining process can help ensure that models stay updated without requiring manual intervention. Automated pipelines can be set up to periodically retrain the model with fresh data, validate its performance, and deploy it to production if it meets predefined performance criteria.

Challenges in Monitoring and Maintaining Models

Despite best practices, several challenges can arise in the process of monitoring and maintaining deployed models:

1. **Model Staleness**: Over time, if a model isn't regularly retrained, its predictions can become outdated. Detecting and addressing model staleness is crucial to maintaining accuracy and relevance.

2. **Data Privacy**: Continuous monitoring requires access to production data, which can raise privacy concerns, especially when dealing with sensitive information. It's important to ensure that monitoring practices comply with privacy regulations and that data is anonymized when necessary.

3. **Model Interpretability**: Monitoring models that are inherently complex, such as deep neural networks, can be challenging due to their black-box nature. Ensuring that these models remain interpretable and transparent in production is a key challenge, especially in regulated industries.

4. **Retraining Frequency**: Determining how often to retrain a model can be difficult. Retraining too frequently can lead to unnecessary resource consumption, while retraining too infrequently can cause the model's performance to degrade.

Monitoring and maintaining deployed machine learning models are crucial for ensuring that models continue to perform well and provide value over time. By tracking data drift, performance metrics, bias, and scalability, organizations can ensure their models remain accurate, fair, and scalable.

Tools like Prometheus, Grafana, Evidently AI, and SageMaker Model Monitor help automate this process, while best practices like regular retraining, version control, and A/B testing ensure that models can evolve with changing data and business needs.

In today's fast-paced environments, machine learning models need constant attention to remain effective. By implementing a robust monitoring and maintenance strategy, organizations can ensure that their machine learning models continue to provide reliable, scalable, and fair predictions in real-world applications.

7.5 Scaling and Optimizing Models for Production Environments

Deploying machine learning models in production is a significant achievement, but ensuring these models can scale and operate efficiently in real-world environments is equally important. Production environments often deal with large volumes of data and concurrent user requests, requiring models to make predictions quickly, handle increasing loads, and remain cost-effective. **Scaling** and **optimizing** machine learning models are essential for maintaining performance, reliability, and cost-efficiency as the demands of the system grow.

In this section, we will explore the challenges of scaling machine learning models, strategies for optimizing performance, tools and techniques for model scalability, and best practices to ensure that models continue to function optimally in production.

Why Scaling and Optimization Matter in Production

Once a machine learning model is deployed into a production environment, it needs to meet real-time user demands, handle potentially vast amounts of data, and operate efficiently within system constraints. The goal of scaling and optimization is to ensure that the model can:

1. **Handle Increased Traffic**: As user interactions with the application increase, the model must be able to handle a growing number of requests without degrading performance.

2. **Deliver Predictions with Low Latency**: For many real-time applications (such as fraud detection, recommendation systems, or autonomous vehicles), the model must provide accurate predictions almost instantaneously. Any delay in predictions can negatively impact the user experience or the effectiveness of the application.

3. **Maintain High Availability**: Production models must be available around the clock, handling thousands or millions of requests. Scaling ensures that models can remain available even during peak traffic periods.

4. **Reduce Costs**: Model scalability must be achieved in a cost-effective manner. Efficient use of compute resources, memory, and storage helps reduce operational costs, especially when models are deployed on cloud platforms.

Key Challenges in Scaling Machine Learning Models

Scaling machine learning models for production environments presents several challenges:

1. **Model Complexity**: As models become more complex, such as deep learning models with millions of parameters, they require more computational resources (e.g., GPUs or TPUs) to make predictions in real-time. Balancing this complexity with performance is a key challenge.

2. **Data Volume**: Production environments often deal with large-scale data streams, requiring models to handle big data efficiently. For example, recommendation systems or real-time bidding platforms must process data in real-time and provide near-instant predictions.

3. **Concurrency**: Web applications, mobile apps, or IoT systems often make multiple concurrent requests to the model. Ensuring the model can handle a large number of simultaneous requests without performance degradation is critical.

4. **Resource Constraints**: Limited CPU, GPU, or memory resources can cause bottlenecks. Ensuring efficient use of these resources while maintaining performance is a core optimization challenge.

5. **Cost Efficiency**: Cloud-based deployments are scalable but can become expensive if not managed properly. Models need to be optimized to ensure they use the least amount of resources while still meeting performance requirements.

Scaling Machine Learning Models: Key Techniques

Scaling a machine learning model involves ensuring that it can handle increasing demands without a drop in performance. Below are some of the main techniques for scaling machine learning models in production.

1. Horizontal and Vertical Scaling

Horizontal scaling (or scaling out) involves adding more instances of the model or infrastructure to handle increasing demand. For example, if one model instance can handle 1,000 requests per second, deploying two instances can theoretically handle 2,000 requests per second. Horizontal scaling is particularly useful for cloud-based deployments because it allows you to spin up additional servers or containers as needed.

Vertical scaling (or scaling up) involves increasing the resources (CPU, RAM, or GPU) of the existing infrastructure to handle more requests or data. For example, upgrading from a single-core to a multi-core server can improve the model's ability to process data in parallel.

- **When to use horizontal scaling**: When you need to handle more requests than a single machine can manage. Horizontal scaling is more common in cloud environments where autoscaling features allow you to dynamically add or remove instances based on demand.

- **When to use vertical scaling**: When a single model instance needs more computational power to process predictions efficiently. Vertical scaling is ideal for applications that require powerful hardware, such as GPU-accelerated deep learning.

2. Model Parallelism

Model parallelism involves splitting a machine learning model across multiple devices (e.g., GPUs) to improve performance. This is especially important for large models that cannot fit into the memory of a single machine. By distributing the model's computations across multiple devices, you can reduce latency and increase throughput.

Data parallelism is another strategy that distributes the input data across multiple devices. Each device processes a portion of the data in parallel and then combines the results. This is useful when processing large datasets, such as image or video data, where the model can process batches of data simultaneously on multiple GPUs.

3. Load Balancing

Load balancing is crucial in scaling models, particularly when multiple instances of the model are deployed across servers or containers. A load balancer distributes incoming requests evenly across the available model instances, ensuring that no single instance is overloaded.

Load balancing helps:

- Improve the performance of the system by evenly distributing requests.

- Ensure high availability and fault tolerance by automatically redirecting traffic to healthy instances when one instance fails.

Cloud platforms like AWS, Google Cloud, and Azure offer built-in load balancing features, making it easier to scale models horizontally.

4. Asynchronous Inference

In real-time applications, waiting for the model to complete its prediction before continuing the workflow can introduce delays. **Asynchronous inference** allows the application to send a request to the model and continue processing other tasks while waiting for the prediction to return. This can significantly reduce perceived latency, especially in applications where predictions are not immediately critical.

Asynchronous inference can be implemented by using:

- **Message queues** (e.g., RabbitMQ or Kafka) that queue requests and process them asynchronously.

- **Event-driven architectures** where the model responds to specific triggers rather than handling predictions sequentially.

5. Model Caching

Model caching involves storing frequently used predictions in a cache so that the model does not have to recompute the same result multiple times. This is particularly useful in applications where certain inputs are requested repeatedly.

For example, in a recommendation system, certain products or categories may be requested frequently by users. Instead of recomputing the recommendation for these inputs each time, the model can return the cached result, reducing the computation time and improving the overall response time.

Popular caching solutions include:

- **Redis**: An in-memory data structure store used for caching frequently accessed data.

- **Memcached**: Another high-performance distributed memory caching system.

Optimizing Model Performance

Once the model is scaled, optimization ensures that it performs efficiently and provides high-quality predictions. Here are some techniques to optimize machine learning models for production environments.

1. Model Compression and Quantization

Model compression refers to techniques used to reduce the size of a machine learning model without sacrificing too much accuracy. Smaller models use fewer resources and can be deployed on devices with limited computational power, such as mobile phones or IoT devices.

Quantization is a specific model compression technique that reduces the precision of the model's parameters (e.g., from 32-bit floating point to 8-bit integers). This reduces the model's memory footprint and speeds up computation without significantly impacting accuracy.

Quantization techniques include:

- **Post-training quantization**: Applied after the model is trained and reduces the precision of the weights and activations.

- **Quantization-aware training**: Trains the model with lower precision, allowing it to adapt to reduced precision during training, which can lead to better accuracy when quantized.

2. Model Pruning

Model pruning removes unnecessary weights or neurons from a neural network to make it smaller and faster. This is especially useful for deep learning models, where not all weights or neurons contribute significantly to the final prediction.

Pruning can be done by identifying and removing weights or neurons that have minimal impact on the model's performance. After pruning, the model can be fine-tuned to maintain accuracy.

3. Batch Inference

For scenarios where the application doesn't require real-time predictions, **batch inference** is an efficient way to optimize the model's performance. In batch inference, multiple input requests are processed together in a batch, reducing the overhead of processing each request individually.

This approach is especially useful for applications such as offline reporting, recommendation systems, and fraud detection, where predictions can be made in bulk during non-peak hours and stored for future use.

4. GPU Acceleration

For models that require heavy computation, such as deep learning models, **GPU acceleration** can significantly improve performance. GPUs are optimized for parallel processing, making them ideal for tasks like matrix multiplication, which is a core operation in many machine learning algorithms.

Cloud platforms like AWS, Google Cloud, and Microsoft Azure provide **GPU instances** that can be used to accelerate model inference in production. Leveraging GPUs can reduce the time it takes to process predictions, especially for large models handling real-time requests.

5. Optimizing Data Preprocessing

In many production environments, the bottleneck in model performance isn't the model itself but the data preprocessing pipeline. Optimizing data preprocessing steps can have a significant impact on the overall system performance. Techniques include:

- **Parallelizing data preprocessing**: Split the data preprocessing tasks across multiple CPU cores or machines to reduce latency.

- **Using optimized libraries**: Use high-performance libraries like **NumPy, Pandas**, or **Dask** for data manipulation and transformation, as they are optimized for speed and scalability.

Tools for Scaling and Optimizing Machine Learning Models

Several tools and frameworks are available to help with scaling and optimizing machine learning models in production. These tools can help automate the scaling process, optimize resource usage, and ensure that models perform efficiently in real-world environments.

1. TensorFlow Serving

TensorFlow Serving is a high-performance system for serving machine learning models in production. It allows for **multi-version** deployment, meaning you can serve multiple versions of the same model and test them against each other. TensorFlow Serving also supports **batching, gRPC APIs**, and **RESTful APIs**, making it easy to integrate with web applications and cloud platforms.

2. TorchServe

TorchServe is an open-source model serving framework developed for PyTorch models. It provides features like multi-model serving, logging, metrics, and support for model versioning. TorchServe makes it easier to deploy and scale PyTorch models in production.

3. Kubernetes and Kubeflow

Kubernetes is an open-source platform for automating the deployment, scaling, and management of containerized applications. **Kubeflow** extends Kubernetes to support machine learning workflows. It helps deploy, monitor, and scale machine learning models efficiently across distributed environments. With features like autoscaling, you can dynamically scale the number of model instances based on incoming traffic.

4. AWS SageMaker

AWS SageMaker provides fully managed services for deploying machine learning models at scale. It offers features like **auto-scaling**, **multi-model deployment**, and **A/B testing**, making it easy to serve large-scale models on the cloud. SageMaker also provides tools for monitoring model performance, drift detection, and automated retraining.

5. Ray Serve

Ray Serve is a scalable model-serving library built on **Ray**, a framework for distributed computing. Ray Serve allows you to deploy machine learning models and scale them across clusters, with built-in support for batching, asynchronous inference, and load balancing.

Best Practices for Scaling and Optimizing Models

Here are some best practices to ensure your machine learning models are scalable and optimized for production environments:

1. **Start with a Simple Model**: Begin with a less complex model that meets your performance requirements. If necessary, add complexity later. A simpler model is easier to scale and optimize.

2. **Monitor Performance Metrics**: Set up monitoring tools to track key performance metrics like latency, throughput, CPU/GPU utilization, and memory usage. This helps identify bottlenecks and optimize resource allocation.

3. **Use Autoscaling**: Take advantage of cloud platforms' autoscaling features to dynamically adjust the number of instances based on demand. This ensures efficient resource usage without over-provisioning.

4. **Version Control for Models**: Always version your models, especially when updating or retraining. This ensures you can revert to previous versions if a new model underperforms.

5. **Optimize Data Pipelines**: Ensure that your data pipelines are optimized for speed and efficiency, as preprocessing often accounts for a significant portion of the total prediction time.

Scaling and optimizing machine learning models for production environments are crucial to ensure that models perform efficiently, handle increasing traffic, and remain cost-effective.

By employing strategies such as horizontal and vertical scaling, model compression, GPU acceleration, and load balancing, you can ensure your models deliver high-quality predictions in real-time without bottlenecks.

With the right tools and best practices, your machine learning models can seamlessly transition from development to production, providing value to users while maintaining performance, reliability, and cost-effectiveness in ever-changing environments.

Chapter 8: Advanced Topics in Machine Learning

8.1 Reinforcement Learning: Fundamentals and Applications

Reinforcement learning (RL) is an exciting branch of machine learning, distinct from supervised and unsupervised learning, where agents learn to make decisions by interacting with an environment. Unlike traditional models where a dataset provides all the information upfront, reinforcement learning revolves around the idea of trial and error.

agent interacts with an environment, takes actions, and learns from the consequences of those actions by receiving rewards or penalties. Over time, the goal of the agent is to maximize cumulative rewards by improving its decision-making process.

In this section, we'll explore the **fundamentals of reinforcement learning**, its key concepts, popular algorithms, and **real-world applications** that demonstrate the power of RL in complex decision-making scenarios.

Fundamentals of Reinforcement Learning

Reinforcement learning can be understood by breaking down its core elements. At its heart, RL involves an **agent** that interacts with an **environment** to achieve a **goal**. The agent learns how to act by receiving feedback from the environment, typically in the form of rewards or penalties, and the agent's objective is to maximize its cumulative reward over time.

Here are the key components of reinforcement learning:

1. Agent

The **agent** is the learner or decision-maker. It takes actions in the environment and learns from the outcomes of those actions. In a real-world example, the agent could be a robot learning to navigate a maze or a program playing a game like chess.

2. Environment

The **environment** is everything the agent interacts with. It responds to the actions taken by the agent and provides feedback in the form of rewards or penalties. The environment could be a physical space, a game, or a simulated system.

3. State

The **state** represents the current situation or configuration of the environment. The agent observes the state of the environment to make informed decisions. For example, in a video game, the state could be the current location of the player, the remaining time, and the positions of obstacles or enemies.

4. Action

An **action** is what the agent does in response to a given state. The agent selects an action from a set of possible actions based on the state of the environment. In a robot's case, the actions might be "move forward," "turn left," or "pick up object."

5. Reward

The **reward** is the feedback signal the agent receives after taking an action. Rewards are numerical values that indicate how good or bad the outcome of the action was. The agent's goal is to maximize its cumulative reward over time. A positive reward encourages the agent to repeat the action, while a negative reward discourages it.

6. Policy

A **policy** is the strategy the agent uses to determine its actions based on the current state. In reinforcement learning, the policy can either be deterministic (always choosing the same action for a given state) or stochastic (choosing actions based on a probability distribution).

7. Value Function

The **value function** estimates the total expected rewards that can be accumulated from a given state. It helps the agent understand which states are desirable and should be pursued. A **state-value function** gives the expected reward for being in a certain state, while an **action-value function** (also known as **Q-value**) gives the expected reward for taking a particular action in a given state.

8. Exploration vs. Exploitation

In reinforcement learning, the agent faces a fundamental trade-off between **exploration** and **exploitation**:

- **Exploration:** Trying new actions to discover their effects on the environment. This helps the agent learn more about the environment and find potentially better strategies.

- **Exploitation:** Using the knowledge the agent already has to choose the action that maximizes the immediate reward. The challenge is to balance exploration (gathering more information) and exploitation (making the best decision with known information).

Types of Reinforcement Learning

Reinforcement learning can be categorized into two main types: **model-based** and **model-free** learning.

1. Model-Based Reinforcement Learning

In **model-based RL**, the agent builds or uses a model of the environment to predict the outcomes of its actions. The model helps the agent simulate and plan future actions based on expected rewards. Model-based RL is advantageous when the environment is stable, and the agent can use the model to make more informed decisions. However, building an accurate model of the environment can be difficult or computationally expensive.

2. Model-Free Reinforcement Learning

In **model-free RL**, the agent does not try to build a model of the environment. Instead, it learns through direct interaction with the environment. Model-free RL methods rely on trial and error to learn an optimal policy. This approach is more commonly used in complex or dynamic environments where building an accurate model is impractical.

Popular Reinforcement Learning Algorithms

Several algorithms have been developed to solve reinforcement learning problems, each with different approaches to learning policies and value functions. Here are some of the most widely used algorithms:

1. Q-Learning

Q-Learning is a popular model-free reinforcement learning algorithm. It focuses on learning the **Q-value**, which is the expected cumulative reward for taking a specific action in a specific state and then following the optimal policy thereafter. Q-Learning updates its Q-values using the **Bellman equation**, allowing the agent to eventually converge on an optimal policy.

The main advantages of Q-Learning are its simplicity and effectiveness in environments with discrete state and action spaces. However, in environments with large or continuous state spaces, Q-Learning becomes computationally expensive.

2. Deep Q-Networks (DQN)

In more complex environments with large state spaces (such as video games), traditional Q-Learning becomes inefficient. **Deep Q-Networks (DQN)** combine Q-Learning with deep learning to approximate the Q-values using a neural network. This allows the agent to handle high-dimensional states, such as images, making DQN particularly effective in environments like Atari games.

3. Policy Gradient Methods

Policy gradient methods directly optimize the policy, rather than learning a value function. These methods use gradient descent to improve the agent's policy by maximizing the expected reward. Policy gradients are particularly useful in continuous action spaces, where Q-Learning struggles.

A common policy gradient method is **REINFORCE**, which updates the policy based on the rewards received from entire episodes of interactions. **Actor-Critic** methods improve upon policy gradients by using a value function (the critic) to help the policy (the actor) make better decisions.

4. Proximal Policy Optimization (PPO)

Proximal Policy Optimization (PPO) is a state-of-the-art policy gradient algorithm designed to improve stability and efficiency. PPO strikes a balance between exploring new actions and exploiting known good actions, using a mechanism that limits how much the policy can change in each update step. This prevents the model from over-updating and ensures smoother learning.

5. SARSA (State-Action-Reward-State-Action)

SARSA is another model-free reinforcement learning algorithm, similar to Q-Learning. However, unlike Q-Learning, which learns the optimal action-value function (assuming the best possible future action is always taken), SARSA updates its values based on the actual actions taken by the agent. SARSA is considered an "on-policy" algorithm, meaning it learns from the actions it is currently taking, rather than the optimal actions.

Applications of Reinforcement Learning

Reinforcement learning has gained popularity in recent years due to its success in solving complex problems across various domains. Here are some notable applications of RL:

1. Game Playing

One of the most famous applications of reinforcement learning is in **game playing**, particularly in board games like chess, Go, and video games. Reinforcement learning agents, such as **AlphaGo** (developed by DeepMind), have achieved superhuman performance in these games by learning optimal strategies through self-play.

In video games, reinforcement learning has been used to train agents to play games like Atari and StarCraft, where the environment is complex, dynamic, and requires long-term planning.

2. Robotics

In **robotics**, reinforcement learning is used to teach robots how to perform tasks such as object manipulation, navigation, and locomotion. By interacting with their environment, robots can learn to perform these tasks autonomously, adapting to different scenarios without explicit programming.

For example, a robotic arm can learn to pick up objects of various shapes and sizes through reinforcement learning, adjusting its actions based on feedback from sensors and cameras.

3. Autonomous Vehicles

Reinforcement learning plays a significant role in the development of **autonomous vehicles**, where the agent (the vehicle) must navigate through complex, dynamic environments while avoiding obstacles and making decisions in real-time. RL is used to train autonomous vehicles to understand how different actions (e.g., turning, accelerating, or braking) impact future outcomes (e.g., safety, speed, or efficiency).

4. Recommendation Systems

In **recommendation systems**, reinforcement learning is used to optimize user experience by suggesting relevant items based on user interactions. RL algorithms can continuously update recommendations based on user feedback (such as clicks or purchases) to improve future recommendations. This dynamic approach is more adaptive than traditional recommendation algorithms, allowing for personalization that evolves over time.

5. Finance

Reinforcement learning is increasingly being applied in **finance**, particularly in areas like portfolio management and trading. RL-based trading algorithms can learn to optimize trading strategies by interacting with the financial markets, seeking to maximize returns while minimizing risks. These systems can adapt to changing market conditions and learn from historical data to make informed decisions in real-time.

6. Healthcare

In **healthcare**, reinforcement learning has been used to optimize treatment strategies and personalize medical care. For example, RL can be used to design adaptive treatment plans for chronic diseases by learning from patient responses to different interventions. In clinical trials, reinforcement learning can help optimize trial designs to improve patient outcomes while reducing costs.

Challenges and Limitations of Reinforcement Learning

While reinforcement learning has shown great promise in many domains, it also comes with its challenges and limitations:

1. **Sample Efficiency**: RL algorithms often require a large number of interactions with the environment to learn an optimal policy. This can be computationally expensive and time-consuming, particularly in real-world applications where obtaining data is costly.

2. **Exploration-Exploitation Trade-off**: Finding the right balance between exploration and exploitation is a key challenge in reinforcement learning. Too much exploration can waste time on suboptimal actions, while too much exploitation can prevent the agent from discovering better strategies.

3. **Sparse Rewards**: In many environments, the agent may receive rewards only occasionally, making it difficult to learn the relationship between actions and rewards. Techniques like **reward shaping** or **hierarchical reinforcement learning** can help address this issue.

4. **Safety and Ethics**: In critical applications like healthcare or autonomous driving, ensuring that reinforcement learning agents make safe and ethical decisions is crucial. Missteps during exploration can have harmful consequences, requiring additional safeguards.

5. **Computational Resources**: Many RL algorithms, especially those involving deep learning, require significant computational power, often relying on GPU or cloud computing resources. This can be a barrier for smaller organizations or projects with limited resources.

Reinforcement learning is a powerful tool for solving complex decision-making problems, with applications ranging from game playing to autonomous systems and healthcare. By leveraging trial and error, RL agents can learn optimal strategies in dynamic environments where traditional machine learning techniques struggle.

As RL continues to evolve, advancements in algorithms, computational efficiency, and real-world applications will likely unlock even more potential across various industries. Despite its challenges, the future of reinforcement learning is promising, offering innovative solutions to some of the most complex problems in AI and beyond.

8.2 Generative Models: GANs and Variational Autoencoders

Generative models have gained significant traction in machine learning, enabling the creation of new data points similar to those from an existing dataset. Unlike traditional discriminative models, which focus on classifying or predicting outcomes based on input data, **generative models** learn the underlying data distribution to generate new samples that resemble the training data. These models have unlocked impressive advancements in areas like image synthesis, text generation, and data augmentation.

Two of the most popular and widely used generative models are **Generative Adversarial Networks (GANs)** and **Variational**

Autoencoders (VAEs). Both offer unique approaches to learning data distributions and generating realistic data, though they differ fundamentally in how they are designed and trained.

In this section, we will explore the fundamentals of GANs and VAEs, how they work, and the applications that highlight their transformative potential.

What Are Generative Models?

Before diving into GANs and VAEs, it's important to understand what generative models are and why they are so powerful. A **generative model** is a type of model that learns to model the probability distribution of the input data so that it can generate new, similar samples.

Generative models answer questions like:

- "Given a dataset of images, can we generate new images that look realistic?"

- "Given a dataset of sentences, can we generate coherent text that mimics human language?"

The goal of generative models is to learn the true data distribution so that new data points can be sampled from it. Some common examples of generative tasks include:

- **Image Generation**: Creating new images that resemble real-world objects or scenes.

- **Text Generation**: Generating human-like text based on language models.

- **Data Imputation**: Filling in missing data points in datasets by generating plausible values.

- **Style Transfer:** Changing the style of an image while preserving its content, such as turning a photograph into a painting.

Generative Adversarial Networks (GANs)

Generative Adversarial Networks (GANs), introduced by Ian Goodfellow and his team in 2014, are one of the most exciting and widely used generative models in recent years. GANs consist of two neural networks—the **generator** and the **discriminator**—that are trained simultaneously in a competitive, game-like setting.

How GANs Work

The architecture of a GAN revolves around two key components:

1. **Generator:** The generator's task is to produce fake data that resembles the real data. It starts with random noise (often from a uniform or Gaussian distribution) and generates new data points that are supposed to mimic the real dataset. The generator does not have direct access to the actual data but learns from the feedback provided by the discriminator.

2. **Discriminator:** The discriminator is a binary classifier that distinguishes between real data (from the training set) and fake data (produced by the generator). Its job is to identify whether a sample is real or fake. It learns to detect the differences between the actual data and the fake data generated by the generator.

The two networks are locked in a **min-max game:**

- The **generator** tries to fool the discriminator by producing data that is increasingly similar to the real data.

- The **discriminator** tries to become better at distinguishing real data from fake data.

The objective of GAN training is to find a balance where the generator produces data that is so convincing that the discriminator cannot tell the difference between real and generated data. In mathematical terms, the training of GANs is framed as a minimax optimization problem:

$$\min_G \max_D \mathbb{E}_{x \sim p_{data}(x)}[\log D(x)] + \mathbb{E}_{z \sim p_z(z)}[\log(1 - D(G(z)))]$$

Where:

- GGG is the generator.

- DDD is the discriminator.

- $pdata(x) p\_\{data\}(x) pdata(x)$ is the distribution of real data.

- $pz(z) p\_z(z) pz(z)$ is the distribution of noise (usually Gaussian or uniform) used as input to the generator.

Training GANs

The training process of a GAN involves alternating between the following steps:

1. **Training the discriminator**: The discriminator is trained to correctly classify real and fake data. It is

updated to maximize the likelihood of correctly identifying real samples and minimizing the likelihood of being fooled by the generator.

2. **Training the generator:** The generator is trained to produce fake data that can fool the discriminator. It is updated to minimize the probability that the discriminator correctly identifies the generated data as fake.

This process continues until the generator becomes good enough that the discriminator can no longer reliably differentiate between real and generated data.

Challenges in Training GANs

While GANs have produced remarkable results in many domains, they can be notoriously difficult to train due to several challenges:

- **Mode Collapse:** One of the major challenges in training GANs is **mode collapse**, where the generator learns to produce a limited variety of samples, essentially generating the same or similar outputs repeatedly, while ignoring other modes of the data distribution.

- **Non-convergence:** Since GANs involve two networks with opposing goals, their training can be unstable. In some cases, the generator and discriminator do not converge, and the training oscillates or diverges.

- **Sensitivity to Hyperparameters:** GANs are sensitive to hyperparameter tuning, such as learning rates, optimizer settings, and the architecture of the networks. Finding the right configuration often requires significant experimentation.

Applications of GANs

GANs have found success in a wide range of applications, particularly in areas involving visual data. Some notable applications include:

1. **Image Generation**: GANs have been used to generate high-quality, realistic images from random noise. Examples include generating faces of people who do not exist, landscapes, and architectural designs.

2. **Deepfakes**: GANs have been used to create realistic **deepfakes**, which are AI-generated videos where the faces of people are swapped or modified in videos. While deepfakes have raised ethical concerns, they are also used in industries like film and entertainment.

3. **Super-Resolution**: GANs can be used for **image super-resolution**, where low-resolution images are enhanced to higher resolutions while retaining fine details.

4. **Image-to-Image Translation**: GANs can perform tasks like converting sketches to real images, turning black-and-white photos into color, or transferring artistic styles from one image to another. The **Pix2Pix** and **CycleGAN** architectures are popular examples of this.

5. **Text-to-Image Generation**: GANs can generate images based on text descriptions. For instance, given a description like "a bird with blue feathers and a long tail," the model can generate an image matching that description.

Variational Autoencoders (VAEs)

Variational Autoencoders (VAEs), introduced by Kingma and Welling in 2013, are another class of generative models that combine the power of deep learning and probabilistic reasoning. VAEs aim to learn a latent representation of the input data and then generate new data by sampling from the learned latent space.

How VAEs Work

VAEs are based on the structure of traditional **autoencoders**, which consist of two components:

1. **Encoder:** The encoder compresses the input data into a lower-dimensional **latent space**. In VAEs, the encoder maps the input data to a probability distribution over the latent space, rather than a single point.

2. **Decoder:** The decoder reconstructs the data from the latent representation. In VAEs, the decoder samples from the latent distribution to generate new data points.

The key difference between VAEs and traditional autoencoders is that VAEs impose a probabilistic structure on the latent space. Instead of encoding an input to a single point, the encoder learns to map the input to a **probability distribution**, typically a Gaussian distribution. This allows for controlled sampling from the latent space to generate new data.

Variational Inference

The VAE framework uses **variational inference** to approximate the true posterior distribution of the latent variables. The goal is to maximize the **evidence lower bound (ELBO)**, which ensures that the model learns both a meaningful latent representation and a way to generate data from that representation.

The loss function for VAEs consists of two terms:

1. **Reconstruction Loss**: Measures how well the decoded output matches the original input data. This term ensures that the generated samples resemble the training data.

2. **KL Divergence**: Encourages the latent space to follow a standard Gaussian distribution. This regularization term ensures that the learned latent space is smooth and continuous, making it easier to generate new samples.

Advantages of VAEs

1. **Continuous Latent Space**: The continuous and smooth latent space in VAEs allows for interpolation between data points. This means that you can smoothly transition between two generated samples by interpolating between their latent representations.

2. **Probabilistic Interpretation**: VAEs provide a probabilistic interpretation of the data generation process, allowing for more flexibility in generating diverse data samples.

Applications of VAEs

VAEs have been used in a variety of applications, particularly where latent space representations are useful. Some common applications include:

1. **Image Generation**: Like GANs, VAEs can generate new images from latent representations, though they tend to produce slightly blurrier images compared to GANs.

2. **Data Imputation**: VAEs can be used to fill in missing data by sampling from the learned latent space and reconstructing plausible data points for the missing entries.

3. **Anomaly Detection**: By learning the distribution of the normal data, VAEs can detect anomalies by comparing how well the model can reconstruct a given input. Poor reconstruction indicates that the input is likely an anomaly.

4. **Latent Space Exploration**: VAEs allow for meaningful exploration of the latent space, enabling tasks like image morphing, where two images can be blended together by navigating through the latent space.

GANs vs. VAEs: Key Differences

While both GANs and VAEs are generative models, they have some fundamental differences in their approach and performance:

1. **Training Stability**: VAEs are typically easier to train compared to GANs, which often suffer from training instability due to the adversarial nature of the generator and discriminator. VAEs use standard optimization techniques, making them more stable but often less powerful in generating realistic outputs.

2. **Output Quality**: GANs tend to generate sharper and more realistic outputs, especially for images. VAEs, on the other hand, can sometimes produce blurrier outputs because they aim to reconstruct data while regularizing the latent space.

3. **Latent Space**: VAEs provide a continuous, structured latent space that can be easily interpreted and sampled from. This makes them well-suited for tasks that require smooth transitions between generated samples. GANs, while capable of generating realistic data, do not offer as easily interpretable or smooth latent spaces.

4. **Probabilistic Modeling**: VAEs are based on probabilistic models and explicitly model the data distribution, allowing them to generate a wider variety of data. GANs, on the other hand, focus on directly learning to generate samples without modeling the underlying probability distribution explicitly.

Generative models like **GANs** and **VAEs** have revolutionized the field of machine learning, enabling systems to create realistic images, videos, text, and more. While GANs excel at producing high-quality, sharp images, VAEs offer the advantage of a continuous latent space that can be explored and manipulated more easily.

Both models have their strengths and weaknesses, and their choice depends on the specific task at hand. GANs are ideal for tasks that require ultra-realistic outputs, while VAEs are more suited for applications requiring smooth latent space manipulation and probabilistic interpretations.

Generative models have immense potential across industries, from creative fields like art and music to practical applications like data augmentation, anomaly detection, and drug discovery, making them one of the most exciting areas of development in modern AI.

8.3 Natural Language Processing (NLP) and Text Mining

Natural Language Processing (NLP) is a subfield of artificial intelligence (AI) that focuses on the interaction between computers and human languages. It involves designing systems that can understand, interpret, and generate human language in a valuable way.

As language is one of the most complex forms of data, NLP combines linguistics, computer science, and machine learning to allow machines to process and analyze vast amounts of natural language data, such as text and speech.

Text mining, on the other hand, is a specific application within NLP that involves extracting useful information and patterns from large volumes of textual data. It involves processing and analyzing unstructured text data to discover valuable insights, trends, and relationships.

In this section, we will explore the fundamentals of NLP, the common techniques and models used in the field, and the applications of NLP and text mining in real-world scenarios.

What is Natural Language Processing (NLP)?

Natural Language Processing allows machines to comprehend, interpret, and generate human language in a way that is both meaningful and useful. This capability is essential in a world where vast amounts of data are generated in text form—think emails, social media posts, customer reviews, news articles, and books.

NLP involves several challenges:

- **Syntax:** Understanding the structure of sentences (grammar).

- **Semantics:** Understanding the meaning behind the words and sentences.

- **Context:** Interpreting meaning based on the context in which words are used.

- **Ambiguity:** Handling polysemy (words with multiple meanings), homonyms, and idiomatic expressions that can lead to different interpretations.

NLP tasks can be categorized into **low-level** tasks (such as tokenization and part-of-speech tagging) and **high-level** tasks (such as text summarization, translation, and question answering).

Key NLP Techniques and Concepts

Here are some of the most common techniques and concepts in NLP:

1. Tokenization

Tokenization is the process of breaking down a piece of text into smaller units, called tokens. Tokens can be words, subwords, or even characters. Tokenization is the first step in most NLP tasks, as it converts unstructured text into structured data that can be analyzed by algorithms.

- **Word-level tokenization:** Splitting text into individual words.

- **Subword tokenization:** Breaking down words into smaller units, which is especially useful for languages with complex morphology (e.g., stemming or lemmatization).

2. Part-of-Speech (POS) Tagging

POS tagging assigns a part of speech (such as noun, verb, adjective, etc.) to each word in a sentence. This helps in understanding the syntactic structure of a sentence. For example, in the sentence "The dog barks," the POS tags would identify "dog" as a noun and "barks" as a verb.

3. Named Entity Recognition (NER)

Named Entity Recognition (NER) is a technique used to identify and classify named entities in text, such as people, organizations, dates, and locations. For example, in the sentence "Google was founded by Larry Page and Sergey Brin," NER would classify "Google" as an organization and "Larry Page" and "Sergey Brin" as people.

4. Dependency Parsing

Dependency parsing identifies the grammatical structure of a sentence and determines how words in a sentence are related to each other. It helps in understanding the roles played by different words within a sentence, such as identifying the subject, object, and verb.

5. Sentiment Analysis

Sentiment analysis is a technique used to determine the emotional tone behind a text, such as whether a sentence or review expresses positive, negative, or neutral sentiment. Sentiment analysis is widely used in social media monitoring, customer feedback analysis, and brand reputation management.

6. Text Classification

Text classification involves assigning predefined categories or labels to a given piece of text. This can include tasks such as spam detection in emails, categorizing news articles into topics, or classifying reviews into positive or negative sentiments.

7. Machine Translation

Machine translation is the process of automatically translating text from one language to another. Popular machine translation systems include **Google Translate** and **DeepL**, which use advanced NLP techniques to produce accurate translations.

8. Text Summarization

Text summarization involves creating a condensed version of a longer piece of text while retaining its key information. There are two main types of text summarization:

- **Extractive summarization**: Selecting important sentences or phrases from the original text to form the summary.

- **Abstractive summarization**: Generating new sentences that summarize the original text, often using machine learning techniques.

9. Speech Recognition and Synthesis

NLP extends to processing spoken language through **speech recognition** (converting spoken language into text) and **speech synthesis** (converting text into spoken language). Speech recognition systems like **Siri**, **Google Assistant**, and **Alexa** rely on NLP to understand and respond to spoken commands.

Common NLP Models and Architectures

NLP models have evolved significantly over time, from simple rule-based systems to sophisticated deep learning architectures that rely on large amounts of data. Below are some of the most common NLP models and techniques used today.

1. Bag of Words (BoW)

The **Bag of Words (BoW)** model is one of the simplest NLP models. It represents a text document as an unordered set of words, disregarding grammar and word order. Each word is assigned a frequency count or binary presence indicator in the document. While BoW is easy to implement, it has limitations in capturing the meaning of sentences, as it lacks context and order.

2. TF-IDF (Term Frequency-Inverse Document Frequency)

TF-IDF is an improvement over BoW and helps address the issue of common but uninformative words (like "the" or "is"). **Term Frequency (TF)** measures how frequently a word appears in a document, while **Inverse Document Frequency (IDF)** downweights words that are common across many documents, emphasizing words that are more unique to a specific document.

3. Word Embeddings

Word embeddings are a more sophisticated way of representing words as vectors in a high-dimensional space. Unlike BoW or TF-IDF, word embeddings capture semantic relationships between words. For example, words like "king" and "queen" or "Paris" and "France" are placed closer together in the vector space because they have similar meanings or relationships.

Popular word embedding techniques include:

- **Word2Vec**: Learns word representations by predicting the surrounding words in a sentence (using either a continuous bag of words or skip-gram model).

- **GloVe**: Constructs word vectors by factoring in the global co-occurrence statistics of words across a large corpus.

- **FastText**: Extends Word2Vec by considering subword information, allowing it to handle out-of-vocabulary words better.

4. Recurrent Neural Networks (RNNs) and LSTMs

Recurrent Neural Networks (RNNs) are a class of neural networks designed to handle sequential data, making them ideal for processing text. **Long Short-Term Memory (LSTM)** networks, a variant of RNNs, are particularly effective in learning long-range dependencies in text by addressing the vanishing gradient problem faced by traditional RNNs.

RNNs and LSTMs are widely used for tasks like machine translation, text generation, and speech recognition.

5. Transformer Models

Transformers have revolutionized NLP, providing a more efficient and scalable approach to modeling sequential data. Unlike RNNs, **Transformers** do not rely on sequential processing; instead, they use a mechanism called **self-attention** to capture relationships between words in a sentence, regardless of their distance from one another.

The most popular transformer-based model is **BERT (Bidirectional Encoder Representations from Transformers)**, which learns contextualized representations of words by considering both the left and right context in a sentence. Other notable transformer models include **GPT (Generative Pretrained Transformer)** and **T5 (Text-to-Text Transfer Transformer)**.

Transformer models have set new benchmarks in various NLP tasks, such as question answering, text generation, and summarization.

What is Text Mining?

While NLP focuses on understanding and processing language, **text mining** is the process of extracting useful information, patterns, and insights from large sets of unstructured text data. Text mining transforms unstructured text into structured data, which can then be analyzed for decision-making, pattern discovery, and predictive modeling.

Text mining involves several key tasks:

- **Information extraction**: Identifying specific pieces of information from text, such as dates, names, or locations.

- **Topic modeling**: Discovering the hidden thematic structure in large collections of documents, such as identifying topics in news articles or research papers.

- **Sentiment analysis**: Determining the emotional tone of text, whether it's positive, negative, or neutral.

- **Document clustering**: Grouping similar documents together based on their content.

- **Text classification**: Assigning predefined categories or labels to a document, such as categorizing emails as spam or non-spam.

Applications of NLP and Text Mining

NLP and text mining have a wide range of applications across various industries, revolutionizing how organizations process and analyze language data.

Below are some notable applications:

1. Search Engines

Search engines like **Google** rely heavily on NLP to understand and process user queries, rank web pages, and provide relevant search results. NLP techniques like tokenization, named entity recognition, and word embeddings are essential in matching search queries with relevant content.

2. Chatbots and Virtual Assistants

Chatbots like **Siri**, **Alexa**, and **Google Assistant** use NLP to interpret user commands and provide appropriate responses. These systems understand natural language inputs, perform actions like setting reminders or playing music, and engage in simple conversations with users.

3. Sentiment Analysis in Social Media

Sentiment analysis is widely used to analyze public opinion on social media platforms like Twitter and Facebook. By classifying user posts as positive, negative, or neutral, companies can monitor brand reputation, track public opinion during events or crises, and adjust their marketing strategies accordingly.

4. Customer Support Automation

Many companies use NLP-driven chatbots and automated response systems to handle customer support requests. These systems can answer frequently asked questions, troubleshoot issues, and provide solutions without human intervention, improving customer service efficiency.

5. Text Summarization for News and Research

NLP-powered summarization tools are used to create concise summaries of lengthy documents, news articles, or research papers. This is especially valuable in industries like journalism, legal, and academic research, where professionals need to stay updated with large volumes of information.

6. Healthcare

NLP plays a critical role in healthcare, particularly in extracting insights from medical records, research articles, and clinical notes. It helps in automating the extraction of medical information, analyzing patient data for diagnoses, and improving decision support systems.

7. Document Classification and Legal Text Mining

In legal and financial industries, NLP is used to classify documents, extract key information from contracts, and identify patterns in legal cases. This enables faster legal research, contract analysis, and compliance monitoring.

8. Recommendation Systems

NLP is used in e-commerce platforms and content streaming services to analyze user reviews and preferences. By understanding customer feedback, recommendation systems can suggest products, movies, or articles based on user preferences and behavior.

Challenges in NLP and Text Mining

Despite its progress, NLP faces several challenges:

1. **Ambiguity:** Human language is inherently ambiguous. Words can have multiple meanings (polysemy), and sentences can be interpreted in various ways depending on the context.

2. **Context Understanding:** Understanding the context in which words are used is crucial for accurate interpretation. Many models struggle to grasp the subtle nuances of meaning in different contexts, especially for tasks like sentiment analysis or question answering.

3. **Language Variety:** Handling multiple languages, dialects, and linguistic variations is another challenge in NLP. Models trained on one language may not work as well on others, especially languages with complex grammar and syntax rules.

4. **Sarcasm and Irony:** Detecting sarcasm, irony, and humor in text is particularly difficult for NLP models because these often rely on contextual clues that may not be explicitly stated.

5. **Domain-Specific Language:** Many industries use domain-specific language or jargon, which can make it difficult for general-purpose NLP models to understand and process specialized texts accurately.

Natural Language Processing and Text Mining have revolutionized the way we process, understand, and interact with vast amounts of textual data. From search engines and virtual assistants to sentiment analysis and healthcare applications, NLP enables machines to comprehend and generate human language, creating new opportunities across industries.

Whether it's text classification, summarization, machine translation, or information extraction, NLP and text mining provide essential tools for unlocking insights from unstructured text, helping organizations make data-driven decisions and enhancing human-machine interaction.

8.4 Time Series Forecasting with Machine Learning

Time series forecasting is a crucial task in many industries, where predicting future values of a variable based on its historical data can lead to better decision-making, optimized resource allocation, and increased efficiency. A time series is a sequence of data points collected at consistent time intervals—such as daily stock prices, weekly sales figures, or hourly weather conditions. Time series forecasting aims to model these patterns and project future trends.

Traditionally, statistical methods like ARIMA (AutoRegressive Integrated Moving Average) and Exponential Smoothing were the go-to techniques for time series forecasting. However, the rise of machine learning has opened new possibilities, enabling models to capture complex patterns and relationships in time series data that may not be immediately evident to classical methods.

In this section, we will explore the fundamentals of time series forecasting, common challenges, key machine learning models used for time series prediction, and real-world applications of time series forecasting in various industries.

What is Time Series Forecasting?

Time series forecasting involves predicting future values based on historical data. The data is sequential, meaning that each observation is associated with a specific timestamp. Time series data is prevalent across many domains, including finance, retail, energy, healthcare, and meteorology.

In a time series forecasting problem, the model attempts to learn the underlying temporal patterns and trends within the data, such as:

- **Trends**: Long-term upward or downward movement in the data.

- **Seasonality**: Recurring patterns within specific time intervals (e.g., daily, monthly, yearly).

- **Cyclic behavior**: Fluctuations that are not of fixed frequency but occur over a longer period.

- **Noise**: Random fluctuations that cannot be explained by any known pattern.

The goal of time series forecasting is to model these patterns to predict future observations, helping businesses plan for the future, anticipate changes, and make informed decisions.

Key Characteristics of Time Series Data

Time series data has unique characteristics that distinguish it from other types of data. Understanding these characteristics is essential when designing models for forecasting.

1. Temporal Dependency

Unlike typical regression problems where observations are assumed to be independent, time series data exhibits **temporal dependency**. Each data point is dependent on previous observations, meaning that past values provide crucial information for predicting future values. For example, the price of a stock today is influenced by its prices over the last few days.

2. Stationarity

A **stationary** time series has statistical properties (mean, variance, autocorrelation) that remain constant over time. Many forecasting models work better on stationary data, so techniques like **differencing** and **log transformations** are often applied to make time series data stationary before modeling.

3. Trend and Seasonality

Trends represent the long-term direction of the data, while **seasonality** refers to regular, periodic fluctuations. For instance, retail sales might increase during holidays and decline afterward. Machine learning models must account for these patterns to produce accurate forecasts.

4. Exogenous Variables

In many real-world problems, external factors (known as **exogenous variables**) can influence the time series. For example, weather conditions might affect energy consumption, or marketing campaigns might drive changes in sales. Including these variables in the model can improve forecasting accuracy.

Challenges in Time Series Forecasting

Time series forecasting poses several unique challenges that distinguish it from other types of prediction problems:

1. Autocorrelation

Time series data often exhibits **autocorrelation**, where a data point is correlated with its past values. Capturing these dependencies is crucial for accurate forecasting but can complicate model design, especially in non-linear cases.

2. Non-Stationarity

Many time series are non-stationary, meaning their statistical properties (such as mean and variance) change over time. Non-stationary time series are more difficult to model, and machine learning models may require preprocessing steps like differencing or scaling to handle this issue.

3. Multiple Time Series

In many cases, multiple time series must be forecasted simultaneously. For example, a retail company may need to predict sales for various products, each with its own patterns. Handling multiple time series and learning cross-series relationships can be challenging.

4. Seasonality and Irregular Events

Time series data often contains seasonal patterns, but it may also be affected by irregular events like holidays, promotions, or economic shocks. Capturing these events and their effects on the time series can be difficult, but failing to account for them can lead to poor forecasts.

5. Long-term Forecasting

Predicting several time steps ahead (e.g., sales predictions for the next year) is more complex than making short-term predictions. As the forecast horizon increases, model uncertainty grows, and small errors can accumulate, leading to significant deviations in predictions.

Time Series Forecasting with Machine Learning

Machine learning models have become popular for time series forecasting because they can capture complex, non-linear relationships in the data. Some machine learning models, such as decision trees and neural networks, can handle multivariate time series and incorporate exogenous variables. Additionally, machine learning models can be more robust when it comes to dealing with noise and irregular patterns in the data.

Here are some of the most common machine learning approaches used in time series forecasting:

1. Linear Regression for Time Series

Linear regression can be applied to time series data by creating **lag features** that represent the previous values of the time series as input features for the model. For example, to predict the value at time ttt, you might use the values at times $t-1t\text{-}1t-1$, $t-2t\text{-}2t-2$, and so on as input features.

While linear regression assumes a linear relationship between past values and the target, it can serve as a simple baseline model for time series forecasting.

2. Decision Trees and Ensemble Methods

Decision trees, **Random Forests**, and **Gradient Boosting Machines (GBM)** can handle non-linear relationships in time series data. These models work well when there are complex interactions between variables, including exogenous variables.

- **Random Forest**: An ensemble of decision trees trained on different subsets of the data. Random forests are robust against overfitting and can capture complex patterns in time series data.

- **Gradient Boosting Machines (GBM)**: Models that build trees sequentially, each tree trying to correct the errors of the previous one. Popular variants include **XGBoost** and **LightGBM**.

These models handle time series forecasting by creating lag features and sometimes additional features such as moving averages or time-based features (e.g., day of the week, month).

3. Support Vector Machines (SVMs)

Support Vector Machines (SVMs) can be applied to time series forecasting by converting the problem into a regression task (called **Support Vector Regression**, or SVR). SVR models aim to predict the next value in the series by fitting a regression line that minimizes the error within a defined margin. SVMs are particularly useful in datasets with smaller sizes and can handle non-linear data by using kernel functions.

4. Neural Networks and Deep Learning

Neural networks are highly effective for time series forecasting, especially when capturing complex, non-linear patterns over time. Deep learning methods like **Recurrent Neural Networks (RNNs)** and **Long Short-Term Memory (LSTM)** networks have been designed specifically to handle sequential data.

- **Recurrent Neural Networks (RNNs)**: RNNs are designed to capture temporal dependencies in time series data. They maintain a memory of previous inputs, making them suitable for forecasting tasks where past values affect future outcomes.

- **Long Short-Term Memory (LSTM)**: A type of RNN that addresses the vanishing gradient problem common in traditional RNNs. LSTMs are particularly effective in capturing long-range dependencies in time series data. They use **memory cells** to store information over long sequences, making them ideal for tasks where historical context plays a crucial role in predictions.

- **Gated Recurrent Units (GRUs)**: GRUs are another type of RNN that are similar to LSTMs but with a simpler architecture. They also excel at capturing temporal dependencies in time series data while being less computationally expensive than LSTMs.

- **Convolutional Neural Networks (CNNs)**: While CNNs are traditionally used for image processing, they can also be applied to time series forecasting by treating the time series as a one-dimensional input. CNNs can capture short-term patterns and interactions within time series data.

5. Autoencoders

Autoencoders are a type of neural network used for unsupervised learning and dimensionality reduction. In time series forecasting, **Sequence-to-Sequence Autoencoders** can be used to learn a compressed representation of the time series, which is then used to generate future predictions. This approach is especially useful when dealing with high-dimensional data or long sequences.

6. Hybrid Models

In practice, combining machine learning models with classical time series models like ARIMA can result in improved forecasting performance. For example, a hybrid model might use ARIMA to capture the linear components of a time series and a neural network to capture the non-linear components.

7. Transformers for Time Series

The **Transformer** architecture, which revolutionized natural language processing (NLP), is increasingly being applied to time series forecasting. Transformers use a **self-attention mechanism** to model dependencies between time steps, regardless of their distance in the sequence. Transformers can capture long-range dependencies without the limitations of RNNs and LSTMs, making them promising for time series forecasting tasks that involve complex, long-term patterns.

Preprocessing Time Series Data

Preprocessing is a critical step in time series forecasting because raw data often needs transformation before it can be fed into machine learning models. Common preprocessing techniques include:

- **Scaling**: Machine learning models often benefit from scaled data (e.g., Min-Max Scaling or Standardization) to ensure features are on similar scales.

- **Differencing**: Helps to remove trends and make a time series stationary, which is important for some models like ARIMA.

- **Smoothing**: Techniques like moving averages or exponential smoothing can help reduce noise and highlight trends in the data.

- **Creating Lag Features**: Lag features represent the previous time steps and are commonly used in machine learning models to capture temporal dependencies.

- **Seasonality Decomposition**: Decomposing the time series into trend, seasonality, and residual components can help the model focus on each aspect individually.

Evaluation Metrics for Time Series Forecasting

Evaluating the performance of time series models requires specialized metrics, as traditional classification metrics (like accuracy) are not suitable. Common evaluation metrics for time series forecasting include:

- **Mean Absolute Error (MAE)**: Measures the average magnitude of the errors in a set of predictions, without considering their direction.

- **Mean Squared Error (MSE)**: Measures the average squared difference between the predicted and actual values. MSE penalizes larger errors more heavily than smaller ones.

- **Root Mean Squared Error (RMSE)**: The square root of MSE, which brings the error metric back to the same scale as the target variable. It is sensitive to large errors.

- **Mean Absolute Percentage Error (MAPE)**: Measures the percentage error between the predicted and actual values, making it useful for evaluating models when different time series have different scales.

- **R-squared**: Measures the proportion of variance in the target variable that is explained by the model. R-squared provides a sense of how well the model fits the data.

Applications of Time Series Forecasting

Time series forecasting is applied in a wide range of industries where predicting future trends is essential for decision-making. Here are some real-world applications:

1. Finance and Stock Market Prediction

Time series forecasting is widely used in finance to predict stock prices, interest rates, and economic indicators. Accurate forecasts can guide investment decisions, risk management, and portfolio optimization.

2. Supply Chain Management and Inventory Forecasting

In supply chain management, time series forecasting helps businesses predict demand for products, optimize inventory levels, and plan for production schedules. Retailers and manufacturers rely on accurate forecasts to ensure they have the right amount of stock to meet demand without overstocking.

3. Weather Forecasting

Meteorologists use time series forecasting to predict weather conditions, including temperature, rainfall, wind speed, and more. Accurate weather forecasts are critical for agriculture, disaster preparedness, and transportation.

4. Energy Demand Forecasting

Utility companies use time series forecasting to predict electricity demand, allowing them to balance supply and demand efficiently. Energy forecasting is essential for grid management and optimizing energy generation.

5. Healthcare

In healthcare, time series forecasting can predict patient admission rates, monitor disease progression, and forecast demand for medical resources. This helps hospitals allocate staff, beds, and equipment more effectively.

6. Traffic Prediction

Time series forecasting is used to predict traffic congestion and optimize transportation networks. Predictive models help manage traffic flow, reduce congestion, and improve public transportation scheduling.

7. Sales and Revenue Forecasting

Businesses use time series forecasting to predict future sales and revenue based on historical trends, seasonal patterns, and external factors such as marketing campaigns or economic conditions. These forecasts guide budgeting, staffing, and marketing strategies.

Time series forecasting is a powerful tool for predicting future trends based on historical data, enabling businesses and organizations to make informed decisions.

While traditional statistical methods like ARIMA and Exponential Smoothing have long been the mainstay of time series forecasting, machine learning models such as decision trees, neural networks, and transformers have significantly expanded the capabilities of time series analysis.

The ability to capture complex, non-linear patterns, account for exogenous variables, and handle large datasets has made machine learning models invaluable in tackling time series forecasting challenges.

However, selecting the right model, preprocessing data appropriately, and accounting for trends, seasonality, and irregular events remain critical for success in real-world applications.

Chapter 9: Case Studies and Real-World Implementations

9.1 Predictive Analytics in Healthcare

Predictive analytics in healthcare refers to the use of data, statistical algorithms, and machine learning techniques to identify the likelihood of future outcomes based on historical data. In healthcare, predictive analytics has the potential to revolutionize how patient care is delivered, improve outcomes, reduce costs, and enhance the efficiency of the entire healthcare system.

By predicting patient risks, disease progression, and resource allocation, healthcare providers can make more informed decisions and take proactive steps to improve patient outcomes.

In this section, we will explore the fundamentals of predictive analytics, the role of machine learning in healthcare, key use cases, challenges, and how predictive analytics is shaping the future of healthcare.

What is Predictive Analytics in Healthcare?

Predictive analytics in healthcare leverages data from various sources, including patient records, medical devices, diagnostic tools, and genomic data, to anticipate future health outcomes. By identifying patterns and correlations in these datasets, predictive models can provide insights into how likely certain events are to occur.

For example, predictive analytics can be used to estimate the likelihood of a patient being readmitted to the hospital, predict the progression of chronic diseases, or anticipate demand for medical resources during an outbreak.

Predictive analytics is especially valuable in healthcare because early intervention can save lives and reduce the burden on healthcare systems. Predictive models enable healthcare providers to move from reactive care (treating illnesses after they occur) to proactive care (anticipating issues before they become serious problems).

Key Components of Predictive Analytics

Predictive analytics involves several critical components that make it effective in healthcare:

1. **Data Collection**: Predictive analytics relies on large datasets to uncover meaningful patterns. In healthcare, these datasets come from sources such as electronic health records (EHRs), patient surveys, diagnostic tests, medical devices (e.g., wearable sensors), and even genetic data. Collecting and aggregating high-quality data is the first step in developing reliable predictive models.

2. **Data Integration:** Healthcare data is often scattered across different systems, such as EHRs, lab results, imaging data, and pharmacy records. Integrating these disparate sources of data is critical to creating a comprehensive view of a patient's health. Advanced data integration techniques allow for more accurate predictions.

3. **Feature Engineering:** In machine learning, **feature engineering** is the process of selecting and transforming raw data into meaningful features that can improve the performance of predictive models. In healthcare, features may include patient demographics (age, gender), medical history, lab results, or social determinants of health (e.g., socioeconomic status, lifestyle factors).

4. **Machine Learning Models:** Predictive analytics in healthcare relies on machine learning algorithms to detect patterns in data and make predictions. Models such as **decision trees, logistic regression, support vector machines, random forests,** and **neural networks** are commonly used. These models can be trained to predict a range of healthcare outcomes, from disease progression to patient readmission rates.

5. **Outcome Predictions:** Once trained, predictive models provide insights into potential future events. In healthcare, predictions may include:

   o The likelihood of a patient developing a chronic condition (e.g., diabetes, heart disease).

   o The probability of hospital readmission within a specified timeframe.

- o The risk of adverse drug reactions or complications following surgery.

- o Predicting the spread of infectious diseases within a population.

6. **Actionable Insights**: The ultimate goal of predictive analytics is to provide **actionable insights** that help healthcare providers make better decisions. These insights can be used to personalize treatment plans, allocate resources more efficiently, and design preventative care strategies.

The Role of Machine Learning in Predictive Healthcare

Machine learning has become a powerful tool in predictive healthcare because it can process vast amounts of data, identify hidden patterns, and make accurate predictions without being explicitly programmed. Below are some key ways in which machine learning contributes to predictive healthcare:

1. **Risk Prediction Models**: Machine learning algorithms can develop risk prediction models to identify patients at high risk for certain conditions. For example, by analyzing historical data, models can predict which patients are most likely to develop heart disease based on factors like age, blood pressure, cholesterol levels, and lifestyle habits.

2. **Disease Progression Forecasting**: Predictive analytics can help forecast how a disease will progress over time for individual patients. This is particularly important in chronic diseases like diabetes or cancer, where early detection and intervention can significantly improve outcomes.

3. **Readmission Risk Prediction:** Predicting which patients are likely to be readmitted to the hospital within 30 days of discharge is a critical challenge in healthcare. Machine learning models can analyze patient data (including previous admissions, comorbidities, and treatments) to identify high-risk patients and design targeted interventions to reduce readmission rates.

4. **Personalized Treatment Recommendations:** Predictive analytics can be used to tailor treatment plans based on a patient's unique characteristics. For example, machine learning models can predict how a patient might respond to a particular medication or therapy, enabling personalized care. This is particularly useful in oncology, where the genetic profile of a tumor can inform treatment decisions.

5. **Predictive Diagnostics:** Machine learning models can assist in early diagnosis by identifying patterns in diagnostic images (such as X-rays, MRIs, or CT scans) or lab results. For example, models trained on medical images can help detect early signs of conditions like cancer, heart disease, or stroke.

6. **Population Health Management:** At a population level, predictive analytics can be used to identify health trends, predict disease outbreaks, and allocate resources more effectively. Public health officials can use predictive models to identify high-risk populations, design targeted interventions, and optimize vaccination campaigns.

Key Use Cases of Predictive Analytics in Healthcare

Predictive analytics is already being applied in many areas of healthcare, delivering real-world benefits by improving patient care and operational efficiency. Here are some key use cases:

1. Predicting Hospital Readmissions

Hospital readmissions are a significant concern for healthcare providers, as they can lead to higher costs and worse patient outcomes. Predictive analytics can help hospitals identify patients at high risk of readmission within 30 days of discharge.

By analyzing factors such as medical history, treatment plans, and social determinants of health, models can identify vulnerable patients and prompt healthcare teams to implement preventive measures (e.g., follow-up appointments, medication adjustments, or home care services).

For example, a predictive model could determine that a patient with chronic obstructive pulmonary disease (COPD) and multiple previous hospitalizations has a high likelihood of readmission. The care team can then provide closer monitoring, arrange home visits, or modify the patient's medication to prevent readmission.

2. Chronic Disease Management

Predictive analytics plays a critical role in managing chronic diseases such as diabetes, hypertension, and heart disease. Machine learning models can predict the likelihood of a patient developing complications based on real-time data from wearable devices, lab results, and historical medical records.

For example, in diabetes management, predictive models can track blood glucose levels, lifestyle factors (e.g., physical activity, diet), and medication adherence to predict the risk of complications like diabetic retinopathy or kidney disease. This enables healthcare providers to take early action and prevent further deterioration in the patient's health.

3. Sepsis Prediction

Sepsis is a life-threatening condition caused by the body's extreme response to infection, and it requires rapid intervention to prevent organ failure or death. Predictive analytics can help detect the early signs of sepsis by continuously monitoring patient data, such as vital signs, lab results, and infection markers. Machine learning algorithms can identify patterns that indicate sepsis risk and alert healthcare providers to take immediate action.

For example, hospitals use predictive models that analyze patient data from electronic health records (EHRs) to identify sepsis risk factors, allowing clinicians to administer antibiotics or other interventions earlier and reduce mortality rates.

4. Early Cancer Detection

Early detection of cancer dramatically increases the chances of successful treatment and survival. Predictive analytics can be used to analyze diagnostic images (such as mammograms, MRIs, or CT scans) or genetic data to detect early signs of cancer that may not be visible to the human eye.

For instance, machine learning models trained on thousands of mammogram images can help radiologists identify small tumors that might otherwise go unnoticed, allowing for earlier diagnosis and treatment.

5. Predictive Modeling in Emergency Care

Emergency departments (EDs) often face challenges related to patient flow, overcrowding, and resource allocation. Predictive analytics can forecast ED patient volume based on historical patterns, time of day, weather conditions, and local events. This allows hospitals to anticipate surges in patient arrivals and optimize staffing levels, reducing wait times and improving patient outcomes.

Predictive models can also prioritize patients based on the severity of their conditions, ensuring that those with the most critical needs receive immediate attention.

6. Pharmaceutical Research and Drug Development

In pharmaceutical research, predictive analytics is used to identify promising drug candidates, predict the effectiveness of treatments, and optimize clinical trial designs. By analyzing vast amounts of genetic, biological, and clinical data, machine learning models can identify molecular targets for new drugs or predict which patients are most likely to respond to certain therapies.

For example, in cancer treatment, predictive models can help identify which patients are most likely to benefit from immunotherapy based on their tumor's genetic profile.

7. Predicting Disease Outbreaks

Predictive analytics is also used at the population level to monitor and predict disease outbreaks. By analyzing data from sources such as hospital admissions, social media, and environmental sensors, public health officials can predict the spread of infectious diseases like influenza, COVID-19, or malaria. These predictions enable timely public health interventions, such as vaccination campaigns, travel restrictions, or resource allocation to high-risk areas.

Challenges of Predictive Analytics in Healthcare

Despite its potential, predictive analytics in healthcare faces several challenges that need to be addressed to maximize its effectiveness:

1. Data Quality and Availability

Predictive models rely on large volumes of high-quality data to make accurate predictions. However, healthcare data is often incomplete, unstructured, or inconsistent. Additionally, data is frequently siloed across different systems (e.g., EHRs, insurance databases, lab systems), making it difficult to integrate and analyze. Ensuring data quality and interoperability between systems is essential for reliable predictive analytics.

2. Bias in Data and Models

Predictive models can be biased if they are trained on non-representative or incomplete data. For example, if a model is trained on data from predominantly one demographic group, it may not perform well for patients from other groups. Addressing bias in data and algorithms is critical to ensure that predictive analytics benefits all patients equitably.

3. Ethical Concerns and Privacy

The use of predictive analytics in healthcare raises ethical concerns, particularly around patient privacy and data security. Healthcare providers must ensure that patient data is handled securely and that predictions are used in ways that align with ethical standards. Additionally, the transparency of predictive models is important—clinicians need to understand how predictions are made and ensure that they can be trusted.

4. Interpretability of Models

Many machine learning models, particularly complex ones like deep learning, are often seen as "black boxes" because their inner workings are difficult to interpret. In healthcare, model interpretability is crucial, as clinicians need to understand the reasoning behind a prediction to make informed decisions. Researchers are working on developing interpretable models that provide more transparency and trustworthiness.

The Future of Predictive Analytics in Healthcare

The future of predictive analytics in healthcare is bright, with continued advancements in data collection, machine learning algorithms, and computing power. The integration of AI and predictive analytics into healthcare workflows has the potential to transform patient care, leading to more personalized and proactive treatment strategies.

Emerging areas of growth include:

- **Genomic and Precision Medicine**: Predictive models will increasingly incorporate genetic and genomic data, allowing for more personalized treatments based on an individual's unique genetic makeup.

- **Wearables and Remote Monitoring**: With the rise of wearable devices and IoT sensors, real-time health monitoring will become more prevalent, enabling continuous data collection and prediction of health events outside of clinical settings.

- **AI-Augmented Diagnostics**: AI and predictive analytics will assist clinicians in diagnosing complex diseases faster and with greater accuracy, reducing diagnostic errors and improving patient outcomes.

Predictive analytics in healthcare has the potential to reshape the healthcare landscape by enabling more proactive, personalized, and efficient care. From predicting disease progression and hospital readmissions to identifying high-risk patients and optimizing resource allocation, predictive analytics is already delivering real-world benefits across the healthcare industry.

While challenges around data quality, model bias, and ethical concerns remain, the continued integration of predictive analytics into healthcare workflows promises to improve patient outcomes, reduce costs, and make healthcare systems more efficient.

9.2 Machine Learning in Finance: Fraud Detection and Algorithmic Trading

Machine learning has become a transformative force in the financial sector, offering sophisticated tools to solve complex problems, streamline operations, and improve decision-making processes.

Two areas in which machine learning has had a particularly profound impact are **fraud detection** and **algorithmic trading**. In both domains, the ability of machine learning models to analyze vast amounts of data, detect patterns, and make predictions is invaluable in mitigating risks and optimizing financial operations.

In this section, we'll explore how machine learning is applied in these two key areas of finance—fraud detection and algorithmic trading—covering the fundamental principles, techniques used, and real-world applications that showcase the power of these technologies.

Machine Learning for Fraud Detection

Fraud detection is one of the most critical challenges in the financial sector. Whether it's detecting fraudulent credit card transactions, insurance fraud, or identifying money laundering activities, companies need reliable tools to spot suspicious activities early.

Traditional rule-based fraud detection systems, while useful, often fall short in terms of flexibility and scalability. This is where machine learning comes into play.

Machine learning-based fraud detection systems are more adaptive, can handle large-scale data in real time, and evolve as new types of fraud emerge. By leveraging historical data and advanced pattern recognition techniques, machine learning models can detect anomalies that may indicate fraud and flag suspicious transactions or activities for further investigation.

Key Steps in Fraud Detection Using Machine Learning

Fraud detection using machine learning generally follows a structured pipeline, from data collection to model deployment and continuous improvement. Below are the main steps:

1. **Data Collection**

   o Fraud detection requires vast amounts of historical transaction data, including information on both legitimate and fraudulent transactions. This data typically includes transaction amounts, locations, times, user profiles, and other features. Data from external sources, such as social media, can also be integrated to enrich the dataset.

   o In addition to financial transactions, metadata like device ID, IP address, and geolocation data can help detect anomalies.

2. **Data Preprocessing**

o **Cleaning**: The data is preprocessed to remove any inconsistencies, duplicates, or missing values.

o **Normalization**: Transaction amounts and other numerical features may need to be normalized to ensure that no feature disproportionately affects the model.

o **Feature Engineering**: Useful features such as transaction frequency, transaction patterns, or user behavior profiles are extracted. This step often involves generating aggregated features like daily transaction counts, average amounts, and the time gap between consecutive transactions.

3. **Anomaly Detection vs. Classification**

o **Anomaly Detection**: In unsupervised learning, models are trained to detect anomalies— transactions that deviate significantly from the normal behavior of a user or a system. **Clustering algorithms** (like K-Means or DBSCAN) or **autoencoders** can be used to detect outliers that may represent fraudulent activity.

o **Classification**: In supervised learning, the model is trained on a labeled dataset, where each transaction is tagged as either "fraudulent" or "legitimate." The model learns to classify future transactions based on these labels. Common classification models used for fraud detection include **Logistic Regression, Random Forests, Gradient Boosting Machines**

(GBM), and **Support Vector Machines (SVMs)**.

4. **Model Training**

   o The chosen machine learning model is trained on historical data. Models like **Random Forests** or **XGBoost** are often used for their ability to handle imbalanced datasets (since fraudulent transactions typically represent only a small fraction of total transactions).

   o **Imbalanced datasets** pose a significant challenge in fraud detection, as the number of fraudulent transactions is often much smaller than legitimate ones. Techniques like **SMOTE** (Synthetic Minority Over-sampling Technique) or **undersampling** the majority class can help balance the dataset during model training.

5. **Model Evaluation**

   o The performance of a fraud detection model is often measured using metrics such as **Precision, Recall, F1 Score,** and **Area Under the ROC Curve (AUC-ROC)**. Precision ensures that when a transaction is flagged as fraudulent, it is likely to be fraud. Recall ensures that most fraudulent transactions are detected.

   o **False positives** (legitimate transactions flagged as fraudulent) must be minimized to avoid inconveniencing customers, while **false negatives** (missed fraudulent transactions) can lead to financial losses.

6. Deployment and Continuous Monitoring

- After training, the model is deployed into production, where it processes live transaction data in real time, flagging potentially fraudulent activities.

- Fraudsters continuously adapt to detection techniques, so it's essential to monitor the model's performance and periodically retrain it with new data to adapt to emerging fraud patterns.

Machine Learning Techniques for Fraud Detection

Several machine learning techniques are particularly useful for fraud detection:

1. **Supervised Learning**: In this approach, models are trained on a labeled dataset. Some commonly used algorithms include:

   - **Logistic Regression**: A binary classification algorithm used to model the probability of a transaction being fraudulent based on its features.

   - **Random Forests**: An ensemble method that constructs multiple decision trees and aggregates their predictions, making it robust and accurate for fraud detection.

   - **Gradient Boosting Machines (GBM)**: Algorithms like **XGBoost** or **LightGBM** are widely used due to their ability to handle imbalanced datasets and their superior predictive power.

2. **Unsupervised Learning**: In cases where labeled data is limited or unavailable, unsupervised learning methods can detect anomalies:

   o **K-Means Clustering**: Used to cluster similar transactions together, with anomalies being transactions that fall outside the normal clusters.

   o **Isolation Forests**: An anomaly detection method that isolates anomalies by randomly partitioning data.

3. **Deep Learning**: Neural networks, particularly **autoencoders** and **recurrent neural networks (RNNs)**, have been used to detect fraud by learning complex, non-linear relationships in transaction data.

4. **Graph-Based Approaches**: Fraud often involves networks of transactions or actors (e.g., money laundering rings). **Graph-based machine learning** can model the relationships between entities in a transaction network and identify suspicious patterns.

Real-World Applications of Fraud Detection

- **Credit Card Fraud Detection**: Credit card companies use machine learning models to flag suspicious transactions in real time. For instance, if a user's credit card is suddenly used in a different country, the system may flag the transaction and alert the user.

- **Insurance Fraud**: Machine learning models can detect suspicious claims by analyzing patterns in claims data and identifying anomalies or unusual behaviors. This can include inflated claims, false medical diagnoses, or staged accidents.

- **Money Laundering Detection:** Financial institutions use machine learning to detect money laundering schemes by analyzing transaction histories, identifying unusual patterns, and tracing the flow of funds across accounts.

Machine Learning for Algorithmic Trading

Algorithmic trading involves using automated trading strategies powered by computer algorithms to execute trades at high speeds and volumes. In this space, machine learning has become a game-changer by enabling algorithms to analyze vast amounts of financial data, detect patterns, and make informed decisions about when to buy or sell assets.

Machine learning models can identify profitable opportunities, minimize risks, and optimize trading strategies based on historical data and real-time market conditions.

How Algorithmic Trading Works

Algorithmic trading relies on pre-defined rules or instructions, known as algorithms, to execute trades. These algorithms can be based on technical indicators, price movements, or complex financial models. Machine learning models enhance algorithmic trading by making the system adaptive, capable of learning from past data, and predicting future price movements or market trends.

The basic workflow for applying machine learning in algorithmic trading involves:

1. **Data Collection and Preprocessing**

   o The first step in algorithmic trading is gathering large volumes of data. This includes historical stock prices, financial statements, news articles, market sentiment data (e.g., from social media), and economic indicators. High-frequency trading (HFT) strategies also require real-time data feeds.

   o Data preprocessing involves cleaning, normalizing, and transforming raw data into formats that can be fed into machine learning models. Time series data (such as stock prices) often needs to be structured with lagged features, moving averages, or volatility indicators.

2. **Feature Engineering**

   o In algorithmic trading, **features** are derived from raw market data to serve as inputs to machine learning models. Common features include:

     ▪ **Technical Indicators**: Moving averages, relative strength index (RSI), and Bollinger Bands.

     ▪ **Volatility Measures**: Standard deviation, beta, or the average true range.

     ▪ **Sentiment Analysis**: Extracting sentiment from news articles, financial reports, or social media to gauge market sentiment.

     ▪ **Volume Trends**: Analyzing the trading volume for specific securities to detect potential breakouts or reversals.

3. Model Selection

- o Various machine learning models can be employed in algorithmic trading, including:

  - **Linear and Logistic Regression:** Simple models that predict future price movements based on past data and trends.

  - **Random Forests and Gradient Boosting:** These models excel at identifying patterns in complex datasets, making them suitable for predicting stock price movements.

  - **Neural Networks:** Deep learning models, such as **LSTMs (Long Short-Term Memory networks)**, can model the sequential nature of stock price data and predict future prices based on historical trends.

  - **Reinforcement Learning (RL):** RL algorithms are particularly useful for trading strategies, as they learn to make decisions by interacting with the environment (i.e., the market) and maximizing cumulative rewards (profits).

4. Training the Model

- o Once the features are created, the machine learning model is trained on historical data. In the training phase, the model learns to predict the future price movements of assets or the likelihood of certain trading opportunities.

- o Models are typically trained to maximize a certain metric, such as return on investment (ROI) or **Sharpe ratio** (a measure of risk-adjusted returns).

5. **Backtesting**

- o Before deploying the model in live trading, it is tested on historical data using **backtesting**. This helps evaluate how the trading strategy would have performed in the past. Backtesting allows traders to assess the profitability, risk, and robustness of their models under real market conditions.

6. **Deployment and Live Trading**

- o Once the model has been validated through backtesting, it is deployed in live trading. The model monitors real-time data, makes predictions about market movements, and executes trades automatically based on pre-set rules.

Machine Learning Techniques for Algorithmic Trading

1. **Supervised Learning:** Supervised learning models are trained on historical price data to predict future price movements or classify trading signals. Algorithms like **Random Forests, XGBoost,** and **Support Vector Machines (SVMs)** are often used to detect patterns in financial data and forecast market trends.

2. **Reinforcement Learning (RL)**: In algorithmic trading, reinforcement learning can be used to develop trading strategies by interacting with the market. The agent (trader) learns to make decisions (buy, sell, hold) that maximize cumulative profits over time. Popular RL algorithms like **Q-learning** and **Deep Q-Networks (DQN)** are applied to optimize trading strategies dynamically.

3. **Neural Networks and Deep Learning**: **LSTM** networks and other types of recurrent neural networks (RNNs) are particularly effective for handling time series data like stock prices. LSTMs can capture long-term dependencies in price data, making them ideal for predicting future trends based on historical patterns.

4. **Sentiment Analysis and Natural Language Processing (NLP)**: Sentiment analysis, often powered by machine learning and NLP, is used to gauge market sentiment by analyzing news articles, financial reports, and social media posts. Positive sentiment can signal buying opportunities, while negative sentiment can indicate potential sell-offs.

Real-World Applications of Algorithmic Trading

- **High-Frequency Trading (HFT)**: HFT strategies use algorithms to execute trades at incredibly high speeds, often within microseconds. Machine learning models can optimize these strategies by predicting short-term price fluctuations and adjusting trades accordingly.

- **Market Making**: In market making, algorithms constantly buy and sell securities to provide liquidity to the market. Machine learning models can optimize the pricing and volume of trades to minimize risk and maximize profits.

- **Arbitrage Trading**: Machine learning models can identify arbitrage opportunities—instances where price discrepancies exist between different markets—and execute trades to profit from these differences.

- **Momentum Trading**: Machine learning models are used to predict the continuation of a market trend (either upward or downward) and execute trades based on the assumption that the trend will persist.

Challenges of Machine Learning in Finance

Despite the potential of machine learning in fraud detection and algorithmic trading, there are several challenges:

1. **Data Quality and Availability**: High-quality, clean, and relevant data is crucial for building accurate models. In finance, obtaining reliable, real-time data can be difficult, and poor-quality data can lead to inaccurate predictions and losses.

2. **Overfitting**: In financial markets, machine learning models are prone to overfitting, especially when trained on noisy or volatile data. Overfitting can result in a model that performs well on historical data but fails in live trading environments.

3. **Market Complexity**: Financial markets are influenced by a wide range of factors, including geopolitical events, economic indicators, and market sentiment. Capturing the complexity of these interactions in machine learning models is a significant challenge.

4. **Changing Market Conditions**: Financial markets are dynamic, and models trained on historical data may not perform well under new market conditions (e.g., during a financial crisis). Continual monitoring and retraining of models are essential.

5. **Regulatory Concerns**: The use of machine learning in finance is subject to strict regulatory oversight. Financial institutions must ensure compliance with laws related to transparency, fairness, and data privacy.

The Future of Machine Learning in Finance

As machine learning algorithms continue to evolve, their impact on fraud detection and algorithmic trading will likely grow even stronger. Advances in **deep learning, reinforcement learning**, and **natural language processing** will lead to more sophisticated models capable of making faster, more accurate predictions.

Additionally, as real-time data sources expand and computational power increases, machine learning-driven trading strategies and fraud detection systems will become more robust, adaptable, and efficient.

Machine learning has fundamentally transformed the financial industry, offering unprecedented capabilities in fraud detection and algorithmic trading. In fraud detection, machine learning models are adept at identifying suspicious activities and adapting to new fraud patterns, ensuring the security of financial systems.

In algorithmic trading, machine learning allows for the development of complex trading strategies that can adapt to market conditions in real time, optimizing profitability and minimizing risk.

9.3 Image Recognition and Computer Vision Applications

Image recognition and **computer vision** are two of the most impactful areas of artificial intelligence (AI), enabling machines to interpret and analyze visual data from the world. From autonomous vehicles to facial recognition, these technologies have revolutionized how machines interact with the physical environment.

By leveraging advanced machine learning algorithms, particularly deep learning, computers can now perform tasks such as identifying objects in images, detecting faces, understanding scenes, and even analyzing medical imagery.

In this section, we will explore the fundamentals of image recognition, its relationship to computer vision, and a range of real-world applications in industries as diverse as healthcare, automotive, retail, and entertainment.

What is Image Recognition?

Image recognition refers to the process by which a computer system identifies objects, features, or patterns in digital images. It involves using machine learning algorithms, often in the form of **convolutional neural networks (CNNs)**, to classify images or detect specific objects within them. Image recognition forms the backbone of many modern AI-driven applications, allowing machines to interpret visual data and make decisions based on that data.

For example, when you upload a picture to social media, image recognition algorithms may identify and tag the people in the photo, detect landmarks, or recognize certain objects like cars, animals, or buildings.

Image recognition is a key task within the broader field of **computer vision**, which encompasses more complex visual tasks such as object detection, image segmentation, and scene understanding.

What is Computer Vision?

Computer vision is a field of AI that enables computers to interpret and make decisions based on visual data, such as images or videos. It involves a range of tasks beyond just identifying objects, such as understanding their position, depth, movement, and context within an environment.

Key tasks in computer vision include:

- **Object Detection**: Identifying and locating objects within an image or video frame.

- **Image Segmentation**: Dividing an image into multiple segments or regions for more detailed analysis.

- **Facial Recognition**: Identifying and verifying human faces in images.

- **Pose Estimation**: Estimating the positions and orientations of objects or humans in a scene.

- **Scene Understanding**: Interpreting the broader context of a scene, including relationships between objects and their environment.

Computer vision has many real-world applications, ranging from **autonomous vehicles** and **robotics** to **healthcare diagnostics** and **security surveillance**.

How Does Image Recognition Work?

Image recognition relies heavily on deep learning, particularly **convolutional neural networks (CNNs)**. CNNs are a class of neural networks specifically designed for processing and analyzing visual data.

Here's how the process typically works:

1. **Image Preprocessing**: Before feeding the image into the neural network, it may be preprocessed. This involves normalizing pixel values, resizing the image, or converting it to grayscale if necessary.

2. **Feature Extraction**: CNNs automatically learn to extract important features from images. Early layers in the CNN detect basic features like edges, corners, and textures. Deeper layers progressively capture more complex structures, such as shapes and patterns that define specific objects.

3. **Convolutional Layers**: These layers apply filters (kernels) to the image to detect different features. Each filter is responsible for identifying a specific feature (e.g., horizontal edges, vertical edges) and producing a **feature map** that highlights where the feature appears in the image.

4. **Pooling Layers**: Pooling layers reduce the dimensionality of the feature maps, making the network more efficient and less prone to overfitting. **Max pooling** is the most common type, which selects the maximum value from a region of the feature map.

5. **Fully Connected Layers**: After passing through several convolutional and pooling layers, the image is flattened

into a one-dimensional vector, which is then passed through fully connected layers. These layers are responsible for making the final classification or prediction.

6. **Classification**: Finally, the output layer uses a softmax or sigmoid activation function to classify the image into one or more categories (e.g., "dog," "cat," "car"). The output is a probability score for each class.

The strength of CNNs lies in their ability to automatically learn hierarchical features from images, making them highly effective for image classification and recognition tasks.

Key Techniques in Computer Vision

Beyond image recognition, computer vision encompasses several key techniques that allow machines to perform more advanced visual tasks:

1. Object Detection

Object detection involves not only identifying objects in an image but also determining their location using bounding boxes. Unlike image classification, which assigns a label to the entire image, object detection specifies where each object is within the image.

Popular object detection models include:

- **YOLO (You Only Look Once)**: A fast and efficient real-time object detection model that processes the entire image in a single pass.

- **Faster R-CNN (Region-based Convolutional Neural Network)**: A two-stage object detection model that first identifies potential object regions and then classifies them.

2. Image Segmentation

Image segmentation divides an image into different segments or regions, where each pixel is assigned a label corresponding to the object it belongs to. Segmentation is especially useful in applications where understanding pixel-level details is critical, such as medical imaging or autonomous driving.

Two main types of segmentation include:

- **Semantic Segmentation**: Assigns each pixel to a predefined class (e.g., road, pedestrian, vehicle).

- **Instance Segmentation**: Differentiates between individual instances of objects, even if they belong to the same class (e.g., multiple cars in an image).

Mask R-CNN is a popular model for instance segmentation.

3. Facial Recognition

Facial recognition is used to identify or verify individuals based on facial features. It has applications in security, authentication, and social media tagging. Facial recognition systems typically involve:

- **Face detection**: Identifying the location of faces within an image.

- **Face alignment**: Adjusting the orientation and scale of the detected face.

- **Feature extraction**: Extracting unique facial features such as the distance between the eyes, nose, and mouth.

- **Classification**: Matching the extracted features against a database to identify or verify the person.

4. Pose Estimation

Pose estimation involves detecting the positions and orientations of objects or humans in an image or video. Human pose estimation identifies key points of the body (e.g., joints, limbs) and tracks their movement over time, which is useful in motion analysis, sports analytics, and gaming.

5. Optical Character Recognition (OCR)

Optical Character Recognition (OCR) converts images of text into machine-readable text. OCR is widely used for digitizing documents, license plate recognition, and reading text in natural scenes. With advances in deep learning, OCR systems have become more accurate at recognizing text in diverse environments.

6. Scene Understanding

Scene understanding refers to interpreting the overall context of an image, including the relationships between objects and their environment. This includes tasks like **image captioning**, which generates textual descriptions of an image, and **scene classification**, which categorizes entire scenes (e.g., "beach," "city street," "forest").

Applications of Image Recognition and Computer Vision

Image recognition and computer vision technologies are applied across a wide range of industries, transforming how businesses operate and improving efficiency, safety, and user experience. Here are some prominent real-world applications:

1. Autonomous Vehicles

Computer vision is a cornerstone technology in the development of **autonomous vehicles**. Self-driving cars rely on image recognition and object detection to perceive their surroundings. Cameras mounted on the vehicle detect other cars, pedestrians, traffic signs, and lane markings, enabling the vehicle to navigate safely.

LiDAR and computer vision work in tandem to create a detailed 3D representation of the environment, allowing autonomous vehicles to make real-time decisions about speed, direction, and obstacle avoidance.

2. Healthcare and Medical Imaging

In healthcare, computer vision plays a critical role in **medical imaging** and diagnostics. AI models can analyze images from **X-rays**, **MRIs**, and **CT scans** to detect early signs of diseases such as cancer, tumors, and other abnormalities. For example:

- **Image segmentation** is used to identify and isolate regions of interest (e.g., tumors in a scan).

- **Object detection** models can highlight anomalies such as fractures or organ damage.

By automating these tasks, computer vision assists radiologists and medical professionals in making faster, more accurate diagnoses.

3. Retail and E-Commerce

Image recognition has transformed the **retail** and **e-commerce** industries by enabling visual search and automated product tagging. For example:

- **Visual search** allows users to search for products by uploading images rather than typing keywords. AI algorithms analyze the image and return similar products available on the retailer's website.

- **Product tagging** automates the process of identifying items in an image, such as clothing, accessories, or home decor, and associating them with product categories and brands.

In physical stores, computer vision is used for **inventory management** and **loss prevention** by analyzing camera feeds to detect when products need restocking or when suspicious activities occur.

4. Security and Surveillance

Facial recognition and **object detection** technologies are widely used in security and surveillance. Cameras equipped with computer vision algorithms can monitor public spaces, identify potential security threats, and alert authorities in real time. This is particularly valuable in airports, stadiums, and other high-security environments.

Additionally, computer vision is used in **biometric authentication** systems, allowing users to unlock devices or gain access to secure areas using facial recognition.

5. Agriculture

In **agriculture**, computer vision is used to monitor crop health, detect pests, and optimize yield. Drones equipped with cameras and computer vision models can scan large fields, identify areas of disease, and provide insights into soil quality and irrigation needs. These technologies help farmers make data-driven decisions that improve efficiency and reduce waste.

6. Manufacturing and Quality Control

In **manufacturing**, computer vision systems are employed to automate quality control processes. Cameras and image recognition models can inspect products for defects, ensuring that only high-quality items are shipped to customers. For example, computer vision can detect imperfections in electronics, automotive parts, or textiles during the production process.

Computer vision is also used in **robotic automation**, enabling robots to "see" and manipulate objects in manufacturing environments, improving productivity and precision.

7. Entertainment and Media

The **entertainment** industry uses computer vision for tasks such as facial recognition in video games, augmented reality (AR) experiences, and visual effects in films. For instance, AR applications like **Snapchat filters** use facial recognition to overlay digital effects on live video.

In **sports analytics**, computer vision is used to track player movements, analyze gameplay, and provide real-time insights into performance.

8. Education

In the **education** sector, computer vision is applied in applications like **automated grading**, **student engagement tracking**, and **online proctoring**. For example, during online exams, AI systems can monitor students via webcam to detect cheating behaviors using facial recognition and eye-tracking technologies.

Challenges in Image Recognition and Computer Vision

Despite their successes, image recognition and computer vision systems face several challenges:

1. **Data Quality**: Training computer vision models requires large, high-quality datasets with accurately labeled images. Poor-quality data can lead to unreliable predictions or biased models.

2. **Variability in Images**: Variations in lighting, perspective, or occlusion can make it difficult for models to consistently recognize objects or people in images. Improving robustness against these variations is a key area of research.

3. **Computational Resources**: Training deep learning models for image recognition requires significant computational power, often requiring GPUs or cloud-based computing resources, which can be costly.

4. **Bias and Fairness**: Computer vision systems can inherit biases from the training data, leading to issues like misidentification or underperformance for certain demographic groups. Addressing these biases is essential to ensure fairness in applications like facial recognition or security.

5. **Ethical Concerns**: The use of computer vision in surveillance and facial recognition raises privacy and ethical concerns, especially when it comes to mass surveillance or unauthorized use of biometric data.

The Future of Image Recognition and Computer Vision

As technology advances, we can expect several key developments in image recognition and computer vision:

1. **Edge Computing**: The rise of **edge computing** will allow more computer vision applications to run locally on devices, reducing the need for cloud-based processing and enabling real-time decision-making in areas like autonomous vehicles and drones.

2. **3D Vision**: Emerging techniques for **3D vision** will allow computer vision systems to better understand depth, object orientation, and the spatial relationships between objects, further enhancing applications like robotics and augmented reality.

3. **Explainable AI**: There is growing demand for **explainable AI**, where computer vision systems not only make predictions but also provide interpretable explanations for their decisions. This will be critical in industries like healthcare, where transparency is necessary.

4. **Generalization**: Future research will focus on improving the ability of computer vision models to generalize across different environments, lighting conditions, and perspectives, making them more adaptable to real-world applications.

Image recognition and computer vision have fundamentally transformed how machines interact with and interpret the visual world. From autonomous vehicles and healthcare diagnostics to retail, agriculture, and entertainment, these technologies are revolutionizing industries by enabling automation, enhancing decision-making, and improving efficiency.

9.4 Recommender Systems: Personalizing User Experiences

Recommender systems have become a critical tool for personalizing user experiences in digital environments. From streaming services like Netflix to e-commerce platforms like Amazon, recommender systems help users discover relevant content and products by analyzing their preferences, behaviors, and interactions.

These systems enhance user engagement, increase customer satisfaction, and drive sales by offering tailored recommendations based on an individual's past interactions and the preferences of similar users.

In this section, we will explore the fundamentals of recommender systems, the types of recommendation algorithms, their real-world applications, and the challenges involved in building effective recommendation engines.

What is a Recommender System?

A **recommender system** is a type of information filtering system designed to predict the preferences of users and recommend items (such as products, movies, articles, or music) that are likely to interest them. The goal of a recommender system is to present users with personalized suggestions that enhance their experience and help them navigate large datasets or catalogs more efficiently.

Recommender systems are ubiquitous in modern online platforms, helping users discover new items that they may not have found on their own. Examples include:

- Netflix recommending movies or TV shows based on viewing history.

- Amazon suggesting products that are frequently bought together.

- Spotify creating personalized playlists based on a user's listening habits.

Types of Recommender Systems

There are three main types of recommender systems: **content-based filtering**, **collaborative filtering**, and **hybrid models**. Each approach uses different techniques to generate recommendations, and the choice of method depends on the type of data available and the specific goals of the recommendation engine.

1. Content-Based Filtering

Content-based filtering recommends items to users based on the attributes of the items themselves and the user's past preferences. This approach assumes that if a user liked a particular item, they would likely enjoy other items with similar characteristics. For example, if a user likes action movies, a content-based recommender would suggest other action movies based on the attributes (genre, director, actors) of previously liked movies.

How It Works:

- **Item profiles** are created by extracting key features from each item (e.g., genre, actors for movies, or keywords for articles).

- **User profiles** are built by analyzing the items a user has interacted with or rated positively.

- The system matches items with similar attributes to those that the user has liked, generating recommendations based on these similarities.

Advantages:

- Content-based filtering does not rely on other users' data, making it effective for users with unique tastes.

- It can recommend niche items that may not be popular with the general user base.

Disadvantages:

- **Limited discovery**: Content-based systems tend to recommend items similar to what the user has already seen, limiting opportunities for discovery.

- **Cold start problem**: New users and new items with no prior data may be difficult to recommend effectively.

Example:

A content-based recommender on a news platform might suggest articles related to topics the user has previously read, such as science or technology, by analyzing keywords and matching similar content.

2. Collaborative Filtering

Collaborative filtering recommends items based on the preferences of other users who share similar tastes. Instead of analyzing the content of the items themselves, collaborative filtering systems focus on the relationships between users and items, identifying patterns of behavior across the user base. There are two main types of collaborative filtering: **user-based** and **item-based**.

How It Works:

- **User-based collaborative filtering** identifies users with similar preferences and recommends items that those similar users have liked. If User A and User B have both enjoyed several of the same movies, the system might recommend a movie that User B has liked but User A hasn't watched yet.

- **Item-based collaborative filtering** recommends items that are similar to those the user has liked, based on the preferences of all users. If many users who liked Movie X also liked Movie Y, the system would recommend Movie Y to a user who enjoyed Movie X.

Advantages:

- **Serendipity**: Collaborative filtering can recommend items that users might not have considered, offering greater discovery and surprise.

- **Scalability**: Collaborative filtering scales well as more users and data are added to the system.

Disadvantages:

- **Cold start problem**: Collaborative filtering struggles with new users (who haven't rated or interacted with many items) and new items (which haven't been rated by many users).

- **Sparsity**: In systems with a large catalog of items, there may be very few common preferences between users, making it difficult to find meaningful patterns.

Example:

On Amazon, collaborative filtering might recommend products based on the purchasing patterns of users with similar shopping habits. If many users who bought a camera also bought a tripod, the system may suggest a tripod to someone who just purchased a camera.

3. Hybrid Models

Hybrid recommender systems combine both content-based and collaborative filtering approaches to overcome the limitations of each method. By leveraging the strengths of both techniques, hybrid models can provide more accurate and diverse recommendations.

How It Works:

- **Weighted hybrid:** The system calculates recommendations from both content-based and collaborative filtering models and then combines them with a weighted score to generate the final recommendation.

- **Switching hybrid:** The system switches between content-based and collaborative filtering approaches based on the availability of data. For example, it may use content-based filtering for new users and collaborative filtering for established users with more data.

- **Feature augmentation hybrid:** Content-based information is used to enhance collaborative filtering recommendations, or vice versa. For example, item features (content) might be used to fill in gaps where collaborative data is sparse.

Advantages:

- **Overcomes cold start problem:** By incorporating content-based features, hybrid systems can recommend new items or for new users more effectively than collaborative filtering alone.

- **Increased accuracy:** Hybrid models can improve the accuracy of recommendations by combining multiple data sources.

Example:

Netflix uses a hybrid recommender system that combines content-based filtering (analyzing the genres and actors of shows a user has watched) with collaborative filtering (analyzing viewing patterns of similar users) to recommend TV shows and movies.

Techniques Used in Recommender Systems

Several machine learning techniques are used to build recommender systems, including:

1. Matrix Factorization

Matrix factorization is a popular technique for collaborative filtering. It decomposes the user-item interaction matrix into lower-dimensional matrices representing latent factors for users and items. These latent factors capture the underlying characteristics of users and items that explain their interactions.

- **Singular Value Decomposition (SVD)** is a commonly used matrix factorization method. It reduces the dimensionality of the user-item matrix, allowing for more efficient predictions of missing ratings.

Matrix factorization is widely used in platforms like Netflix, where user ratings for movies are predicted based on the learned latent factors.

2. Neural Networks

Neural networks have become increasingly popular in modern recommender systems due to their ability to model complex, non-linear relationships in data. **Deep learning** techniques are often used to combine multiple input features (user preferences, item attributes, and collaborative information) to generate highly personalized recommendations.

For example, **deep collaborative filtering** models use neural networks to learn user-item interactions, while **convolutional neural networks (CNNs)** can be applied to image-based recommender systems to recommend products based on visual similarity.

3. Association Rule Mining

Association rule mining is used to discover relationships between items in large datasets, making it useful for market basket analysis. This technique identifies patterns, such as "customers who bought item X often bought item Y," and uses these patterns to generate recommendations.

For example, Amazon's recommendation engine suggests "Frequently Bought Together" items based on association rules.

4. Factorization Machines

Factorization machines are a generalization of matrix factorization that can model interactions between all possible features (users, items, and side information like time or location). They are highly flexible and can incorporate both collaborative and content-based data.

5. Content-Based Techniques

In content-based systems, **TF-IDF (Term Frequency-Inverse Document Frequency)** and **word embeddings** (like Word2Vec or GloVe) are often used to represent text data, such as movie descriptions or product reviews, allowing the system to match items with similar textual features.

Real-World Applications of Recommender Systems

Recommender systems are used in a wide range of industries to enhance user experience, increase engagement, and drive business outcomes. Below are some of the most common applications:

1. E-commerce

E-commerce platforms like Amazon and eBay use recommender systems to personalize the shopping experience by suggesting products based on user preferences, browsing history, and purchase behavior. Common recommendations include:

- **Personalized product suggestions** on the homepage.

- **Cross-sell and up-sell** recommendations during the checkout process (e.g., "Frequently Bought Together").

- **Trending items** and **best-sellers** based on current user behavior.

Recommender systems in e-commerce drive sales by improving product discovery and encouraging users to make additional purchases.

2. Entertainment and Media

Streaming platforms like Netflix, YouTube, and Spotify rely

heavily on recommender systems to suggest personalized content. These platforms analyze users' viewing or listening history and the preferences of similar users to recommend movies, TV shows, music tracks, and podcasts.

For example, Netflix's recommendation system is responsible for a significant portion of user activity on the platform, helping users find shows they're likely to enjoy without spending too much time searching.

3. Social Media

Social media platforms like Facebook, Instagram, and Twitter use recommender systems to curate personalized feeds for users. These systems recommend posts, friends, events, and ads based on users' interests, interactions, and social connections.

For instance, Instagram's "Explore" page recommends images and videos based on the user's previous likes and the engagement history of similar users.

4. News and Content Platforms

Recommender systems are widely used in news platforms like Google News or Medium to suggest articles and blogs tailored to users' reading habits and preferences. Content-based filtering plays a key role here, as the system matches the topics and keywords of articles with the user's reading history.

5. Online Advertising

In the world of online advertising, recommender systems are used to serve personalized ads based on a user's browsing behavior, purchase history, and demographics. Ad targeting algorithms are designed to maximize relevance, increasing the chances of clicks and conversions.

For example, Google Ads and Facebook Ads use sophisticated recommender systems to display ads that are tailored to each user's interests and online activity.

6. Healthcare

In healthcare, recommender systems are being used to recommend treatment plans, suggest medical content to patients, and support clinical decision-making. These systems analyze patient records, medical history, and clinical data to recommend personalized treatments, medications, or preventative measures.

For instance, a healthcare provider might recommend a personalized fitness plan or dietary changes based on a patient's health records and wearable device data.

Challenges in Recommender Systems

While recommender systems have become highly sophisticated, they face several challenges:

1. Cold Start Problem

The cold start problem occurs when there is insufficient data about new users or new items to make accurate recommendations. Without historical data, it is difficult for collaborative filtering systems to generate meaningful recommendations for new users or products. Hybrid models that incorporate content-based filtering can help mitigate this issue.

2. Scalability

As the number of users and items grows, scaling recommender systems to handle large datasets becomes a challenge. Efficient algorithms and distributed computing techniques are required to ensure that recommendations are generated in real time, especially for platforms with millions of users.

3. Data Sparsity

In systems with a vast catalog of items (such as large e-commerce platforms), user-item interactions can be sparse, meaning that there are relatively few data points compared to the total number of possible interactions. Data sparsity can hinder the effectiveness of collaborative filtering models.

4. Bias and Fairness

Recommender systems can introduce biases in their suggestions, often recommending popular or mainstream items more frequently than niche products. Additionally, if the training data is biased, the system may perpetuate social, racial, or gender biases. Ensuring fairness and diversity in recommendations is a growing area of concern.

5. Privacy Concerns

Recommender systems require access to user data, including browsing behavior, purchase history, and social interactions. Protecting user privacy and ensuring compliance with regulations like GDPR (General Data Protection Regulation) is crucial when implementing recommendation systems.

The Future of Recommender Systems

As technology continues to evolve, several trends are shaping the future of recommender systems:

1. **Context-Aware Recommendations**: Future systems will incorporate contextual information, such as the time of day, location, or weather, to make more relevant recommendations. For example, a music app might

suggest different playlists based on whether the user is at home, at the gym, or commuting.

2. **Explainable Recommendations:** Users are increasingly interested in understanding why a recommendation was made. Providing transparent and explainable recommendations (e.g., "We recommended this because you liked X") can increase user trust and engagement.

3. **Deep Learning in Recommenders:** Deep learning models are becoming more prominent in recommender systems, enabling more accurate and dynamic recommendations by learning complex patterns in user-item interactions.

4. **Cross-Domain Recommendations:** As users interact with multiple platforms (e.g., social media, e-commerce, and entertainment), future recommender systems may combine data across domains to provide more holistic and accurate recommendations.

5. **Personalized Recommendations in Real Time:** With advances in real-time data processing and edge computing, recommender systems will become faster and more responsive, delivering highly personalized recommendations instantly based on the latest user interactions.

Recommender systems have revolutionized the way users discover content, products, and services, becoming an essential component of many digital platforms. By personalizing the user experience, these systems enhance engagement, drive sales, and improve customer satisfaction.

Whether through content-based filtering, collaborative filtering, or hybrid models, recommender systems have proven to be invaluable in industries ranging from e-commerce and entertainment to healthcare and social media.

9.5 Machine Learning for Autonomous Systems and Robotics

Machine learning plays a crucial role in the development of **autonomous systems** and **robotics**, enabling machines to perceive their environment, make decisions, and perform complex tasks without human intervention. These technologies are at the core of self-driving cars, drones, industrial robots, and intelligent home assistants.

By integrating machine learning algorithms with robotics, we are moving towards systems that can learn from their experiences, adapt to new environments, and improve their performance over time.

In this section, we will explore how machine learning is applied in autonomous systems and robotics, covering key concepts, algorithms, real-world applications, and the challenges faced in building autonomous systems that can safely and efficiently navigate the world.

What Are Autonomous Systems and Robotics?

Autonomous systems are machines or software that can perform tasks independently without the need for direct human control. They often operate in dynamic and unpredictable environments, requiring the ability to perceive, plan, and make decisions in real time. **Robotics** refers to the design and development of robots—physical machines that can perform tasks autonomously or semi-autonomously.

When combined with machine learning, robots and autonomous systems become more adaptable and intelligent, allowing them to process sensory data (like images, sound, or touch), learn from experiences, and make decisions based on real-time input. Examples of autonomous systems include:

- **Self-driving cars**: Autonomous vehicles that use sensors, cameras, and machine learning to navigate roads and avoid obstacles.

- **Drones**: Unmanned aerial vehicles (UAVs) that can perform tasks like aerial photography, surveying, or delivery.

- **Industrial robots**: Machines that perform repetitive tasks like assembly, welding, or material handling in manufacturing plants.

- **Home assistants**: Robots like **Roomba** or **Amazon's Astro** that can clean, monitor homes, or assist with everyday tasks.

The Role of Machine Learning in Autonomous Systems and Robotics

Machine learning is critical for enabling robots and autonomous systems to function in complex, real-world environments. Traditional rule-based systems are limited in their ability to handle uncertainty or adapt to new situations. By using machine learning algorithms, autonomous systems can learn from data, improve their performance over time, and handle the unpredictability of the real world.

Here's how machine learning is applied in autonomous systems and robotics:

1. Perception

Perception is the ability of a robot to understand its environment by interpreting sensory data. Machine learning algorithms, especially those in the realm of **computer vision** and **sensor fusion**, are used to process and analyze data from cameras, LiDAR (Light Detection and Ranging), sonar, radar, and other sensors.

- **Computer vision:** Machine learning models, particularly **convolutional neural networks (CNNs)**, enable robots to recognize objects, detect obstacles, and understand their surroundings through image and video data.

- **Sensor fusion:** Machine learning algorithms combine data from multiple sensors (e.g., cameras, LiDAR, GPS) to provide a more accurate understanding of the robot's environment. This is critical in applications like autonomous driving, where different sensors contribute to a holistic view of the surroundings.

2. Localization and Mapping

For autonomous systems to navigate, they need to understand their position in the environment and build a map of their surroundings. **Simultaneous Localization and Mapping (SLAM)** is a technique used by robots to create a map of an unknown environment while keeping track of their location within it. Machine learning improves SLAM by making it more robust and adaptable in dynamic environments.

- **Localization:** Machine learning models help robots determine their precise location by analyzing data from sensors like GPS, IMUs (Inertial Measurement Units), and cameras.

- **Mapping**: Using sensor data, machine learning algorithms help robots create a map of their environment in real time, identifying obstacles and navigable paths.

3. Planning and Decision Making

Once a robot understands its environment, it needs to decide how to navigate or perform tasks. Machine learning enables robots to make decisions based on past experiences, current conditions, and future goals.

- **Path planning**: Robots use machine learning to calculate the best path to reach a destination while avoiding obstacles. Algorithms like **Dijkstra's algorithm, A***, and **reinforcement learning** are commonly used for path planning.

- **Task planning**: For robots that perform complex tasks (e.g., manufacturing or assembly), machine learning helps determine the most efficient sequence of actions to achieve a goal.

4. Control and Motion

Control systems ensure that robots move accurately and efficiently in their environment. Machine learning helps optimize the control strategies for robots, allowing them to adapt to different conditions (e.g., uneven terrain or changing dynamics).

- **Reinforcement learning**: In robotics, reinforcement learning (RL) is used to train robots to perform tasks by interacting with the environment and learning from the outcomes. RL algorithms reward the robot for achieving its goals and penalize it for errors, allowing it to learn optimal strategies over time.

- **Dynamic control**: Machine learning is used to model the dynamics of robotic systems and improve control over movement, such as grasping objects, maintaining balance, or adjusting speed.

5. Learning from Demonstration

One of the most intuitive ways for robots to learn is by observing human actions. **Learning from demonstration (LfD)**, also known as **imitation learning**, allows robots to learn tasks by observing how humans perform them. This approach is particularly useful in tasks like assembly, cooking, or other activities that involve precise movements and actions.

- **Imitation learning**: In this method, robots are trained to replicate human actions by mimicking the demonstrated behavior. This approach uses supervised learning, where the robot learns from examples provided by humans.

6. Collaboration and Interaction

Autonomous robots often need to collaborate with humans or other robots to complete tasks. Machine learning enables **human-robot interaction (HRI)**, where robots learn to understand and respond to human gestures, speech, or commands. In multi-robot systems, machine learning helps robots communicate and collaborate to achieve shared goals.

- **Human-robot interaction**: Machine learning models, such as natural language processing (NLP) and gesture recognition, allow robots to interpret human instructions and act accordingly.

- **Multi-robot systems**: Machine learning helps robots coordinate with one another in environments where multiple robots work together, such as in warehouses or automated factories.

Machine Learning Algorithms in Autonomous Systems and Robotics

Several machine learning algorithms are widely used in autonomous systems and robotics. Below are some of the key algorithms:

1. Reinforcement Learning (RL)

Reinforcement learning is one of the most popular approaches in robotics because it allows systems to learn from interactions with their environment. In RL, a robot learns by trial and error, receiving rewards or penalties based on its actions. The goal is to maximize cumulative rewards, leading to the discovery of optimal policies for navigation, manipulation, or other tasks.

- **Q-learning**: A common RL algorithm where the agent learns a value function (Q-value) that maps state-action pairs to rewards.

- **Deep Q-Networks (DQN)**: Combines Q-learning with deep learning to handle high-dimensional state spaces (e.g., visual data from cameras).

- **Policy gradient methods**: In contrast to Q-learning, policy gradient methods directly optimize the policy, making them useful in continuous action spaces like robot control.

2. Convolutional Neural Networks (CNNs)

CNNs are widely used in autonomous systems for processing visual data, such as images or video streams. CNNs extract features from images and use them to classify objects, detect obstacles, or recognize faces. CNNs are a crucial component of perception systems in autonomous vehicles, drones, and home robots.

3. Recurrent Neural Networks (RNNs)

RNNs and their variants, such as **Long Short-Term Memory (LSTM)** networks, are used to handle sequential data, such as time-series data from sensors. In robotics, RNNs can model the dynamics of the environment or predict future states based on past observations.

4. Generative Models

Generative models, such as **Generative Adversarial Networks (GANs)** and **Variational Autoencoders (VAEs)**, are used in robotics for tasks like simulation and data augmentation. For example, GANs can generate synthetic images to train vision systems when real-world data is scarce.

5. Bayesian Networks

Bayesian networks are probabilistic graphical models that represent the relationships between variables. They are useful in robotics for dealing with uncertainty and making decisions under uncertain conditions. For example, Bayesian networks can help robots predict the outcome of their actions and update their beliefs based on new observations.

6. Support Vector Machines (SVMs)

SVMs are used in robotics for classification tasks, such as object recognition or gesture classification. SVMs find the optimal hyperplane that separates data into different classes, making them effective for tasks where the goal is to categorize objects or actions.

Real-World Applications of Machine Learning in Autonomous Systems and Robotics

Autonomous systems and robots powered by machine learning are transforming industries and enabling new applications across various sectors. Here are some notable examples:

1. Self-Driving Cars

One of the most well-known applications of machine learning in autonomous systems is **self-driving cars**. Companies like Tesla, Waymo, and Uber rely on deep learning, reinforcement learning, and sensor fusion to enable cars to navigate roads, avoid obstacles, and make real-time decisions. Key tasks include:

- **Object detection and tracking**: Using cameras and LiDAR to detect pedestrians, vehicles, traffic signs, and other objects.

- **Path planning**: Determining the optimal route to a destination while avoiding obstacles and following traffic rules.

- **Control**: Managing acceleration, braking, and steering based on environmental conditions and navigation goals.

2. Drones

Drones, or **unmanned aerial vehicles (UAVs)**, use machine learning for a wide range of applications, including aerial photography, surveillance, delivery, and environmental monitoring. Machine learning enables drones to:

- **Navigate autonomously**: Drones use computer vision and reinforcement learning to fly safely, avoid obstacles, and navigate complex environments without human intervention.

- **Perform object detection**: Drones equipped with cameras and CNNs can detect and track objects on the ground, such as vehicles, animals, or people.

3. Industrial Robotics

In manufacturing and logistics, **industrial robots** perform repetitive tasks such as assembly, welding, material handling, and quality control. Machine learning helps these robots adapt to new tasks, optimize their movements, and collaborate with human workers.

- **Collaborative robots (cobots)**: Cobots work alongside humans in factories, using machine learning to interpret gestures and avoid collisions.

- **Quality control**: Robots equipped with machine vision systems can inspect products for defects, improving the accuracy and efficiency of manufacturing processes.

4. Home Robotics

Home robots, such as vacuum cleaners (e.g., Roomba), personal assistants (e.g., Amazon Astro), and lawn mowers, use machine learning to navigate domestic environments and assist with household tasks. These robots rely on SLAM for mapping and path planning, as well as computer vision for object detection and obstacle avoidance.

5. Healthcare Robotics

Robots are increasingly being used in healthcare to assist with surgery, patient care, and rehabilitation. Machine learning helps healthcare robots:

- **Perform minimally invasive surgeries**: Surgical robots like **da Vinci** use machine learning to assist surgeons with precision tasks, such as stitching or cutting.

- **Assist in rehabilitation**: Robots designed for physical therapy can learn from a patient's movements and adjust their assistance based on the patient's progress.

- **Autonomous healthcare assistants**: Robots can navigate hospital environments, deliver medications, and assist with patient monitoring.

6. Agriculture

In agriculture, autonomous robots are used for tasks such as planting, harvesting, and monitoring crops. Machine learning enables agricultural robots to:

- **Identify plant diseases**: Using computer vision, robots can detect signs of diseases or pests in crops, enabling early intervention.

- **Optimize planting and harvesting**: Machine learning models help robots plan efficient routes for planting seeds or harvesting crops.

Challenges in Machine Learning for Autonomous Systems and Robotics

Despite the progress in autonomous systems and robotics, several challenges remain:

1. Safety and Reliability

Autonomous systems must operate safely, especially in critical applications like self-driving cars or healthcare robots. Ensuring that machine learning models are robust and can handle edge cases (e.g., rare or unexpected events) is a major challenge. **Testing** and **validation** in real-world environments are essential to ensure safety and reliability.

2. Real-Time Decision Making

Many autonomous systems, such as drones or self-driving cars, need to make decisions in real time. Machine learning models must be optimized for low latency and high efficiency to process sensor data and make decisions within milliseconds.

3. Data Scarcity

In some domains, there is a lack of sufficient real-world data to train machine learning models. **Simulations** and **synthetic data** are often used to overcome this challenge, but there can be discrepancies between simulated and real-world environments, leading to **sim-to-real** transfer issues.

4. Uncertainty and Adaptability

Autonomous systems must operate in dynamic and unpredictable environments, where sensor noise, changing conditions, and unexpected obstacles can pose challenges. Machine learning models must be able to handle uncertainty and adapt to new situations without constant retraining.

5. Ethical and Legal Concerns

Autonomous systems, particularly in transportation and healthcare, raise ethical and legal concerns. Questions about accountability, privacy, and the ethical implications of machine decision-making must be addressed before widespread adoption of autonomous technologies.

The Future of Machine Learning in Autonomous Systems and Robotics

The future of autonomous systems and robotics is closely tied to advancements in machine learning. Key trends shaping the future include:

1. **Deep Reinforcement Learning (DRL)**: As DRL continues to evolve, robots will become better at learning complex tasks autonomously, improving their ability to navigate and interact with dynamic environments.

2. **Human-Robot Collaboration**: The rise of **cobots** and human-robot collaboration systems will make it easier for humans and robots to work together in industries like manufacturing, healthcare, and logistics.

3. **5G and Edge Computing**: The deployment of 5G networks and edge computing will enable faster and more efficient communication between robots and cloud systems, allowing for real-time decision-making and data processing.

4. **Explainable AI (XAI)**: As autonomous systems become more widespread, the need for transparency and explainability in decision-making will grow. **Explainable AI** will help ensure that robots and autonomous systems can provide understandable reasons for their actions, especially in safety-critical applications.

5. **Robots as a Service (RaaS)**: The **Robots as a Service (RaaS)** model will enable businesses to access robotic capabilities without the need for large upfront investments. As machine learning-driven robots become more capable, they will be deployed across a wide range of industries, from agriculture to retail.

Machine learning is a driving force behind the development of autonomous systems and robotics, enabling machines to perceive their environment, make intelligent decisions, and perform tasks with increasing autonomy.

From self-driving cars and drones to healthcare robots and industrial automation, machine learning empowers robots to learn from experience, adapt to new situations, and operate in complex, real-world environments.

Chapter 10: Getting Started with Machine Learning Projects

10.1 Choosing the Right Machine Learning Problem

One of the first and most critical steps in developing machine learning solutions is choosing the right problem to solve. Not every business challenge or task is suitable for machine learning, and selecting an appropriate problem directly impacts the success of the solution.

Understanding the problem context, aligning with business goals, assessing the availability of data, and determining the feasibility of the solution are all key factors to consider before embarking on a machine learning project.

In this section, we will explore the steps involved in choosing the right machine learning problem, common types of machine learning problems, and how to evaluate the suitability of a problem for machine learning.

Why Is Problem Selection Important?

Choosing the right machine learning problem is crucial because:

- **Relevance**: The problem must align with business objectives and add value.

- **Data availability**: Machine learning relies on data, so a problem without sufficient or appropriate data may not be solvable using machine learning techniques.

- **Feasibility**: The problem must be solvable within practical constraints, such as time, budget, and computational resources.

- **Impact**: Solving the problem should lead to significant improvements in business processes, customer satisfaction, or operational efficiency.

By selecting the right problem, you can avoid wasting resources on projects that may not deliver value or may be difficult to implement with machine learning.

Steps to Choose the Right Machine Learning Problem

Choosing the right problem involves a structured approach to evaluating business challenges and determining which ones can be effectively addressed using machine learning techniques.

Here's a step-by-step guide to help with this process:

1. Understand the Business Context and Objectives

The first step in choosing a machine learning problem is to deeply understand the business context and objectives. This requires collaboration between data scientists, domain experts, and business stakeholders to clearly define the goals and desired outcomes. Some key questions to ask include:

- What business problems are we trying to solve?

- What metrics or KPIs (Key Performance Indicators) are most important for the business?

- How can machine learning contribute to achieving these goals?

- Is there a specific process that can be automated, optimized, or improved through machine learning?

For example, in an e-commerce setting, business goals might include improving customer retention, increasing sales, or reducing operational costs. Each of these goals could be supported by machine learning, but understanding which goal is the priority helps in selecting the right problem.

2. Identify Problems That Are Data-Driven

Machine learning is inherently data-driven, which means it works best when there are clear patterns, correlations, or trends in data that can be learned from. Therefore, the next step is to identify problems that can benefit from data analysis. Some questions to ask include:

- Is there enough historical data available for this problem?

- Are there clear patterns or relationships in the data that machine learning can model?

- Can the problem be defined in terms of input (features) and output (target)?

If the problem involves a lot of uncertainty, with no clear patterns or relationships, it might be more difficult for machine learning to offer a solution. On the other hand, if the problem is well-defined and there is ample data, it may be suitable for machine learning.

3. Determine the Type of Problem

Once a suitable problem is identified, it's essential to determine what type of machine learning problem it is. Machine learning problems generally fall into one of three categories:

- **Supervised Learning**: The model learns from labeled data, where the outcome (target variable) is known. Common problems include:

    o **Classification**: Predicting discrete categories (e.g., spam or not spam, fraud or no fraud).

    o **Regression**: Predicting continuous values (e.g., predicting house prices, stock prices).

- **Unsupervised Learning**: The model learns from unlabeled data, where there is no known outcome. Common problems include:

    o **Clustering**: Grouping similar items together (e.g., customer segmentation).

- o **Anomaly detection:** Identifying unusual or rare events (e.g., fraud detection without labeled fraud cases).

- **Reinforcement Learning:** The model learns through trial and error, receiving rewards or penalties for actions. Common problems include:

  - o **Decision making:** Optimizing a series of decisions in dynamic environments (e.g., robotics, self-driving cars, personalized recommendations).

By understanding the type of problem, you can select the most appropriate machine learning algorithms and techniques to tackle it.

4. Evaluate Data Availability and Quality

The success of any machine learning project depends heavily on the availability, quality, and relevance of data. Before proceeding with a machine learning problem, evaluate the data you have available:

- **Do you have enough data?** Machine learning models need sufficient data to learn patterns and generalize well. For example, deep learning models often require large datasets, while simpler models like linear regression may perform well with smaller datasets.

- **Is the data relevant to the problem?** Ensure the data includes the features necessary to solve the problem. For instance, if you want to predict customer churn, you need data on customer behavior, purchases, interactions, and demographics.

- **Is the data clean and reliable?** Data preprocessing (handling missing data, removing duplicates, etc.) is crucial for model performance. Assess the quality of the data and whether it needs cleaning or transformation.

- **Do you have labeled data (for supervised learning)?** If the problem is a supervised learning task, labeled data is essential. If labeled data is unavailable, consider whether it can be collected or created.

5. Assess Feasibility and Constraints

Before committing to a machine learning project, evaluate the feasibility of the solution. This includes considering factors like:

- **Time and resources**: Does your team have the expertise and computational resources (e.g., cloud computing, GPUs) to develop and deploy a machine learning solution? More complex problems like deep learning require more resources than simpler models.

- **Model complexity**: Is the problem simple enough to be solved with basic models, or does it require advanced techniques like deep learning or reinforcement learning?

- **Deployment and scalability**: Once the model is built, how will it be deployed in production? Will it scale to handle large volumes of data or real-time predictions?

- **Legal and ethical concerns**: Some machine learning problems, especially those involving personal data (e.g., in healthcare or finance), raise privacy, security, and ethical concerns. Ensure that the solution complies with legal and ethical standards.

6. Estimate Potential Impact

Lastly, consider the potential impact of solving the problem with machine learning. Machine learning projects should deliver tangible value to the business, so assess the potential benefits of implementing a machine learning solution. Key questions to ask include:

- What improvements can be expected from the solution (e.g., increased revenue, reduced costs, improved customer satisfaction)?

- How will solving this problem improve decision-making or operational efficiency?

- What is the return on investment (ROI) for implementing the solution?

If solving the problem is likely to have a significant positive impact on the business, it is a strong candidate for a machine learning project.

Common Examples of Machine Learning Problems

To illustrate how machine learning is applied across different industries, here are some common examples of machine learning problems:

1. Predictive Maintenance in Manufacturing

- **Problem**: Predict when equipment or machinery is likely to fail based on historical sensor data and operational metrics.

- **Type**: Supervised learning (regression or classification).

- **Impact**: Reducing downtime and maintenance costs by predicting failures before they happen.

2. Customer Churn Prediction in Telecom

- **Problem**: Predict which customers are likely to leave (churn) based on usage patterns, customer demographics, and service interactions.

- **Type**: Supervised learning (classification).

- **Impact**: Retaining more customers by proactively addressing the needs of at-risk users.

3. Product Recommendation in E-Commerce

- **Problem**: Suggest relevant products to users based on their browsing history, purchase history, and preferences.

- **Type**: Unsupervised learning (collaborative filtering) or supervised learning (regression).

- **Impact**: Increasing sales and improving user satisfaction through personalized recommendations.

4. Fraud Detection in Finance

- **Problem**: Detect fraudulent transactions by identifying unusual spending patterns or behavior.

- **Type**: Supervised learning (classification) or unsupervised learning (anomaly detection).

- **Impact**: Reducing financial losses and improving security.

5. Medical Diagnosis from Imaging in Healthcare

- **Problem**: Analyze medical images (e.g., X-rays, MRIs) to diagnose conditions like cancer or fractures.

- **Type**: Supervised learning (classification, deep learning with CNNs).

- **Impact**: Improving the accuracy and speed of medical diagnoses.

6. Supply Chain Optimization

- **Problem**: Predict product demand in different regions or seasons to optimize inventory levels and logistics.

- **Type**: Supervised learning (regression).

- **Impact**: Reducing inventory costs and minimizing stockouts.

Challenges in Selecting Machine Learning Problems

Selecting the right machine learning problem also comes with challenges, including:

- **Ill-defined problem statements**: Sometimes, the problem is not clearly defined, making it difficult to apply machine learning. The team must work with stakeholders to clarify the goals.

- **Overfitting expectations**: Business stakeholders may expect machine learning to solve overly complex or ill-suited problems, leading to unrealistic goals.

- **Data issues**: Lack of sufficient or relevant data can hinder the success of a machine learning project. Data collection and preprocessing are crucial steps before modeling.

- **Alignment with business goals**: A technically interesting problem might not always align with the business's strategic priorities, making it less valuable.

Choosing the right machine learning problem is the foundation for a successful machine learning project. By aligning with business goals, understanding the problem type, ensuring the availability of high-quality data, and assessing the feasibility of the solution, you can identify the problems that are most suitable for machine learning.

Careful problem selection ensures that the resulting machine learning solution delivers meaningful, actionable insights that drive business value and improve decision-making.

10.2 Tools and Frameworks for Machine Learning Development

The rise of machine learning has been accompanied by a robust ecosystem of tools and frameworks that make it easier for data scientists, machine learning engineers, and developers to build, train, and deploy machine learning models.

These tools range from programming libraries to end-to-end platforms that provide everything needed for machine learning development, including data processing, model building, and deployment.

In this section, we will explore the most widely used machine learning tools and frameworks, their key features, and the situations in which they are best suited. Understanding these tools is essential for developing efficient and scalable machine learning solutions.

Categories of Tools and Frameworks for Machine Learning

Machine learning tools and frameworks can be broadly categorized into the following groups:

1. **Programming Libraries**

2. **Integrated Development Environments (IDEs) and Platforms**

3. **Cloud-Based Platforms**

4. **Data Management Tools**

5. **Model Deployment Tools**

1. Programming Libraries for Machine Learning

Programming libraries are the foundational tools used to implement machine learning algorithms, build models, and perform data preprocessing. These libraries provide pre-built functions, classes, and routines to simplify the implementation of complex mathematical and statistical tasks.

a. TensorFlow

TensorFlow, developed by Google, is one of the most popular open-source libraries for building and training machine learning models, particularly deep learning models. TensorFlow provides a flexible ecosystem of tools that allow developers to create a wide range of models, from simple regression to complex neural networks.

- **Key Features:**

    o **Scalability**: TensorFlow is designed to run efficiently on both single machines and large distributed clusters.

    o **TensorFlow Serving**: A high-performance system for serving machine learning models in production environments.

- o **TensorFlow Extended (TFX)**: A full framework for end-to-end machine learning, including data validation, model building, deployment, and monitoring.

- o **Keras**: An easy-to-use, high-level API that runs on top of TensorFlow, simplifying the process of building neural networks.

- **Best For**: Deep learning models, distributed machine learning, and production-ready systems.

b. PyTorch

PyTorch, developed by Facebook, is another open-source machine learning library, widely used for deep learning and research in artificial intelligence (AI). PyTorch is known for its flexibility, ease of use, and dynamic computational graph, which allows developers to modify models during runtime.

- **Key Features**:

  - o **Dynamic computation graph**: PyTorch builds computation graphs dynamically, making it ideal for tasks where the model structure needs to change at runtime.

  - o **Autograd**: PyTorch includes automatic differentiation, which simplifies the implementation of complex backpropagation for neural networks.

  - o **TorchScript**: Enables the transition from research models to production by allowing models to be serialized and optimized for production environments.

- o **PyTorch Lightning**: A high-level framework built on top of PyTorch, aimed at reducing boilerplate code and making deep learning research easier.

- **Best For**: Research and experimentation in deep learning, building neural networks, and working with dynamic models.

c. Scikit-learn

Scikit-learn is one of the most popular Python libraries for classical machine learning. It provides simple and efficient tools for data mining and analysis, offering a wide range of algorithms for tasks such as classification, regression, clustering, and dimensionality reduction.

- **Key Features**:

  - o **Broad algorithm support**: Scikit-learn includes a wide array of algorithms, such as decision trees, random forests, support vector machines (SVMs), and k-nearest neighbors (k-NN).

  - o **Feature engineering**: Provides tools for data preprocessing, such as scaling, normalization, and imputation.

  - o **Cross-validation**: Built-in methods for validating models and tuning hyperparameters using grid search and random search.

  - o **Model evaluation**: Tools for calculating metrics such as accuracy, precision, recall, and F1 score.

- **Best For**: Classical machine learning tasks, prototyping, and working with structured data (tabular data).

d. XGBoost

XGBoost (Extreme Gradient Boosting) is an optimized distributed gradient boosting library designed to be highly efficient and scalable. It is widely used for regression, classification, and ranking problems and is known for its performance in machine learning competitions, such as Kaggle.

- **Key Features**:

  o **Speed and performance**: XGBoost is optimized for both memory and computation, making it extremely fast for large datasets.

  o **Regularization**: XGBoost includes regularization techniques to prevent overfitting and improve model generalization.

  o **Tree pruning**: XGBoost uses a more efficient pruning algorithm than standard decision trees, which reduces overfitting and speeds up training.

  o **Distributed processing**: XGBoost supports distributed processing, making it ideal for working with large-scale datasets.

- **Best For**: Tabular data, structured data, boosting algorithms, and competitions like Kaggle.

e. LightGBM

LightGBM (Light Gradient Boosting Machine) is another high-performance gradient boosting framework developed by Microsoft. It is designed to handle large datasets efficiently, making it a popular choice for machine learning competitions and real-world applications.

- **Key Features:**

  - **Leaf-wise tree growth**: LightGBM grows trees leaf-wise, rather than level-wise, which leads to deeper and more efficient trees.

  - **Sparse data handling**: LightGBM is optimized for handling sparse datasets, making it suitable for high-dimensional data.

  - **GPU acceleration**: LightGBM supports GPU training, making it faster for large datasets.

- **Best For**: Large-scale datasets, gradient boosting, and use cases where performance and speed are critical.

f. CatBoost

CatBoost, developed by Yandex, is a gradient boosting algorithm that works especially well with categorical features. It requires minimal data preprocessing and handles categorical variables automatically.

- **Key Features:**

  - **Handling categorical features**: CatBoost automatically processes categorical variables, making it easier to work with datasets containing mixed data types.

  - **Efficient handling of missing values**: CatBoost can handle missing data without the need for imputation.

  - **Fast and scalable**: CatBoost is designed for speed and can handle large datasets efficiently.

- **Best For:** Structured data with many categorical features, gradient boosting, and quick prototyping.

2. Integrated Development Environments (IDEs) and Platforms

IDEs and platforms provide an environment for writing, testing, and debugging machine learning code, offering built-in support for libraries, version control, and collaborative features.

a. Jupyter Notebooks

Jupyter Notebooks is one of the most popular open-source IDEs used by data scientists and machine learning practitioners. It provides an interactive, web-based environment for writing and running Python code, visualizing data, and documenting work.

- **Key Features:**

  - **Interactive coding:** Run code in small increments, view output immediately, and visualize results with graphs and charts.

  - **Support for multiple languages:** Though primarily used for Python, Jupyter supports other languages like R, Julia, and SQL.

  - **Integration with libraries:** Jupyter works seamlessly with libraries like Matplotlib, Seaborn, and TensorFlow for visualizing machine learning models.

  - **Collaborative features:** Jupyter notebooks can be shared easily, allowing for collaboration in research and development.

- **Best For**: Prototyping, data exploration, and developing machine learning models interactively.

b. Google Colab

Google Colab is a cloud-based platform that allows users to write and execute Python code in a Jupyter-like environment. It provides free access to GPUs and TPUs (Tensor Processing Units), making it a popular choice for training machine learning models.

- **Key Features**:

  - **Free GPU/TPU access**: Google Colab provides access to powerful hardware for training deep learning models, without the need for a local setup.

  - **Pre-installed libraries**: Common machine learning libraries like TensorFlow, PyTorch, and Scikit-learn are pre-installed, saving time in setup.

  - **Integration with Google Drive**: Colab allows easy saving and loading of files from Google Drive, enabling users to store datasets and models.

- **Best For**: Running machine learning code on the cloud, deep learning, and GPU-based training.

c. VS Code (with Extensions)

Visual Studio Code (VS Code) is a popular lightweight code editor that, with the help of extensions, can be transformed into a powerful machine learning IDE. Extensions like **Python**, **Jupyter**, and **Pylance** enhance VS Code's functionality, making it suitable for writing, testing, and debugging machine learning code.

- **Key Features**:

  o **Versatility**: Supports a wide range of programming languages and machine learning workflows.

  o **Built-in debugging**: VS Code includes advanced debugging features, making it easier to identify and fix issues in machine learning pipelines.

  o **Git integration**: VS Code offers tight integration with Git for version control, making collaboration easier.

- **Best For**: Developers who want a customizable and feature-rich environment for machine learning development.

3. Cloud-Based Machine Learning Platforms

Cloud-based machine learning platforms offer end-to-end solutions for building, training, and deploying machine learning models. These platforms provide scalable infrastructure and tools for data processing, model training, and monitoring.

a. Amazon SageMaker

Amazon SageMaker is a fully managed service from AWS that provides an integrated environment for building, training, and deploying machine learning models at scale.

- **Key Features**:

  o **Managed training**: Automatically provisions the necessary infrastructure to train models, with support for distributed training and hyperparameter tuning.

o **Built-in algorithms**: SageMaker provides a wide range of built-in algorithms for common tasks like classification, regression, and clustering.

o **SageMaker Studio**: An IDE-like environment for machine learning development, including data preparation, model training, and debugging.

o **Model deployment**: SageMaker simplifies deploying models to production with real-time endpoints, automatic scaling, and monitoring.

- **Best For**: Organizations looking for a scalable, end-to-end platform to handle all aspects of machine learning development, especially those already using AWS services.

b. Google AI Platform

Google AI Platform is a comprehensive machine learning development platform offered by Google Cloud. It provides tools for data preparation, model training, hyperparameter tuning, and deployment, leveraging Google's AI infrastructure.

- **Key Features**:

o **Integration with Google Cloud**: Seamlessly integrates with other Google Cloud services like BigQuery, Dataflow, and Google Cloud Storage.

o **AutoML**: Google's AutoML feature allows users to build custom machine learning models with minimal coding.

- o **TPU support**: Offers support for Tensor Processing Units (TPUs), specialized hardware for accelerating deep learning models.

- o **Managed Jupyter notebooks**: Provides hosted notebooks for model development and experimentation.

- **Best For**: Developers and organizations that want to leverage Google's powerful AI and cloud infrastructure, especially for deep learning and big data projects.

c. Microsoft Azure Machine Learning

Microsoft Azure Machine Learning is a cloud platform that offers a suite of tools for building, training, and deploying machine learning models on Microsoft's Azure cloud infrastructure.

- **Key Features**:

  - o **Automated ML**: Azure ML's AutoML feature automates the process of selecting algorithms, hyperparameters, and model optimization.

  - o **Machine learning pipelines**: Build, test, and deploy machine learning workflows with Azure's integrated pipelines.

  - o **Enterprise-grade security**: Offers robust security features and compliance with enterprise-grade regulations, making it suitable for industries like finance and healthcare.

- **Best For**: Enterprise users looking for a scalable and secure machine learning platform, especially those already using Microsoft's ecosystem of tools and services.

4. Data Management Tools for Machine Learning

Effective data management is crucial for machine learning, as data quality, consistency, and accessibility directly impact model performance.

a. Pandas

Pandas is a Python library used for data manipulation and analysis. It provides data structures like **DataFrames** that allow for easy handling of structured data.

- **Key Features:**

    o **DataFrames**: A powerful data structure for manipulating structured data, similar to Excel or SQL tables.

    o **Data cleaning**: Tools for handling missing data, filtering, and transforming datasets.

    o **Data aggregation**: Functions for summarizing and aggregating data, making it easier to prepare datasets for machine learning models.

- **Best For**: Handling structured data (CSV, Excel, SQL databases) and performing data preprocessing tasks.

b. Dask

Dask is a parallel computing library in Python that extends Pandas and Scikit-learn to handle larger-than-memory datasets. Dask allows users to scale their data science workflows across multiple machines without changing their code significantly.

- **Key Features**:

  - o **Distributed computing**: Dask allows for distributed execution, making it possible to work with datasets that exceed the limits of a single machine.

  - o **Seamless integration**: Dask integrates with Pandas, NumPy, and Scikit-learn, allowing for easy scaling of existing workflows.

  - o **Parallel processing**: Enables parallel computation across multiple cores or machines, speeding up data processing.

- **Best For**: Handling large datasets that don't fit into memory and scaling data processing workflows.

5. Model Deployment Tools

Deploying machine learning models into production environments is a critical step in transforming a machine learning project into a real-world solution. Several tools help automate and streamline the deployment process.

a. TensorFlow Serving

TensorFlow Serving is a flexible, high-performance serving system for machine learning models designed for production environments. It is part of the TensorFlow ecosystem and supports versioned models, allowing for easy updates and rollbacks.

- **Key Features:**

    o **Model versioning:** Allows for deploying and managing multiple versions of models in production.

    o **High performance:** Optimized for low-latency and high-throughput serving of TensorFlow models.

    o **RESTful API:** Provides a RESTful interface for serving predictions to external applications.

- **Best For:** Deploying TensorFlow models in production environments with a focus on scalability and performance.

b. MLflow

MLflow is an open-source platform that helps manage the machine learning lifecycle, from experimentation to deployment. It is language-agnostic and can be used with any machine learning library or framework.

- **Key Features:**

    o **Experiment tracking:** Track and log experiment results, including model parameters, metrics, and artifacts.

    o **Model management:** Centralized model registry for versioning and deploying machine learning models.

    o **Multi-platform support:** MLflow supports deployment on various platforms, including AWS, Azure, and on-premises servers.

- **Best For**: Managing the end-to-end machine learning lifecycle, from experiment tracking to deployment.

c. Docker

Docker is a popular containerization tool used to package machine learning models and their dependencies into containers, ensuring that they can run consistently across different environments.

- **Key Features**:

  - **Containerization**: Encapsulates the model, its dependencies, and runtime environment into a portable container.

  - **Scalability**: Containers can be easily deployed and scaled across cloud environments, making it ideal for production deployment.

  - **Portability**: Ensures that models can run in the same way across different environments, from local machines to cloud servers.

- **Best For**: Deploying machine learning models in production, ensuring consistency across development and production environments.

The machine learning ecosystem offers a wide range of tools and frameworks that support every stage of the development lifecycle, from data preprocessing to model deployment.

Depending on your specific needs—whether you're experimenting with deep learning, building models with structured data, or scaling solutions in production—there is a tool or framework designed to simplify and enhance the machine learning process.

By understanding the strengths and weaknesses of each tool, machine learning practitioners can select the best resources to accelerate their workflows, optimize model performance, and ensure successful deployment in real-world environments.